GREAT SCIENCE PROJECTS

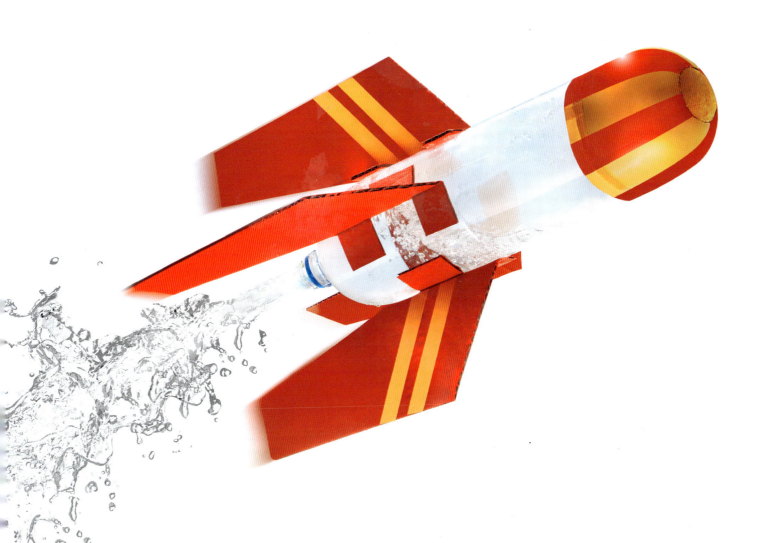

DK LONDON
Editor Zaina Budaly
Art editor Mary Sandberg
Managing editor Rachel Fox
Managing art editor Owen Peyton Jones
Production editor Jacqueline Street-Elkayam
Production controller Meskerem Berhane
Senior jacket designer Stephanie Cheng Hui Tan
Senior jackets coordinator Priyanka Sharma-Saddi
Jacket design development manager Sophia MTT
Publisher Andrew Macintyre
Art director Karen Self
Associate publishing director Liz Wheeler
Publishing director Jonathan Metcalf

Consultant and writer
Jack Challoner

First published in Great Britain in 2023 by
Dorling Kindersley Limited
DK, One Embassy Gardens, 8 Viaduct Gardens,
London, SW11 7BW

The authorised representative in the EEA is
Dorling Kindersley Verlag GmbH. Arnulfstr. 124,
80636 Munich, Germany

Content previously published in *Science Lab*,
Maths Lab, *Home Lab*, *Outdoor Activity Lab*.

Copyright © 2023 Dorling Kindersley Limited
A Penguin Random House Company
10 9 8 7 6 5 4 3 2 1
001–331889–February/2023

A CIP catalogue record for this book
is available from the British Library.
ISBN: 978-0-2415-6994-8

Printed and bound in China

For the curious
www.dk.com

MIX
Paper | Supporting
responsible forestry
FSC™ C018179
FSC
www.fsc.org

This book was made with Forest
Stewardship Council ™ certified paper –
one small step in DK's commitment to a
sustainable future.
For more information go to
www.dk.com/our-green-pledge

GREAT SCIENCE PROJECTS

TRIED AND TESTED EXPERIMENTS FOR ALL BUDDING SCIENTISTS

CONTENTS

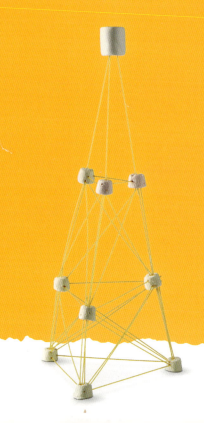

HOW LONG HAVE YOU GOT?

In this table you'll find the projects categorized by the time it takes to complete them. The difficulty level is listed beside each project and the page number. This is useful for when you're in a hurry, or have plenty of time on your hands!

10-20 minutes

Dancing snake	Easy	24		Twirling helicopter	Medium	12
Wonderful water	Easy	84		Spinning whirlpool	Medium	98
Soap-powered boat	Easy	114		Sticky slime	Medium	104
Sturdy sandcastle	Easy	148		Spaghetti tower	Medium	126
Beautiful sun prints	Easy	192		Origami jumping frog	Medium	186
Singing spoons	Easy	196		Lemon battery	Medium	218
Buzzer	Easy	206		Sensational speakers	Medium	222
Harmonica	Easy	226		Brilliant barometer	Medium	232
				Paper sundial	Medium	252

30-45 minutes

Newspaper stool	Easy	130		Erosion bottles	Medium	92
Lucky dip	Easy	280		Pantograph	Medium	180
Bake and share a pizza	Easy	284		Spectroscope	Medium	200
Bottle raft	Medium	38		Rain gauge	Medium	236
Wind turbine	Medium	44		Thermometer	Medium	240
Speed trials	Medium	70		Latitude locator	Medium	256
Soil-free planter	Medium	80		Make your own clock	Medium	306
				Diamond kite	Hard	30

1 hour+

Optical illusions	Easy	268		Tower crane	Hard	52
Maths bingo	Easy	296		Waterwheel	Hard	108
Erupting volcano	Medium	118		Suspension bridge	Hard	134
Lolly stick bird feeder	Medium	272		Geodesic dome	Hard	142
Water rocket	Hard	16		Guitar	Hard	210
				Anemometer	Hard	244

2 hours+

Symmetrical pictures	Medium	154		Fibonacci spiral collage	Medium	300
Tessellating patterns	Medium	160		Automaton	Hard	60
Friendship bracelets	Medium	166		Marble run	Hard	174
Scaling up pictures	Medium	262		Popcorn sale tray	Hard	288

STEM IN THE REAL WORLD

What is STEM? And why is it important? STEM stands for science, technology, engineering, and maths. These subjects often overlap. For example, to build a rocket an engineer needs to understand how forces work (science) and know what materials (technology) to use. In fact, if you look around you, you'll find STEM just about everywhere!

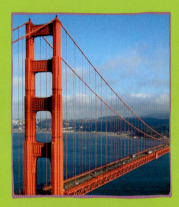

SCIENCE
Science is everything we know about the Universe, and this knowledge keeps on expanding thanks to the curiosity of scientists.

TECHNOLOGY
Engineers use technology to build and operate their machines. For example, a wind turbine is monitored by computer programs.

ENGINEERING
Cities around the world are full of skyscrapers and bridges. Engineers use their understanding of science and maths to build them.

MATHS
From telling the time to weaving fabrics that make clothes, humans have used maths in everyday tasks for thousands of years.

LOOK OUT FOR THESE!

STEM icons
Placed throughout the book are coloured symbols, each representing a STEM subject. They are accompanied by fast facts to help you understand a specific STEM subject at work in your project, so watch out for them as you're going along. With all this knowledge you'll be a STEM expert in no time!

BE CAREFUL

WARNING
This symbol identifies a task that might be dangerous. Be sure to get adult supervision.

A WORD ABOUT GLUES
Several of the projects in this book require the use of glue. We have suggested that you use ordinary PVA glue or glue sticks, but in some cases it will be easier to use a glue gun if you have one, as this glue sets much faster. A glue gun should only ever be used by an adult, and they must be sure to follow the manufacturer's guidelines.

SCIENCE
This symbol points out facts about biology, chemistry, or physics.

TECHNOLOGY
This symbol highlights more information about tools or materials.

ENGINEERING
This symbol directs you to more facts about structures or machines.

MATHEMATICS
This symbol identifies extra information on formulas, shapes, or measurements.

FOREWORD

I wish I had this book when I was growing up. Like most young people, I was really curious about how the world works and what it's made of. I could often be found playing with water and soap, or magnets and torches, building weird structures or exploring sound in imaginative ways. I was trying things out and testing my own ideas, a bit like a real scientist. The activities in this book would have satisfied my curiosity, while also feeding it and guiding it.

I believe the best way to understand something is to do it yourself. Every activity in *Great Science Projects* has simple step-by-step instructions, with helpful tips to guide you along. Before you know it, you'll be launching homemade water rockets high into the air, building a crane, exploring soil erosion, and making colourful friendship bracelets. And once you've completed a project, you'll find a clear explanation of the science.

Science is the way we answer questions about the world. Scientists ask specific questions. Then they work out possible answers, and carry out experiments to see if their answer might be right. Over the past few hundred years, science has helped us to understand the world in incredible detail. Technology is the use of scientific knowledge to make useful things. Engineering is how we apply scientific knowledge to design tools, machines or structures. Maths is an essential part of science, technology and engineering – and, of course, everyday life.

Remember, this book is not only "hands-on": it's also "brain-on". You'll get the best out of it if you keep wondering and thinking as you go. I hope that you enjoy these projects, and that they inspire your curiosity about the amazing world we live in.

Jack Challoner

JACK CHALLONER

FORCES AND MOTION

A force is a push or a pull, and there are forces at work everywhere! Forces can make things move or stop moving, make things speed up, slow down or change direction, or just keep things still. A familiar force is gravity, which pulls everything down towards the ground. Tension is another familiar force. It is created by an object that is being stretched, like a rubber band or a rope. Engineers use forces to set objects into motion, such as helicopter rotors and rockets, and in this chapter, you'll get to build your very own!

SPINNING BLADES

A helicopter's rotor blades are a bit like aeroplane wings – they generate an upward force called lift as they move through the air. But unlike an aeroplane's wing, which must travel forwards with the aeroplane to create lift, a helicopter's rotor rotates rapidly, so it can generate lift even when the helicopter is hovering in one place.

The rotor is twisted slightly so that it meets the air at an angle as it spins.

As it moves through the air, the rotor pushes air downwards.

TWIRLING HELICOPTER

The helicopter is a remarkable form of transport. It can lift off from a standing start, without the need for a runway, and carry out intricate manoeuvres in all directions. Using just a drinking straw and a piece of paper or card, you can make a simple helicopter model to explore the forces produced by helicopter rotors.

STEM YOU WILL USE

• SCIENCE: Air moving over surfaces can create a force called "lift".
• ENGINEERING: Shafts used in mechanical engineering transmit power from one part of a machine to another.

HOW TO MAKE A
TWIRLING HELICOPTER

Follow the instructions to make your own helicopter. It might need a bit of flight testing and adjustment. A snip off each end of the rotor, or a slightly longer straw, could make all the difference. You can also test how different weights of paper and card affect your helicopter's flight.

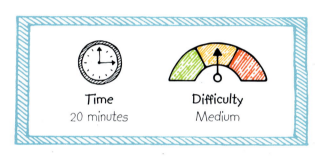

Time
20 minutes

Difficulty
Medium

WHAT YOU NEED

Scissors

Sticky tape

Pencil

Adhesive putty

Biodegradable straw

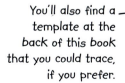
Coloured paper or card

Ruler

1 If you have a bendy straw, cut it off just below the bend. You'll need a straight piece of straw to make your helicopter stable as it flies.

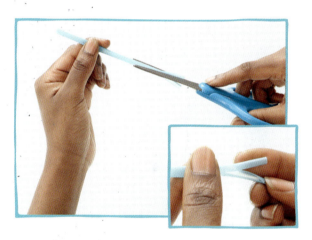

2 Using the scissors, cut into the end of the straight piece of straw to a depth of about 1 cm (½ in). This will create two tabs that will hold the rotor in place.

You'll also find a template at the back of this book that you could trace, if you prefer.

3 To make the rotor, lay the paper or card on a table and draw a rectangle in one corner, 2 cm (¾ in) wide by 14 cm (5½ in) long.

Scissors are force magnifiers – they increase the force that your fingers and thumb provide.

4 Cut out the rectangle you drew on the paper or card, trying not to bend it at this stage.

Measure 1 cm (½ in) in if you want to make sure you are exactly in the centre.

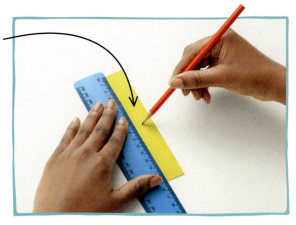

5 Measure halfway along the long side of the rectangle you just cut out – 7 cm (2¾ in) from one end – and make a mark at the centre.

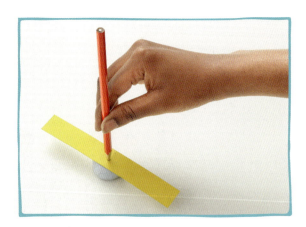

6 Place your rotor on top of the adhesive putty. Use the sharp end of a pencil to make a hole at the centre point you have marked.

Try not to bend the rotor at this stage.

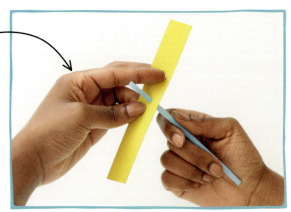

7 Push the cut end of the straw through the hole. If the hole is not quite big enough, carefully make it a bit bigger with the pencil.

8 Bend the two halves of the end of the straw in opposite directions and push them flat onto the rotor. Secure them with tape. Keep the rotor flat.

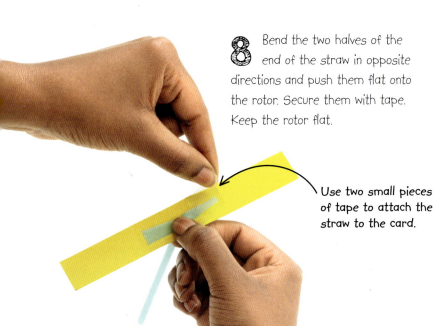

Use two small pieces of tape to attach the straw to the card.

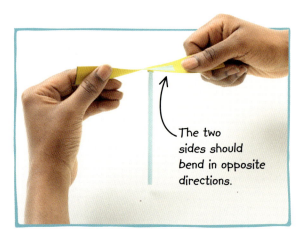

The two sides should bend in opposite directions.

9 Now, finally, you can bend the rotor – otherwise your helicopter won't take off. Gently twist anticlockwise with each hand.

10 Your helicopter is ready! To make it fly, you need to hold the straw between your two palms, push your right palm forwards, and release.

What happens if you push your left palm instead?

Try making your rotor different lengths or widths to see how they affect its flight.

A helicopter rotor pushes air downwards to create upward lift.

The straw is acting as a shaft – a component that transmits power from one part of a machine to another.

HOW IT WORKS

As the helicopter's rotor spins, its angled edges push the surrounding air downwards, creating an area of high pressure air below it (and lower pressure above it). The higher pressure air pushes the rotor upwards. This force is called "lift". Try making different helicopters to find the best combination of the length and width of the rotor, how much it is bent, and the length of the straw.

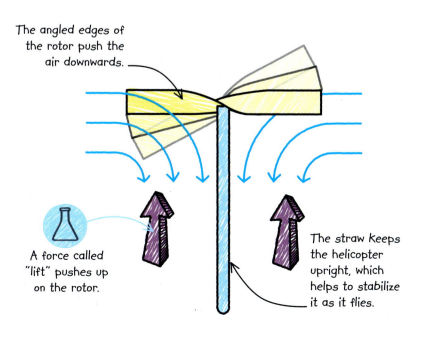

The angled edges of the rotor push the air downwards.

A force called "lift" pushes up on the rotor.

The straw keeps the helicopter upright, which helps to stabilize it as it flies.

REAL WORLD: TECHNOLOGY
UNPILOTED AERIAL VEHICLES

Some unpiloted aerial vehicles, such as UAVs, have rotors similar to your helicopter. Electric motors spin the rotors, generating lift. The faster they turn, the more lift they generate. To make the UAV change direction, the rotors on one side turn faster than the rotors on the other side.

WATER ROCKET

Five... four... three... two... one... blast off! You can make a powerful rocket that shoots up into the air at high speed, without using a drop of rocket fuel! This rocket uses air, water, and muscle power to launch a plastic bottle high into the air. Your rocket won't quite reach the stars, but you'll be impressed at how fast and high it can go. So, gather what you need and prepare for lift-off.

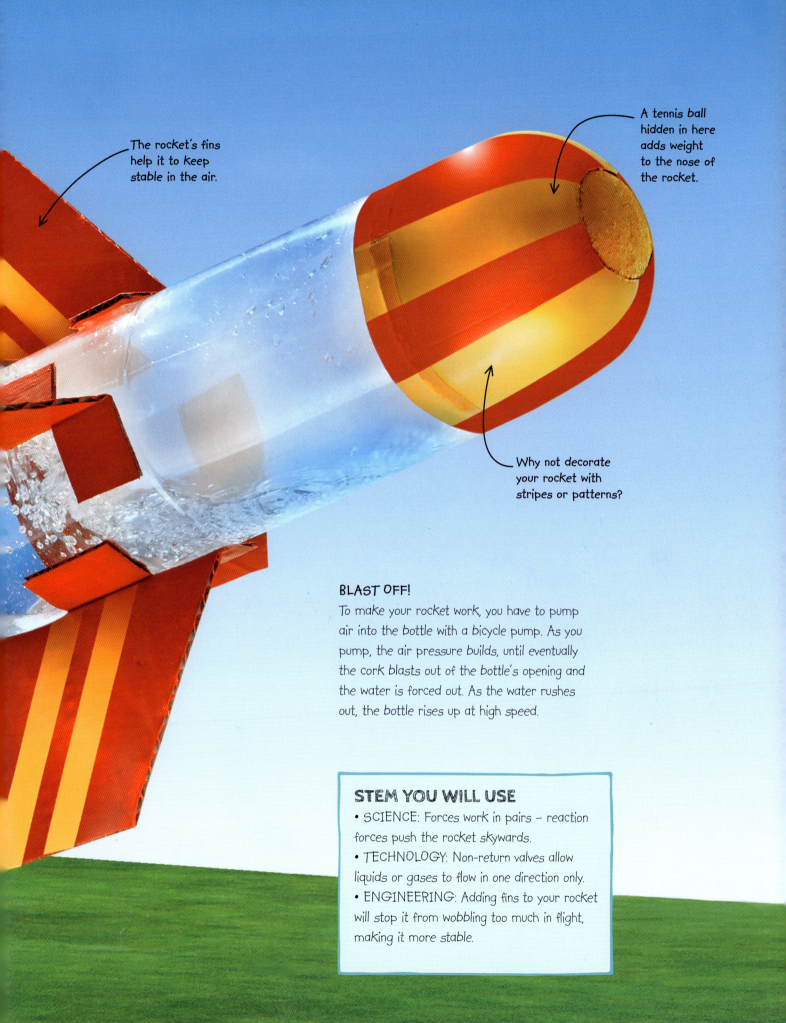

The rocket's fins help it to keep stable in the air.

A tennis ball hidden in here adds weight to the nose of the rocket.

Why not decorate your rocket with stripes or patterns?

BLAST OFF!

To make your rocket work, you have to pump air into the bottle with a bicycle pump. As you pump, the air pressure builds, until eventually the cork blasts out of the bottle's opening and the water is forced out. As the water rushes out, the bottle rises up at high speed.

STEM YOU WILL USE

• SCIENCE: Forces work in pairs – reaction forces push the rocket skywards.
• TECHNOLOGY: Non-return valves allow liquids or gases to flow in one direction only.
• ENGINEERING: Adding fins to your rocket will stop it from wobbling too much in flight, making it more stable.

HOW TO MAKE A
WATER ROCKET

The sky's the limit with this experiment, which uses air pressure to launch your very own water rocket. Two plastic bottles make the rocket – one for the rocket's body and another to make the nose cone at the top of the rocket. Give yourself an open place away from trees, buildings, and people before launching your rocket!

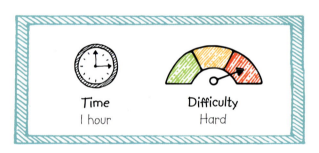

Time
I hour

Difficulty
Hard

WHAT YOU NEED

Adhesive putty

Double-sided tape

Coloured tape

Paint

Tennis ball

Valve

Cork

Foot pump

Small plastic bottle full of water

Ruler

Paintbrush

Felt-tip pen

Cardboard

Card

Scissors

Two large plastic bottles

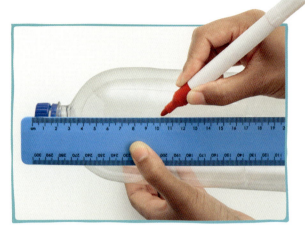

1 With the felt-tip pen, make a mark 10 cm (4 in) down from the cap of one plastic bottle.

2 Wrap the sheet of card around the bottle where you marked it, and draw a straight line around the bottle.

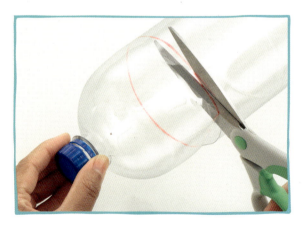

3 Cut all the way along the line you've drawn. Be careful, and if you have any trouble, ask an adult for help.

4 Ask an adult to cut off the very top of the bottle, making sure the hole is smaller than the tennis ball.

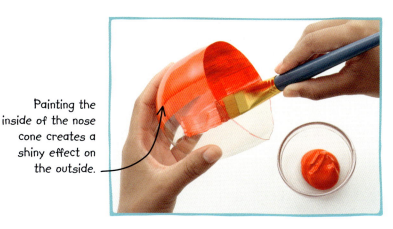

Painting the inside of the nose cone creates a shiny effect on the outside.

5 Paint the inside of the round shape you have made. Your nose cone is nearly complete.

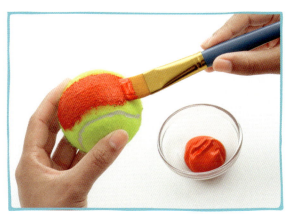

6 Paint the tennis ball. Only part of the ball will show, so you only have to paint half of it.

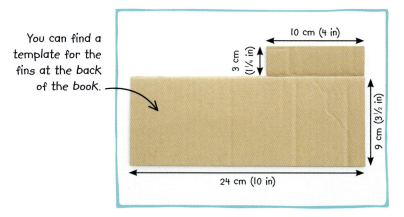

You can find a template for the fins at the back of the book.

10 cm (4 in)

3 cm (1¼ in)

9 cm (3½ in)

24 cm (10 in)

7 Draw two rectangles on cardboard, one on top of the other. Make one 10 cm (4 in) long and 3 cm (1¼ in) wide and the other 24 cm (10 in) long and 9 cm (3½ in) wide. Cut along the outlines, so you end up with a shape like the one above.

The middle rectangle should be about 4 cm (1½ in) wide.

3 cm (1¼ in)   3 cm (1¼ in)

3 cm (1¼ in)

5 cm (2 in)

18 cm (7 in)

8 Draw the shape of a fin on the large rectangle, like the one shown here. Draw two dotted lines on the small rectangle, 3 cm (1¼ in) in from each side.

9 Cut out the fin and then along the dotted lines to create three separate tabs.

The fin is a quadrilateral – a 2D shape with four straight sides.

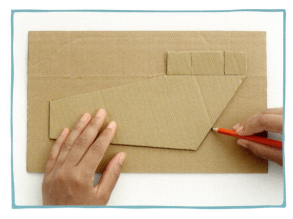

10 Make three more fins. Use the first one as a template to make sure all your fins are the same shape and size.

11 Paint all four fins on both sides and leave them to dry. This design is red, but you could decorate your rocket however you like.

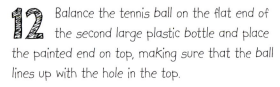

The tennis ball should be placed between the large bottle and the nose cone.

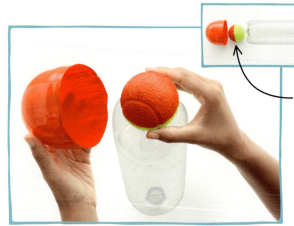

12 Balance the tennis ball on the flat end of the second large plastic bottle and place the painted end on top, making sure that the ball lines up with the hole in the top.

13 Use coloured tape to secure the nose cone in place. Make sure you attach it firmly – you don't want it to fall off in mid-flight!

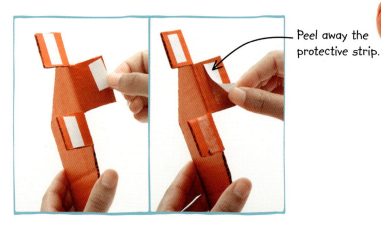

Peel away the protective strip.

14 Fold the fins' top and bottom tabs to the left, and the middle tab to the right. Apply double-sided tape to the underside of each tab.

15 Stick the fins low down on the rocket so that they extend well beyond the neck of the bottle.

The tennis ball in the nose helps to keep the rocket stable in flight.

The fins are really important if you want your rocket to fly straight up, so make sure they are secure.

A non-return valve allows fluid (liquid or gas) to flow in one direction only.

16 Make sure the bottom of each fin lines up with the others so that the rocket can stand up straight. Your rocket should now look something like this.

The cork should be cut just slightly shorter than the length of the valve.

17 Check your cork fits in the opening of your bottle, and then ask an adult to help you cut a quarter off at the thinner end.

18 Push the valve into the middle of the wide end of the cork until it pokes out the other side. Put a piece of adhesive putty on one end, so you don't damage the table.

19 Screw or clip the valve into the foot pump. This is how you'll pump air into the rocket.

20 Turn the rocket upside down and use the small bottle to pour in around 500 ml (18 fl oz) of water. Your rocket should be about one-quarter full.

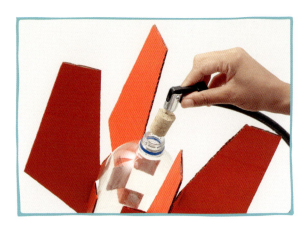

21 Push the cork firmly into the upturned rocket, being careful not to bend the fins. You are nearly ready for launch!

22 Stand the rocket on its fins on level ground and, without knocking the bottle over, begin pumping. Keep going until the rocket blasts off.

Don't point your rocket at friends, and keep your head clear of the top of the rocket – you don't want it to hit you!

What happens if you put more water in the bottle – or less?

The pump contains two valves: one allows air in when you lift your foot, the other releases the air when you push down.

HOW IT WORKS

Forces always work in pairs. For instance, when you row a boat with a pair of oars, the force of the oars pushing the water creates an opposite force that pushes the oars, and so the boat, forwards. This opposite force, called a reaction force, is what makes rockets fly. When you pump air into your rocket, the air pressure inside builds up until it pushes out the cork and then the water with a powerful force. That same air pressure also pushes upwards on the top of the bottle – and it is this force that makes the rocket soar as the water is released. Once all the water has been expelled, and the air pressure returns to normal, the rocket will fall back to Earth.

The reaction force pushes the rocket upwards.

Before you use the pump, the air pressure inside the bottle equals the air pressure outside.

Now that air has been pumped in, the air pressure is higher inside than out.

The higher pressure pushes the water out.

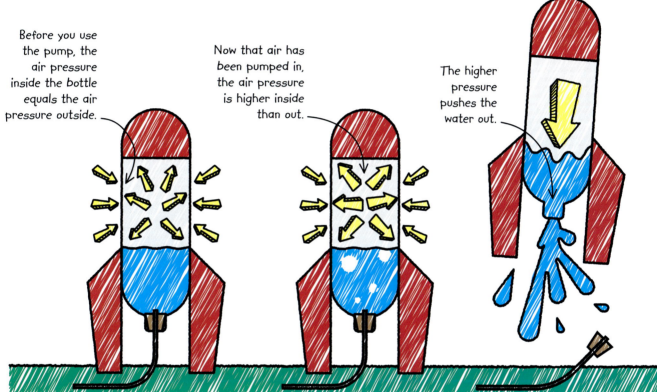

REAL WORLD: TECHNOLOGY
ROCKET FUEL

A real space rocket works in the same way as your water rocket – but it's not a bicycle pump that increases the pressure inside the rocket. Instead, rocket fuel burns very quickly, producing huge amounts of gas. As new gas is produced, it pushes down on the gas already there, forcing it out of the base of the rocket, and that pushes the rocket upwards.

DANCING SNAKE

How would you like to have a new career as a snake charmer and get a writhing serpent to jump up and down and dance as if by magic? You'll have to make use of the invisible forces created by static electricity. You can create this force with nothing more complicated than tissue paper and a balloon. And, as you'll see, static electricity can do other strange things besides taming paper snakes. It can even bend a stream of water!

Your snake responds to amounts of electric charge that are not dangerous.

It could almost be alive! The balloon gives the snake's head a charge of static electricity and makes it rear up.

HEADS UP

When you put your tissue snake on a table or in the bottom of a basket, its head will normally lie flat. Even light material like this is pulled down by the force of gravity. To lift it up, there must be another force acting on it – one that pulls the snake's head upwards, against gravity. That is the force of attraction between electric charges.

For a real snake-charmer effect, you can put your snake in a basket.

HOW TO MAKE A
DANCING SNAKE

You need a steady hand to draw and cut out your snake, but otherwise this experiment is as easy as blowing up a balloon! Once you've discovered what static electricity can do to a tissue snake, you can try other things, too. The tiny electric charge involved in the experiment is completely safe. However, you should never investigate the electricity in power cables and appliances; it can be very dangerous indeed!

Time
15 minutes

Difficulty
Easy

STEM YOU WILL USE

• SCIENCE: There are two types of electric charge: positive and negative. Separating charges creates static electricity, which produces forces that can make objects move.

• ENGINEERING: Tissue paper is thin and lightweight. It responds easily to the small amounts of static electricity generated in this activity.

WHAT YOU NEED

Sticky tape

Balloon

Pens

Scissors

Large plate or bowl

Tissue paper

Don't press too hard with the pen, otherwise you might tear the paper.

1 Unfold the tissue paper, so that it is just one sheet thick. For best results, use the thinnest tissue paper you can find. Lay the paper out flat on a table and put the plate upside down on top. Draw around the plate with a pen.

A spiral is any curve that starts at a central point and grows further away from the point as it circles around it.

2 Now draw a spiral on the paper. The centre of the spiral will be the head of the snake, while the tail will be the pointed part. Make the snake's body the same width all the way round.

5 Now it's time to generate static electricity. Blow up the balloon and tie it off. Then rub it quite hard against something woollen, such as a jumper, for about a minute. If you don't have anything woollen, you can rub the balloon on your hair.

3 Cut carefully around the circle you drew and continue along the line of the spiral. As you go round, your snake will be revealed! Tissue paper crumples up very easily, so try not to grip it too hard with your fingers.

The balloon is now electrically charged.

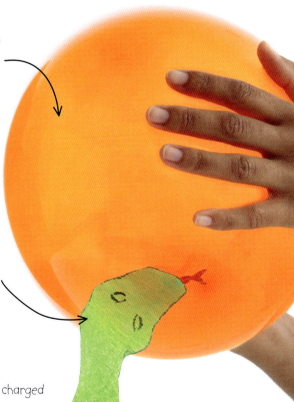

Try moving the balloon closer and further away from the snake to make it dance.

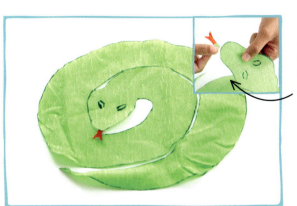

Attach the tongue carefully, then your snake is ready!

4 You can decorate the snake, if you like. Perhaps you could draw on some eyes, or make a small tongue by colouring in some leftover tissue paper with a red pen, then sticking it on. Tape the snake's tail to the table.

6 Hold the charged balloon a few centimetres above the snake and then slowly bring it closer. When the balloon is about 2 cm (¾ in) above the snake's head, the snake will be attracted to the balloon, and will rise up towards it.

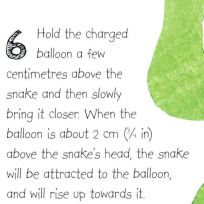

TAKE IT FURTHER

You can explore the forces of static electricity in many ways –
here are just a few fun ways, using objects you can find around the
home. Charge the balloons by rubbing on hair or wool, as before.

BENDING WATER

The invisible forces of static electricity can do
surprising things that seem like magic! See
for yourself how static electricity can bend
water before your very eyes.

1 Turn on a tap to produce a slow but steady
stream of water. Bring an uncharged balloon
close to the running water. What happens? Nothing!

2 Now charge up the balloon and bring it close to
the stream of water. This time the water bends,
attracted by the forces of static electricity.

JUMPING PAPER PEOPLE

Make the people dance! You can use a charged
balloon to attract small pieces of paper on a table.
See how close you have to hold the balloon before
the paper jumps up and down.

Gravity pulls the
paper pieces
down towards
the surface.

1 Cut out lots of small pieces of paper. The round
"confetti" made by a hole punch works well, or you
could make fun shapes like these. Lay them on a table.

The closer
the balloon, the
stronger the force
of attraction.

The charge
on the balloon
charges the
paper pieces.

2 Bring a charged balloon close to the paper pieces.
The pieces will jump up and stick to the balloon.
Some will even fall off and jump up again.

PUSHING BALLOONS

Hang two uncharged *balloons* together and nothing much happens. Yet, when the balloons are charged with *static electricity*, things start to get a little more interesting.

1 Tie string to each of two balloons. Do not charge them yet, but hold both strings between a finger and thumb and let the balloons hang down.

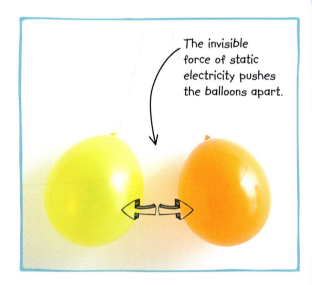

The invisible force of static electricity pushes the balloons apart.

2 Charge both balloons evenly, all over their surfaces. When you dangle them down now, they stay apart, repelled (pushed) by an invisible force.

HOW IT WORKS

Electric charge is carried by tiny particles called protons, which carry a positive (+) charge, and electrons, which carry a negative (-) charge. Charges exert forces on each other: charges of the same type push apart, or repel, while opposite charges pull together, or attract. Normally, there are equal numbers of positive and negative charges everywhere. However, when you rub the *balloon* on wool or your hair it picks up extra electrons, giving the balloon an overall negative charge. This pushes the electrons away in the paper, making the paper's edge positively charged. That is why the paper snake is attracted to the balloon.

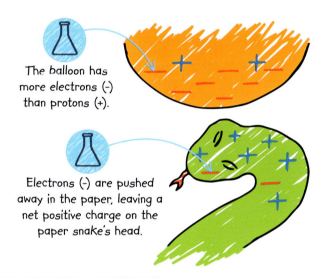

The balloon has more electrons (-) than protons (+).

Electrons (-) are pushed away in the paper, leaving a net positive charge on the paper snake's head.

REAL WORLD: SCIENCE
LIGHTNING STORM

Inside a thundercloud, swirling winds make ice crystals in the cloud rub together, which charges them. The base of this cloud becomes negatively charged, which is attracted to a positively charged ground. This can produce lightning, which takes the shortest route to the ground, often striking trees.

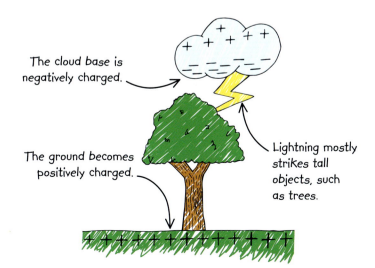

The cloud base is negatively charged.

The ground becomes positively charged.

Lightning mostly strikes tall objects, such as trees.

The part of the kite that catches the wind is called the sail.

This kite has a bridle: a triangular-shaped string arrangement that keeps the kite's sail at a right angle to the flying line.

This is the flying line. Hold tight – it keeps the kite from flying away.

DIAMOND KITE

When a breeze picks up, there's no better way to experience the power of wind than to fly a kite. The wind can take a kite soaring up high, while you're in control of it down on the ground. In this activity, you can make your own colourful kite that really flies, using things you have at home. If you are inspired by flying your kite, there are lots of other designs you can try. What about using different materials to make the sail? How about making a kite that's much bigger, or one that has a much longer string?

STEM YOU WILL USE
- SCIENCE: Wind exerts a force on any surface it hits.
- ENGINEERING: Strings and cables exert a force called tension when they stretch.
- MATHS: Four right angles of 90° make a complete turn.

LET'S GO FLY A KITE
Kite flying can take practice and patience, but you'll find it's worth the effort. A beach is a good place to fly a kite, if it isn't too crowded, because it often has steady breezes. Don't fly a kite in a storm or if it's really windy, and never fly a kite near power lines or airports.

The tail will flutter in the wind.

HOW TO MAKE A
DIAMOND KITE

To make the sail of your kite, which catches the wind, you need to use something light, flat, and flexible. This kite is made from two plastic carrier bags. You'll need two sticks that must be strong but flexible, and lots of string to tether the kite as it climbs into the sky!

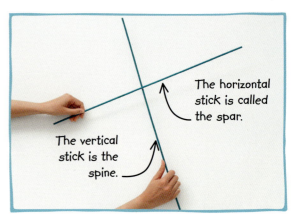

The horizontal stick is called the spar.

The vertical stick is the spine.

1 Place the two sticks at right angles to each other, with the horizontal one (the spar) a little more than halfway up the vertical stick (the spine).

Time
45 minutes

Difficulty
Hard

WHAT YOU NEED

Pencil

Felt-tip pen

Adhesive putty

String

Double-sided tape

Sticky tape

Two garden sticks

Scissors

Ruler

Two plastic carrier bags

2 Cut about 40 cm (16 in) of string, which you'll use to tie the spar and the spine together.

3 Wrap the string a few times around the crossing point, then tie the sticks together. They should still be at right angles to each other, with the spar a little more than halfway up the spine.

A right angle is an angle of 90°. As you can see here, four right angles make one complete turn (360°).

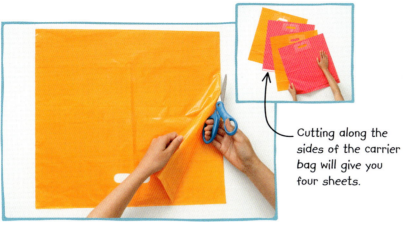

Cutting along the sides of the carrier bag will give you four sheets.

4 Cut open both sides of each carrier bag, and then across the bottom, so that you end up with four pieces the same size and shape.

5 Stick double-sided tape along the bottom of one of the bags. Make it as flat as you can. Peel back the protective strip.

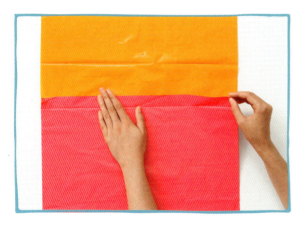

6 Attach a differently coloured piece of plastic by carefully placing it onto the double-sided tape on the first piece and pressing down.

7 Make a patchwork pattern as shown with all four pieces stuck together with double-sided tape. Make each join as smooth as possible.

If the spar and the spine are at right angles, they should line up with the joins.

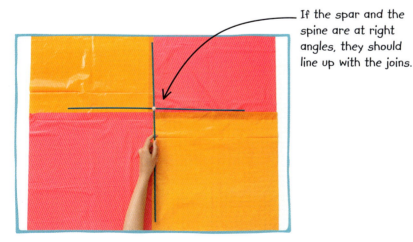

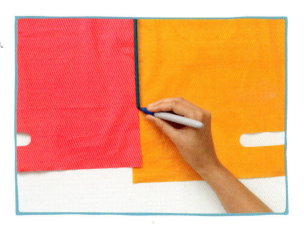

8 Lay the crossed sticks onto the patchwork pattern, so that the point at which the sticks cross is on top of the centre of the plastic pieces.

9 With the sticks still in place, mark the position of each end of each stick with the felt-tip pen. Then put the sticks to one side.

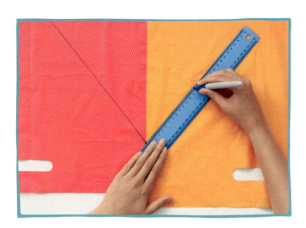

10 Using a ruler and the felt-tip pen, draw straight lines between the four marks you just made to create the outline of your sail.

Keep the leftover pieces – you'll need them to make the tail for your kite.

11 Cut neatly along the straight lines to reveal your diamond-shaped sail.

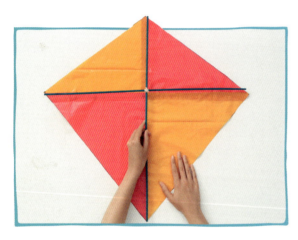

12 Carefully lay the crossed sticks on the sail so that the ends of the sticks line up with the points of the diamond shape.

13 Secure the ends of the sticks to the sail with tape. Make sure they are stuck firmly, otherwise your kite may fall apart in the wind!

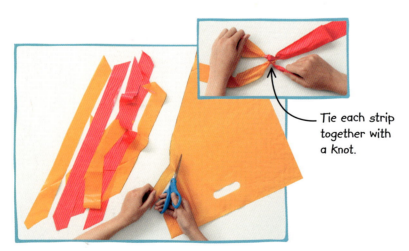

Tie each strip together with a knot.

14 To make the tail, cut strips from the leftover pieces of plastic and tie the strips together, alternating the colours.

15 Knot one end of the tail tightly to the spine, and slide it down to the bottom.

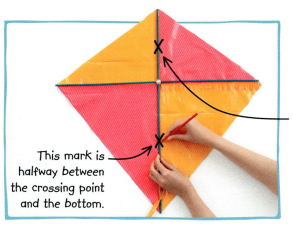

This mark is halfway between the crossing point and the bottom.

Here's the halfway mark between the top of the kite and the crossing point.

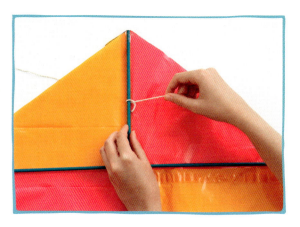

16 Mark one point halfway between the top, or nose, and the crossing point of the kite. Then add a second point halfway between the crossing point and the bottom, or tail. Place adhesive putty underneath and make a small hole in the sail at each mark using the pencil.

17 Cut a piece of string as long as the kite's spine, and pass the ends through the holes in the plastic sheet. Tie the string to the spine at the two points you marked.

This is the point where you will attach the flying line.

A kite is flown at an angle to the wind, so that air is forced underneath it.

This part, which makes the kite fly at an angle, is called the bridle.

18 Turn the kite over and pull the string over to one side, moving your fingers along the string until they are over the spar. Keep hold of the string.

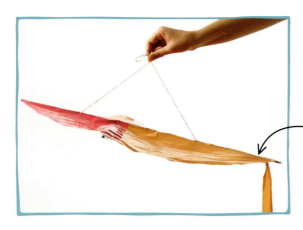

The tail end of the kite should be lower than the nose.

19 Still holding the string, hang your kite from your fingers. It should hang at an angle, with the nose higher than the tail.

Ask an adult for help if you find this too fiddly.

20 Tie a small loop in the string at the point you were holding with your fingers. This is where you will attach the flying line.

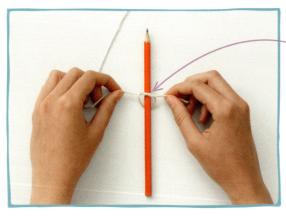

It is friction that prevents the knot from coming undone.

21 Cut a very long piece of string – or perhaps even use the rest of the ball of string. Tie one end to the middle of the pencil, which will be your handle while your kite flies.

22 Wind the entire length of string around the pencil. As the kite climbs higher in the air, you'll be able to let out more string.

23 Tie the other end of the long piece of string to the loop you made in the bridle. Now your kite is ready to fly! On a breezy day, and never in a storm, take your kite out to an open space – on high ground is ideal.

HOW IT WORKS

The wind that lifts your kite is simply moving air. Because your kite is at an angle, the moving air is forced downwards under the sail. As the kite pushes the air downwards, the air pushes the kite upwards – this force is called "lift". While the wind is pushing the kite both upwards and forwards, the flying line that you hold pulls the kite downwards and backwards. The stronger the wind, the more you have to tug on the kite to stop it flying away, but if the wind stops or you let go, gravity will bring the kite back down to earth with a crash.

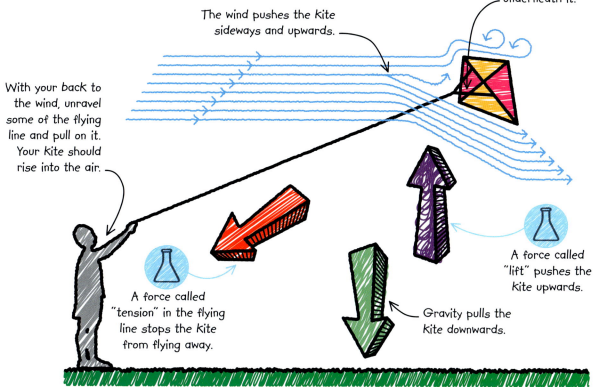

The bridle ensures that the kite flies at an angle to the wind. The angle of the kite forces the wind underneath it.

The wind pushes the kite sideways and upwards.

With your back to the wind, unravel some of the flying line and pull on it. Your kite should rise into the air.

A force called "tension" in the flying line stops the kite from flying away.

A force called "lift" pushes the kite upwards.

Gravity pulls the kite downwards.

REAL WORLD: SCIENCE
KITESURFING

A kitesurfer uses a large sports kite attached to their waist to speed through the sea on a surfboard. A sports kite is a bit more complicated than your kite. It has two strings instead of just one, which allows the person flying it more control. Pulling on one string or the other makes the kite twist and turn, changing its direction as the air flows over each side of the kite differently. The sports kite can lift the kitesurfer high into the air to perform difficult tricks, such as jumps, flips, and spins.

BOTTLE RAFT

This activity could save your life! If you were stranded on a desert island, and you had some large empty barrels, you could make a raft to escape! It's a simple matter of balancing forces. The bowl of pebbles on the lollipop stick platform pushes the raft downwards into the water, but this force is balanced out by the buoyancy, or "upthrust", of the water pressing against the air-filled plastic bottles. Because these forces are equal, the raft floats!

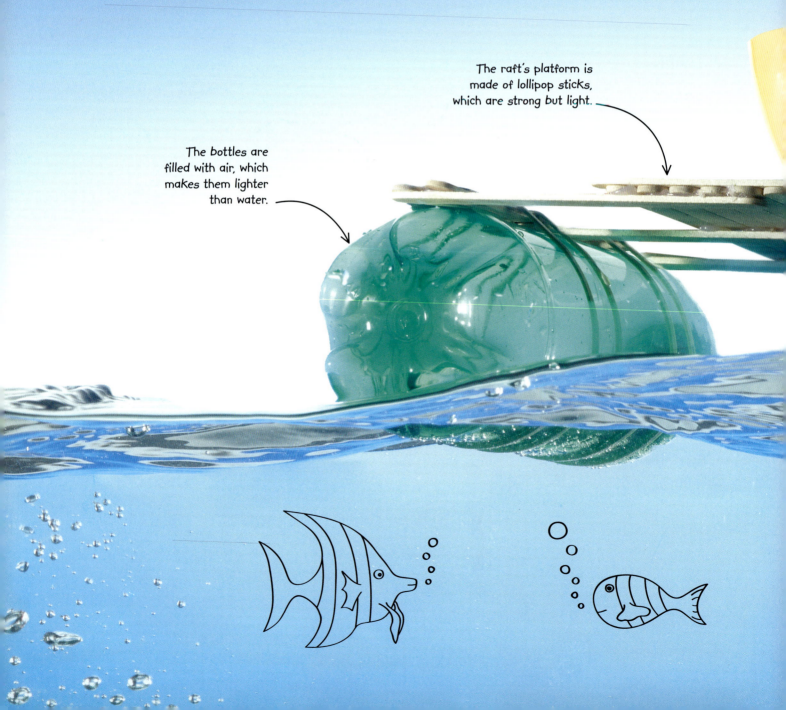

The raft's platform is made of lollipop sticks, which are strong but light.

The bottles are filled with air, which makes them lighter than water.

This bowl of pebbles is acting as a load – a force that the raft's structure can withstand.

When the raft is placed in water, the water pushes upwards on the bottles, with a force called buoyancy, or "upthrust".

HOW TO BUILD A
BOTTLE RAFT

Empty plastic bottles float well in water, but to make an effective raft, you need to build a platform on which to support the load. It's a fairly simple project – the raft's platform is made of lollipop sticks glued together, and it is attached to the bottles with stretched rubber bands.

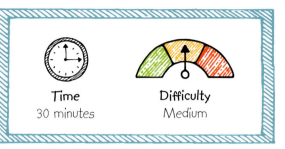

Time
30 minutes

Difficulty
Medium

STEM YOU WILL USE
• SCIENCE: Water pushes upwards on objects placed in it, using a forced called "upthrust".
• ENGINEERING: Every structure can be made stronger by adding more support.

WHAT YOU NEED

Bowl of pebbles

Rubber bands

Glue

23 lollipop sticks

Scales

Two 500 ml (1 pint) bottles

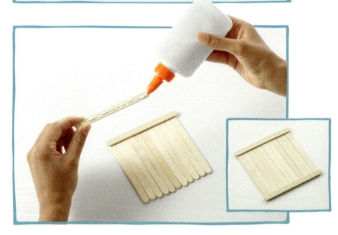

1 Lay eleven lollipop sticks side-by-side. Secure them together by adding glue to two other lollipop sticks and positioning them on either side of the platform.

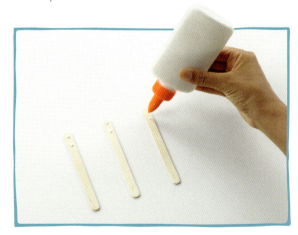

2 Take three lollipop sticks. Space them evenly so that they stretch the length of one lollipop stick. Put glue at the far end of each stick.

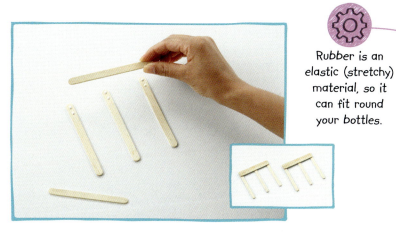

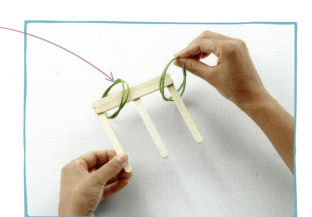

Rubber is an elastic (stretchy) material, so it can fit round your bottles.

3 Press two lollipop sticks on top of the dabs of glue to make an E-shape. Repeat steps 2 and 3 to make a second E-shape.

4 Once the glue on your two E-shapes has dried, slip two rubber bands over the ends of each one.

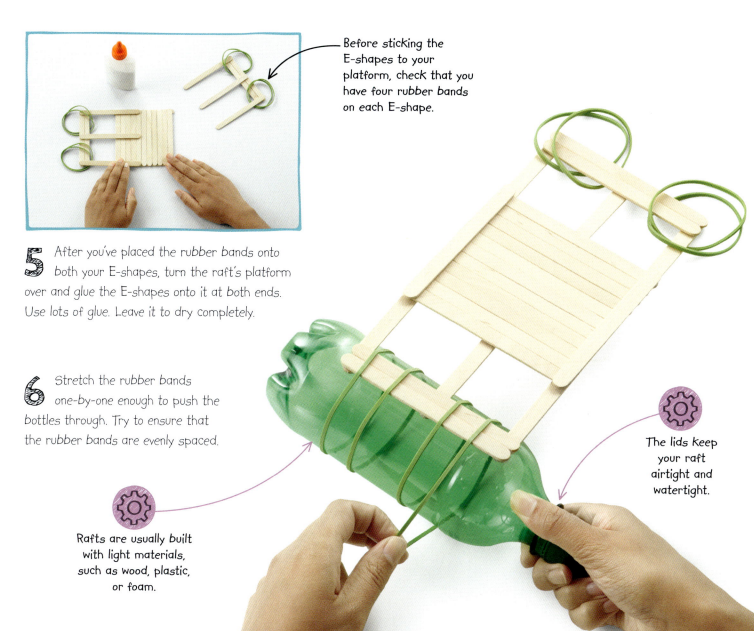

Before sticking the E-shapes to your platform, check that you have four rubber bands on each E-shape.

5 After you've placed the rubber bands onto both your E-shapes, turn the raft's platform over and glue the E-shapes onto it at both ends. Use lots of glue. Leave it to dry completely.

6 Stretch the rubber bands one-by-one enough to push the bottles through. Try to ensure that the rubber bands are evenly spaced.

Rafts are usually built with light materials, such as wood, plastic, or foam.

The lids keep your raft airtight and watertight.

8 Float your raft in the sink or bath, or even on a pond (make sure you have an adult with you). Gently place the bowl of pebbles on top of your raft's platform... can it take the load?

470g

7 Use scales to weigh the bowl and the pebbles, so you can see how heavy a load your raft is able to carry.

The strength of the join between the frame and platform might limit how heavy a load your raft can take – how can you make it stronger?

What would happen if the bottles were filled with water instead of air?

TAKE IT FURTHER

See how much weight your raft can support by experimenting with heavier loads. You could also adapt your raft to make a bridge or even a boat. To make a boat, add a sail to give it propulsion and a rudder underneath to help it steer a straight or curved path.

This large bowl of sand is heavier than the bowl of pebbles. What happens if you put it on your raft?

To support heavier loads, you could use bigger bottles or more bottles to make the raft more buoyant.

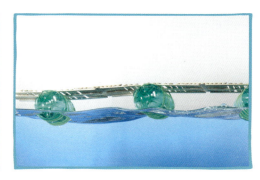

A pontoon is a bridge made by tying boats together. To turn your raft into a pontoon, simply add more platforms and bottles!

HOW IT WORKS

Whether or not an object floats depends on something called density. Density is how much mass (stuff) an object contains relative to its volume (the amount of space it takes up). When you place an object in water, the water pushes it upwards with a force called upthrust. If an object is more dense than water, the upthrust is too weak to support its weight, and the object sinks. That's why small, heavy things like coins and stones sink. Objects with low density, like your air-filled plastic bottles, are less dense than water, so the upthrust supports their weight and makes them float. Any object more dense than water will sink, and any object less dense will float.

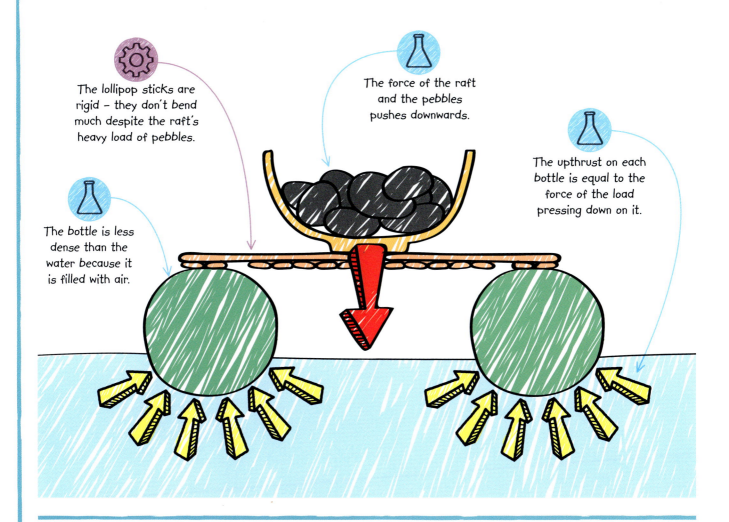

The lollipop sticks are rigid – they don't bend much despite the raft's heavy load of pebbles.

The force of the raft and the pebbles pushes downwards.

The upthrust on each bottle is equal to the force of the load pressing down on it.

The bottle is less dense than the water because it is filled with air.

REAL WORLD: ENGINEERING
SUBMARINES

Submarines can change their buoyancy – that's how they rise to the surface and dive deep. They have tanks that can be filled with water or air. At the surface, they take water into those tanks, increasing their density – so they sink. To rise up, air is pumped into the tanks, reducing their density and allowing them to float up to the surface.

STEM YOU WILL USE

• TECHNOLOGY: A turbine is a device for taking energy from moving gas or liquid.

• ENGINEERING: The energy of wind can come in handy for lifting heavy loads.

• MATHS: The bigger the blades of a turbine, the more energy they capture.

The shaft rotates as the blades move. This motion winds the string, which lifts the bucket.

WIND TURBINE

Have you ever seen huge wind turbines spinning slowly around? The blades are being pushed round by the energy of the wind. Inside each tower is an electrical generator, which converts wind energy into electrical energy to power homes, offices, factories, and schools. You can explore the engineering challenge of extracting energy from the wind by building your own wind turbine, using paper cups to make the blades.

The curved blades deflect the wind. This makes the blades move in the opposite direction.

HOW TO MAKE A
WIND TURBINE

Perhaps the most important feature of a wind turbine is the fact that the blades are at an angle, and so deflect the wind. This turbine's blades are made from paper cups, which are naturally curved, so they deflect the wind and work well. Take time to make your turbine, waiting for the glue to set where necessary.

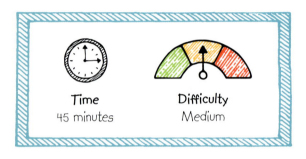

Time
45 minutes

Difficulty
Medium

WHAT YOU NEED

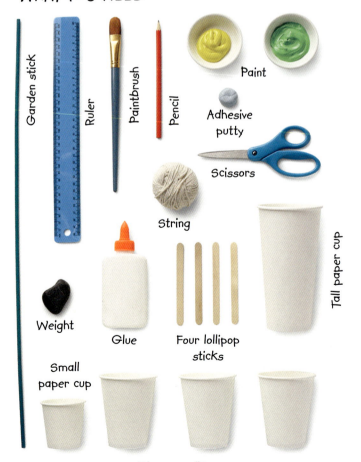

Garden stick

Ruler

Paintbrush

Pencil

Paint

Adhesive putty

Scissors

String

Tall paper cup

Weight

Glue

Four lollipop sticks

Small paper cup

Three medium paper cups

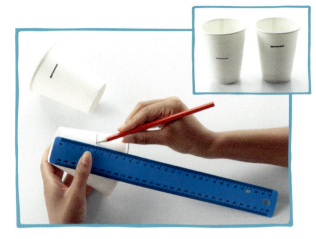

1 Take two medium cups and draw a line on the side of one 7 cm (2¾ in) from the bottom. Draw a line 5 cm (2 in) from the bottom of the other cup.

2 With a pair of scissors, carefully cut around the lines and remove the top parts of both cups. Discard the tops – recycle them if possible.

3 Using the sharp point of the pencil, pierce a hole at the centre of the base of each medium cup. Take care not to pierce yourself!

The shorter cup is upside down.

4 Insert the smaller of the two shortened cups into the larger one. Then squeeze glue into the joint to fix them together and wait for the glue to dry.

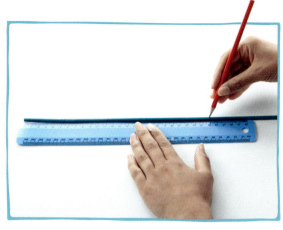

5 Make a pencil mark 25 cm (10 in) from one end of the garden stick.

Use scissors to score the stick.

6 Cut the garden stick at the pencil mark. Score the stick with scissors first, then bend it to snap it. Ask an adult if you find this tricky.

This stick performs the job of the shaft in a real wind turbine, which helps generate electricity.

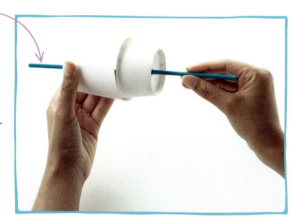

7 Slide the stick through the holes in the bases of the two joined cups.

8 Place the tall, uncut cup upside down and glue a lollipop stick to either side of the base, making sure each one reaches the same distance above the cup.

9 When the glue has dried, spread glue on the inside surfaces of the two lollipop sticks, near their ends.

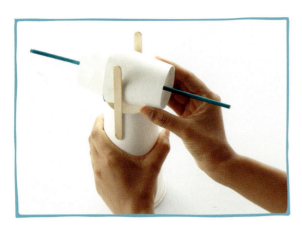

10 Place the joined cups with the stick through the centre between the lollipop sticks. Hold the cups in place while the glue dries.

11 To make the turbine blades, take your remaining medium-sized cup and carefully cut it in half down the side with a pair of scissors.

12 Cut each half in half again so you are left with four equal pieces. Cut the base of each quarter off and recycle these pieces.

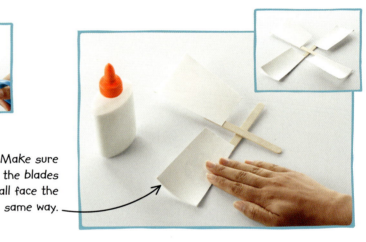

Make sure the blades all face the same way.

13 Place glue at the centre of a lollipop stick and stick it to another to form a cross. Glue the edges of your blades to the lollipop sticks.

On a real wind turbine, the blades on their shaft are able to swing around to face the wind.

14 Stick a piece of adhesive putty to the centre of the cross. The adhesive putty will secure the blades to the shaft.

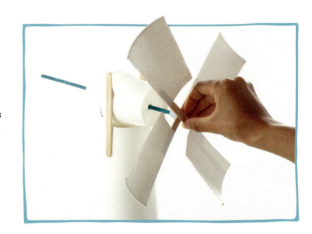

15 To attach the blades to the wind turbine, fix the adhesive putty to the end of the stick in the top of the turbine.

Hold some adhesive putty on the inside of the cup to stop you hurting yourself.

16 Take the small cup and make three equally spaced small holes around the top using a sharp pencil. This will be your load-lifting bucket.

The string will act as the bucket's handle.

17 To connect the bucket to the wind turbine, cut a 12 cm (5 in) piece of string. Thread the string through two of the holes in the bucket and tie a knot at either end to secure it in place.

18 Measure and cut a 40 cm (16 in) piece of string. Thread one end of the string through the third hole in the bucket, then tie it to the middle of the short piece of string.

The wind turbine's blades are curved, helping them to deflect the wind.

The garden stick acts as a pulley, drawing up the string as it turns.

To neaten up the end of the stick, cover it with adhesive putty.

19 Tie the free end of the long string to the garden stick. If you want to be sure it won't slip, secure it with a small piece of tape.

20 Now paint and decorate your wind turbine in your favourite colours and patterns.

The curved blades of this wind turbine transfer some of the kinetic (movement) energy in the wind into rotary (turning) motion in the blades.

Stick some modelling clay inside the base to act as a weight if the wind turbine keeps falling over.

21 Now you can try it out! Put weights in the bucket and see how quickly it rises when you expose the turbine to wind. If there's no wind, you could use a fan or a hairdryer. What happens to the bucket when the wind stops – does it fall back down or does friction hold it in place?

Put different weights in the bucket to see how much your wind turbine can lift.

TAKE IT FURTHER

If you have a fan with different speed settings, investigate how quickly the windmill lifts the bucket as the wind speed increases. Try making different kinds of turbine blade to see which turns fastest. To test your designs fairly, use a fan and make sure you have it on the same speed setting each time. Can you make your turbine lift heavier weights?

LARGER BLADES

To make larger blades for your model simply use a larger cup.

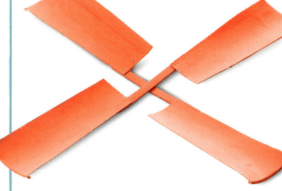

MORE BLADES

Make a cross out of three lollipop sticks and cut up two cups to make more blades.

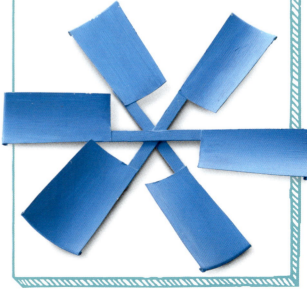

HOW IT WORKS

Wind is simply moving air. It is caused by uneven heating of Earth's surface by the Sun. In hot places, the warm air rises, causing cooler air to be drawn into the space left behind and so creating wind. For instance, land heats up under the Sun more quickly than the sea, so on sunny mornings a breeze often blows from sea to land. Wind turbines harness the kinetic energy of the wind to cause a generator inside the turbine to make electricity.

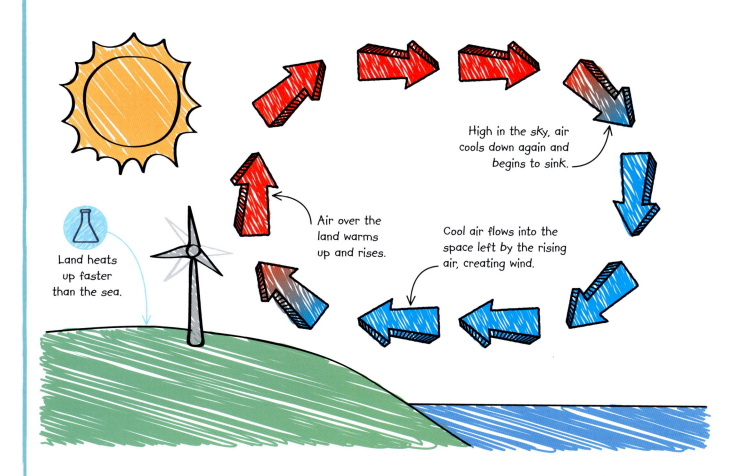

Land heats up faster than the sea.

Air over the land warms up and rises.

High in the sky, air cools down again and begins to sink.

Cool air flows into the space left by the rising air, creating wind.

REAL WORLD: TECHNOLOGY GENERATING POWER

Wind turbines use the kinetic energy in wind to generate power. Wind causes the turbine's blades to turn, which causes a generator in the main shaft of the turbine to spin. The generator produces electrical energy, which can be used to power things. Wind turbines produce the most energy in windy places, such as hilltops and on the coast.

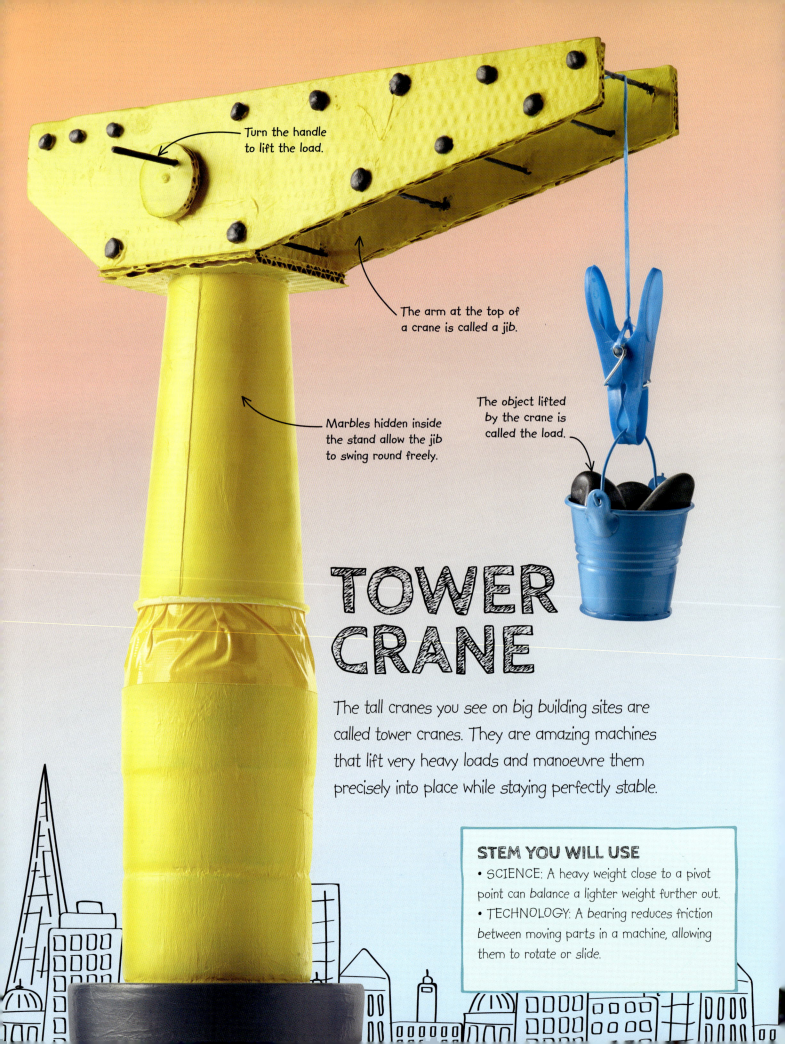

Turn the handle to lift the load.

The arm at the top of a crane is called a jib.

Marbles hidden inside the stand allow the jib to swing round freely.

The object lifted by the crane is called the load.

TOWER CRANE

The tall cranes you see on big building sites are called tower cranes. They are amazing machines that lift very heavy loads and manoeuvre them precisely into place while staying perfectly stable.

STEM YOU WILL USE

- SCIENCE: A heavy weight close to a pivot point can balance a lighter weight further out.
- TECHNOLOGY: A bearing reduces friction between moving parts in a machine, allowing them to rotate or slide.

HOW TO BUILD A
TOWER CRANE

You'll need patience for this build as there are lots of steps. The trickiest part is the jib – the horizontal arm on top of the crane. It's made of two pieces of cardboard held together by toothpicks. The crane's stand is made from heavier materials that keep the whole structure stable.

Time
1 hour and 30 minutes

Difficulty
Hard

Warning
This activity uses small marbles. Don't put them in your mouth.

WHAT YOU NEED

Small container

String

Bottle cap

Paint

Strong tape

Toothpicks

Modelling clay

Adhesive putty

Marbles

Two tall paper cups

Peg with spring

Scissors

Glue

Pencil

Paintbrushes

Wooden skewer

Large flowerpot and saucer

Sand

Large plastic bottle full of water

Ruler

Thick cardboard 40 x 30 cm (16 x 12 in)

Make sure the bottle fits inside the flowerpot.

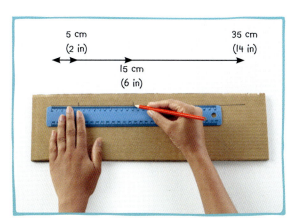

5 cm (2 in)   35 cm (14 in)

15 cm (6 in)

1 Use your ruler to draw a 35 cm (14 in) line on a piece of cardboard, near the top. Then make pencil marks 5 cm (2 in) and 15 cm (6 in) from the left end of the line.

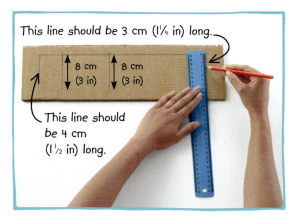

This line should be 3 cm (1¼ in) long.

8 cm (3 in)   8 cm (3 in)

This line should be 4 cm (1½ in) long.

2 Now add four vertical lines: a 4 cm (1½ in) line at the left end, two 8 cm (3 in) lines from your pencil marks, and a 3 cm (1¼ in) line on the right.

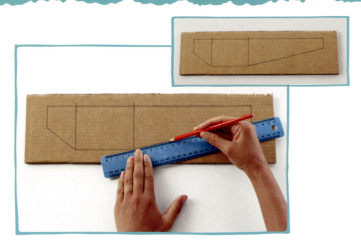

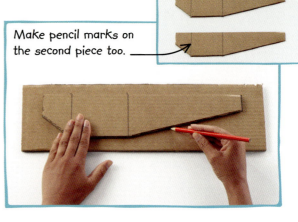

Make pencil marks on the second piece too.

3 Join up the ends of the four vertical lines. The shape you've drawn will form one side of the crane's jib.

4 With scissors, cut out the shape and then use it as a template to make an identical shape on another piece of cardboard.

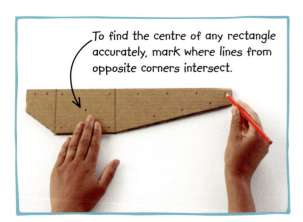

To find the centre of any rectangle accurately, mark where lines from opposite corners intersect.

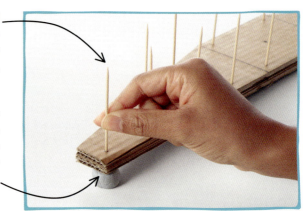

Be careful of the sharp ends of the toothpicks.

Place adhesive putty under the cardboard to protect the table and your fingers.

5 On one of the shapes, add a dot in the middle of the rectangular section. Then draw dots at regular intervals along the edges as shown above.

6 Stack the two pieces of cardboard together. Using the dots as a guide, carefully push toothpicks through both pieces of cardboard.

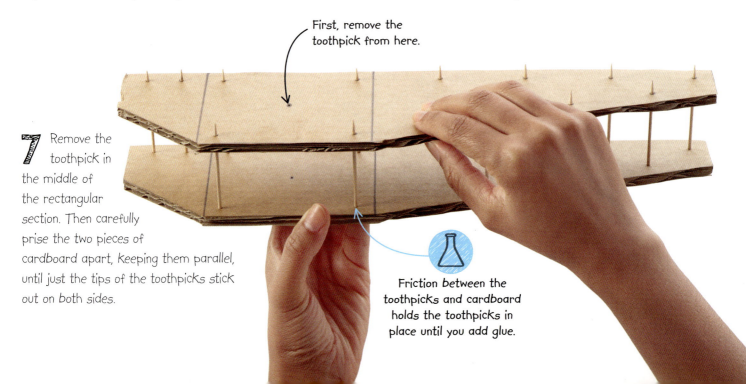

First, remove the toothpick from here.

7 Remove the toothpick in the middle of the rectangular section. Then carefully prise the two pieces of cardboard apart, keeping them parallel, until just the tips of the toothpicks stick out on both sides.

Friction between the toothpicks and cardboard holds the toothpicks in place until you add glue.

Before gluing, check you have removed the toothpick from the rectangular section.

8 Dab glue on the tips of the toothpicks. Do this first on one side and let the glue dry. Then turn the jib over and do the other side.

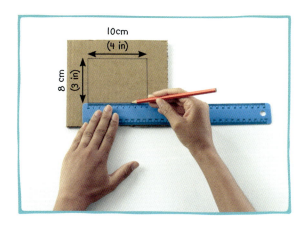

10cm (4 in)

8 cm (3 in)

9 To make the base of your jib, draw a rectangle on a small piece of cardboard that is 8 cm by 10 cm (3 in by 4 in).

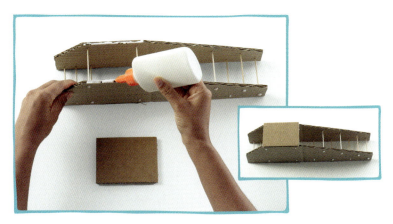

10 Turn your jib upside down and put glue on the short horizontal edges. Press the cardboard rectangle into place and let the glue dry.

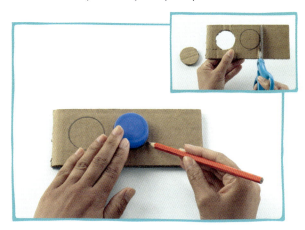

11 To make your crane's handle, draw two identical circles using the bottle cap as a guide. Then carefully cut out the circles.

One of the circles should have a second hole between its middle and edge.

Use adhesive putty to protect the surface.

12 Use a wooden skewer to poke a hole in the middle of each circle. Then, in one of the circles, make an extra hole halfway between the middle and the edge.

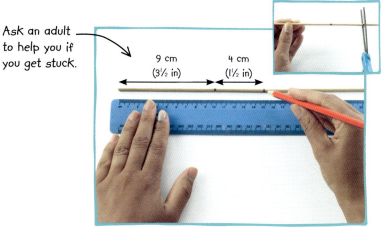

Ask an adult to help you if you get stuck.

9 cm (3½ in)   4 cm (1½ in)

13 Measure and cut the skewer into a 9 cm (3½ in) length and a 4 cm (1½ in) length, by first scoring it with scissors, then snapping it.

The longer piece goes into the centre.

The shorter piece goes into the hole at the side.

The skewer and cardboard form a device called a crank, which you will use to lift the load.

14 Push the two pieces of wooden skewer into the cardboard circle that has two holes. Glue them in position on both sides.

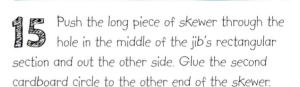

The second cardboard circle attaches to the other end of the skewer on the other side.

15 Push the long piece of skewer through the hole in the middle of the jib's rectangular section and out the other side. Glue the second cardboard circle to the other end of the skewer.

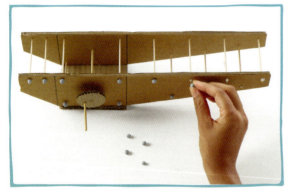

16 Cover both ends of every toothpick with a small ball of adhesive putty, to ensure that no sharp points poke out from the jib.

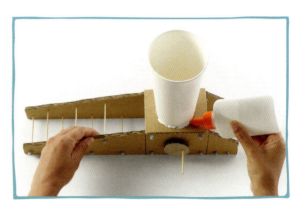

17 Turn the jib upside down and glue the bottom of one of the paper cups to the base. Wait for the glue to dry.

18 Paint your jib and paper cup. Use whatever colours you like. We've chosen yellow for the main structure and grey for the toothpicks and balls of adhesive putty.

Apply two coats of paint for a good finish.

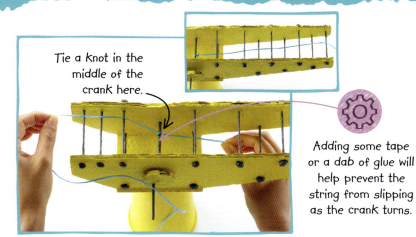

Tie a knot in the middle of the crank here.

Adding some tape or a dab of glue will help prevent the string from slipping as the crank turns.

19 Cut 1 m (3 ft) of string and tie one end to the middle of the crank. Thread the other end between the two rows of toothpicks, as shown.

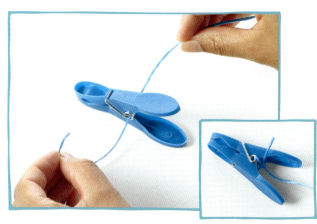

20 Carefully poke the long end of the string through the spring in the peg. Tie a knot to hold it in place.

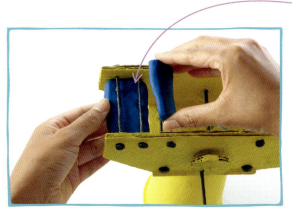

The slabs of modelling clay form a counterweight – a weight that helps balance the load.

21 Make two thick slabs of modelling clay and sandwich them together over the toothpicks at the rear of the jib.

22 Now paint the flowerpot, which will form the crane's heavy base.

23 Take the plastic bottle filled with water and paint it with two coats of paint.

The heavy, sand-filled base keeps the crane stable.

24 Stand the bottle in the flowerpot on top of the saucer and pack sand around it.

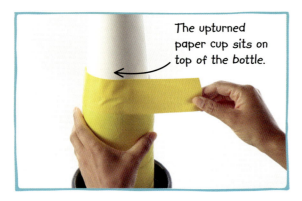

The upturned paper cup sits on top of the bottle.

25 Turn the second paper cup upside down, place it over the bottle, and secure in place with strong tape.

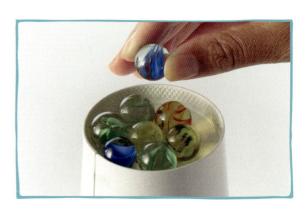

26 Place the marbles inside the lip of the base of the upturned cup. Make sure that there is enough room for the marbles to move a little.

Turn the crank handle to raise and lower the container.

Marbles between the cups act as bearings, reducing friction and allowing the jib to swing round.

Real cranes are anchored to a heavy concrete base for stability. The heavy base of your model does the same job.

27 Mount the crane's jib on the tower by placing the painted cup on top of the marbles. Attach the container with a load inside it to the peg and raise or lower it by turning the handle.

The load pulls downwards on one side of the crane, exerting a turning force, or torque, on the whole crane.

TAKE IT FURTHER

See how heavy a load your crane can lift without toppling over. Try threading the string so it hangs closer to the crane's tower – can the crane lift more now? What happens if you make the wheel of the crank handle bigger, so that your handle moves in a bigger circle? Why not try scaling up the design, so that you can lift a heavier load? Or see what happens if you increase or decrease the weight of the counterweight? Perhaps you could use skewers instead of toothpicks, and use a double thickness of cardboard, for extra strength.

To lift heavy loads, reposition the string so it hangs closer to the tower.

HOW IT WORKS

Tower cranes can lift huge loads without toppling because they can control how far along the jib the load is positioned. Any load pulls downwards on the jib, creating a turning force, or torque. The further along the jib a load is, the greater the torque (the torque equals the load's weight multiplied by its distance from the tower). Large loads are lifted close to the tower, and small loads are lifted further out. As a result, both produce a similar torque, which is roughly balanced by the counterweight. They don't need to be perfectly balanced because the crane is also anchored to the ground.

Distance A   Distance B

Weight A (counterweight)

Weight B (load)

The crane is perfectly balanced when weight B x distance B = weight A x distance A.

REAL WORLD: ENGINEERING CONSTRUCTION CRANES

In a real tower crane, a steel cable hangs from a mobile trolley that can move back and forth along the jib. By varying the position of the trolley, the operator can change the torque created by the load. In your crane, threading the string over different toothpicks does the same thing. A tower crane can lift up to about 20 tonnes – as much as 20 cars.

AUTOMATON

An automaton is a mechanical figure that appears to move of its own accord. In reality, automata are powered by hand, clockwork, or any source of moving energy – also known as kinetic energy. Automata date back more than 2,000 years and were often built to entertain audiences. In this project, you can make a shark automaton that swishes its tail and opens its jaws. These movements are controlled by devices called cams and cranks, which are found in many kinds of machine, including car engines.

The jaw moves up and down.

This wooden skewer forms a push rod – a straight piece that is pushed up and down.

Twisting this skewer round transfers energy to the cam, which transfers it to the shark's mouth, making it open and close.

This circular piece of cardboard is a cam. It rotates off-centre on the skewer, causing the push rod to move up and down.

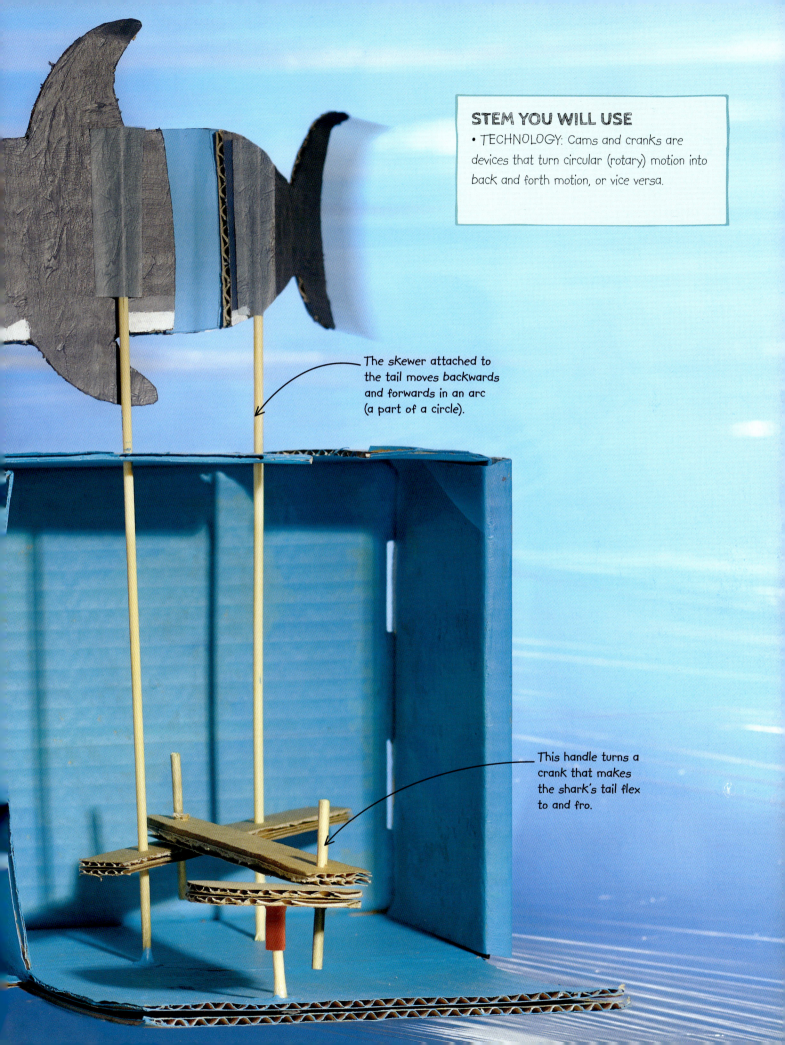

STEM YOU WILL USE
• TECHNOLOGY: Cams and cranks are devices that turn circular (rotary) motion into back and forth motion, or vice versa.

The skewer attached to the tail moves backwards and forwards in an arc (a part of a circle).

This handle turns a crank that makes the shark's tail flex to and fro.

HOW TO MAKE AN
AUTOMATON

This challenging build will take you a while. You'll need plenty of thick cardboard, as this project has lots of small pieces. You can still do this activity if you don't have a cardboard box exactly the same size as ours, but you may have to adjust some of the other pieces you cut.

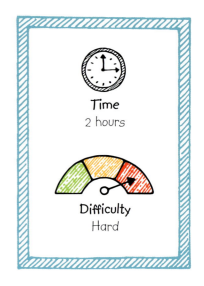

Time
2 hours

Difficulty
Hard

WHAT YOU NEED

Paint

Coloured tape

Scissors

Pencil

Paper straw

String

Adhesive putty

Paintbrushes

Ruler

Five wooden skewers

Glue

Paperclip

Coloured paper

Cardboard box
26 cm x 16 cm x 8 cm
(11 in x 6 in x 3 in)

Lots of thick cardboard

Double-sided tape

1 To make the base of your automaton, draw a rectangle 20 cm by 15 cm (8 in by 6 in) on a small piece of thick cardboard.

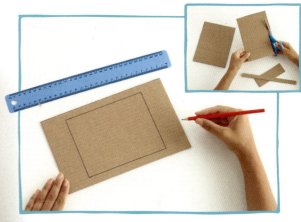

2 On another small piece of cardboard, draw a second rectangle 12 cm by 15 cm (5 in by 6 in). Then cut out both rectangles.

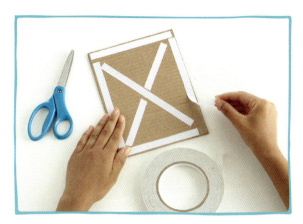

3 Apply double-sided tape across the middle and around the edges of the larger rectangle. Peel the protective strip off the tape.

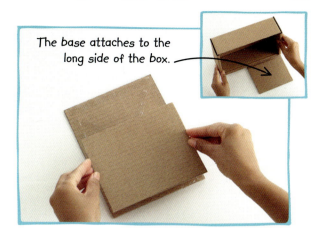

The base attaches to the long side of the box.

4 Stick the two rectangles together, as shown, leaving part of the large rectangle exposed. Place the long side of the box onto the exposed part.

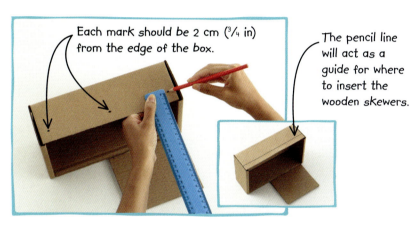

Each mark should be 2 cm (³/₄ in) from the edge of the box.

The pencil line will act as a guide for where to insert the wooden skewers.

5 On the top, make three marks 2 cm (³/₄ in) from the edge in the middle and at both ends. Draw a straight pencil line to join them.

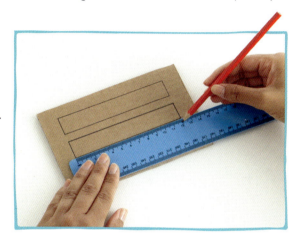

6 To make the mechanism for the automaton's right-hand section, draw two 12 by 2 cm (5 by ³/₄ in) rectangles on cardboard. Cut them out.

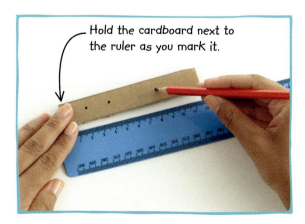

Hold the cardboard next to the ruler as you mark it.

7 Make three dots along the middle of one of the small rectangles, 2 cm, 4 cm, and 8 cm (³/₄ in, 1¹/₂ in, and 3 in) from one end.

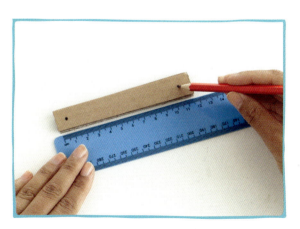

8 On the other small rectangle, make two pencil dots along the middle, 1 cm (¹/₂ in) from each end.

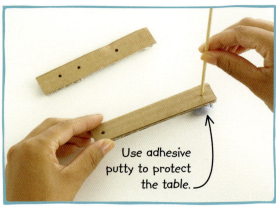

Use adhesive putty to protect the table.

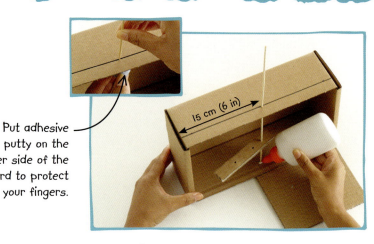

Put adhesive putty on the other side of the card to protect your fingers.

15 cm (6 in)

9 Using a wooden skewer, make holes in the dots you made on the small rectangles.

Ask an adult to help if you find this part tricky.

10 Push the skewer through the top of the box 15 cm (6 in) in from the left, then through the hole in the rectangle with three holes, as shown. Poke the skewer into the base of the box and glue it.

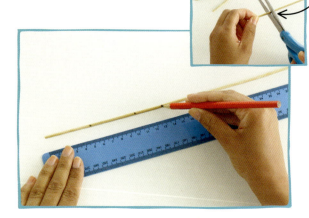

This is the 5 cm (2 in) piece of skewer.

11 Take another skewer and make marks 5 cm, 10 cm, and 13 cm (2 in, 4 in, and 5 in) along it. Use scissors to score and break it at each mark.

12 Push the 5 cm (2 in) piece of skewer through the middle hole. Then place a full-length skewer through the remaining hole.

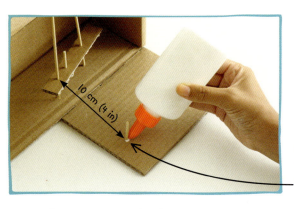

10 cm (4 in)

The distance between the skewer and pencil should be 6 cm (2½ in).

The handle will be placed on top of this piece of skewer.

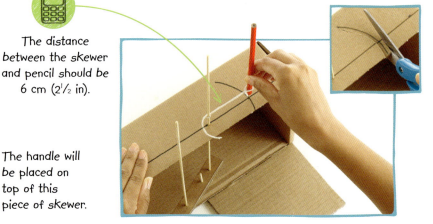

13 Push the 3 cm (1¼ in) piece of skewer into the base so that it is 10 cm (4 in) away from and in line with the skewer that goes through the top of the box. Add glue.

14 Use a short piece of string tied to a pencil to draw an arc around the skewer that goes through the top of the box. Cut a 1 cm (½ in) wide slit along the arc.

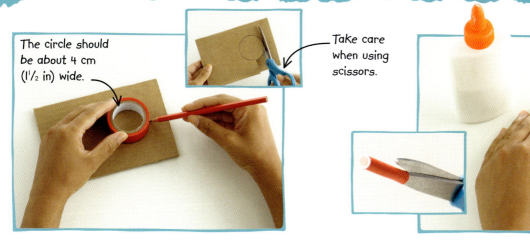

The circle should be about 4 cm (1½ in) wide.

Take care when using scissors.

15 To make the handle for the right-hand section of the automaton, draw round a roll of tape on cardboard to make a circle. Cut it out.

16 Cut a 4 cm (1½ in) length of straw. Cut four slits at one end and fold them out. Glue these flaps down onto the cardboard circle.

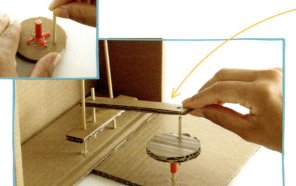

The small rectangle acts as a crank. It turns the handle's rotation movement into a back-and-forth motion.

17 Push the remaining 5 cm (2 in) piece of skewer into the handle close to the edge of the circle. Turn the handle over and place the straw over the small piece of skewer you stuck to the base. Then put the spare rectangle from step 9 over the two small pieces of skewer, as shown.

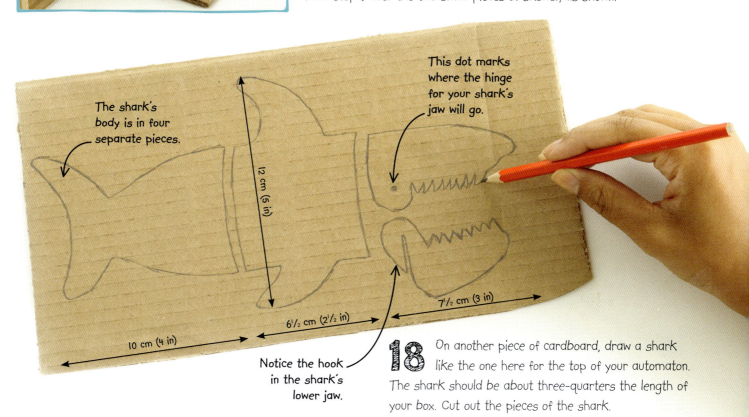

This dot marks where the hinge for your shark's jaw will go.

The shark's body is in four separate pieces.

12 cm (5 in)

Notice the hook in the shark's lower jaw.

10 cm (4 in)

6½ cm (2½ in)

7½ cm (3 in)

18 On another piece of cardboard, draw a shark like the one here for the top of your automaton. The shark should be about three-quarters the length of your box. Cut out the pieces of the shark.

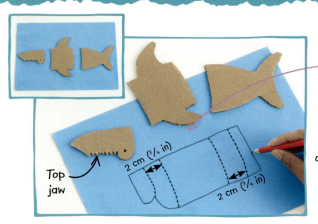

Top
jaw

2 cm (¾ in)

2 cm (¾ in)

This paper
backing will allow
the shark's body
to move freely
once it is attached
to the skewers.

Don't put
double-sided
tape in
the gaps.

19 Place the three shark pieces shown above on coloured paper, with gaps of about 2 cm (¾ in) between them. Draw around them and join the gaps to create the outline shown.

20 Cut out the paper shape. Attach the pieces of the shark's body to the paper using double-sided tape. Be sure to leave 2 cm (¾ in) gaps between the top jaw, the middle, and the tail.

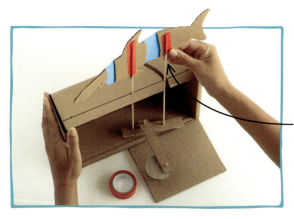

Attach the skewers
to the shark's body
using coloured tape.

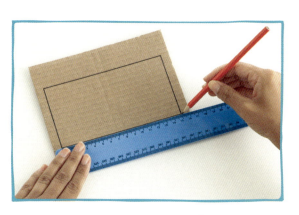

21 Use tape to attach the shark's body and tail to the two skewers that are sticking up from the box. Snip off any excess bits of skewer that stick out above the shark.

22 You now need to add a wall to divide your your automaton into two sections. To do this, measure and cut a rectangle that matches the depth and height of your box.

9 cm (3½ in)

This section will house
the mechanism for
your shark's jaw.

This circle will form
part of a cam – a
device that turns
circular motion into
to-and-fro motion.

The circle should
be about 3½ cm
(1½ in) wide.

23 Glue the rectangle of cardboard 9 cm (3½ in) from the left side of the box. Make sure it doesn't prevent the mechanism on the right from moving freely back and forth.

24 To make the mechanism for your automaton's left-hand section, draw a small circle on a piece of cardboard, using the inside of the coloured tape as a guide, and cut it out.

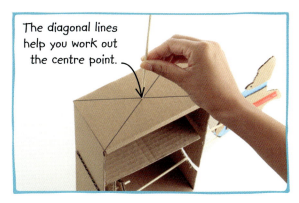

The diagonal lines help you work out the centre point.

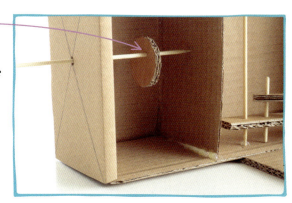

In order to make the cam work, the skewer is off-centre.

25 Turn the box on its right side and draw diagonal lines across the top end to find the centre. Push the pointed end of a skewer through the point where the diagonal lines meet.

26 Turn the box back on its base. Push the skewer through the circle about 1 cm (½ in) from its edge. Then gently push the skewer's tip through the cardboard wall.

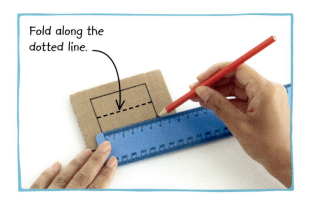

Fold along the dotted line.

This is a push rod. The cam pushes it up and down.

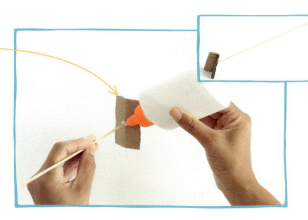

27 Now draw and cut out a 4 cm by 6 cm (1½ in by 2½ in) rectangle, and fold it in half lengthways.

28 Push a skewer through the centre of the folded cardboard rectangle so that it just pokes through. Add a dab of glue and let it dry.

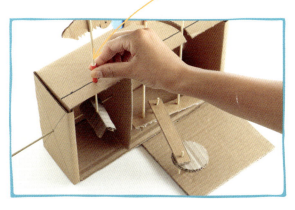

The straw acts as a bushing – a low-friction tube that allows a shaft to turn freely inside it.

This small circle will stop the lower jaw wobbling.

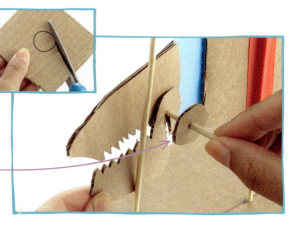

29 Make a hole on the pencil line that lines up with the middle of the jaw. Push a 5 cm (2 in) piece of straw through the hole, then insert the push rod by feeding it up through the straw.

30 To make the hinge for the jaw, cut out a cardboard circle 2 cm (¾ in) wide. Push a short piece of skewer through this and through the dot in the upper jaw. Hook the lower jaw in between.

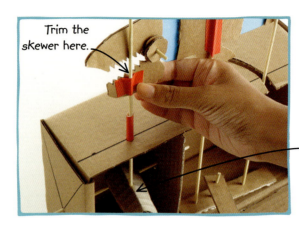

Trim the skewer here.

Rest this cardboard on the circular cam below.

31 Tape the push rod to the shark's lower jaw, making sure the folded piece of cardboard is resting on the cam inside the box. Snip off any excess bits of skewer.

32 To decorate your automaton, draw a fish onto a small piece of cardboard, and cut it out. Straighten a paperclip, tape one end to the fish, and stick the other into the top of the box.

33 Finally, paint your automaton as you like. To make your automaton work, turn the handle to swish the shark's tail and twist the skewer at the side of the box to make the jaw move up and down.

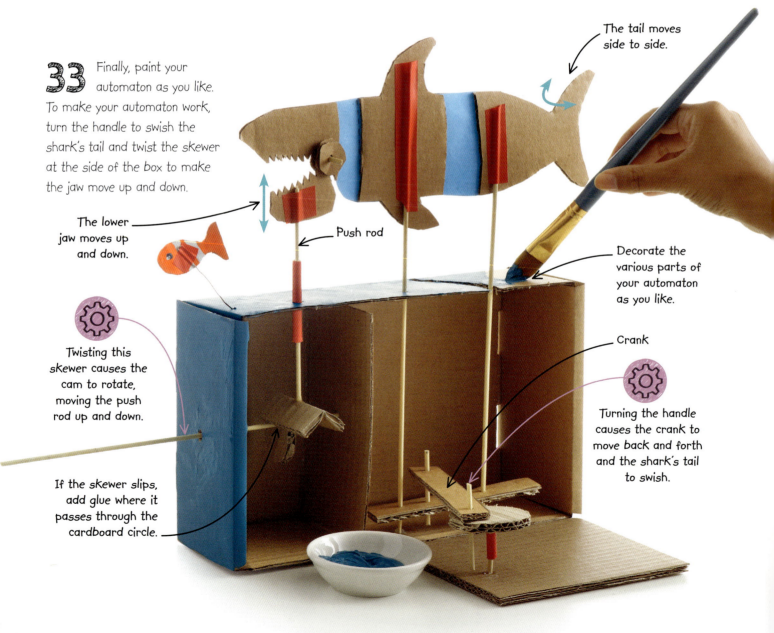

The tail moves side to side.

The lower jaw moves up and down.

Push rod

Decorate the various parts of your automaton as you like.

Crank

Twisting this skewer causes the cam to rotate, moving the push rod up and down.

Turning the handle causes the crank to move back and forth and the shark's tail to swish.

If the skewer slips, add glue where it passes through the cardboard circle.

HOW IT WORKS

When you twirl the skewer at the left side of the automaton, it turns the cam – the cardboard circle that is set off-centre on the skewer. The cam pushes a folded rectangle and the push rod up and down as it rotates, turning circular motion into up-and-down motion.

In the right-hand section the arm attached to the circle is a crank. As the handle turns, one end of the crank moves round with it, pivoting as it goes and pushing the other end in and out. A crank can turn rotation into to-and-fro motion or do the opposite, turning to-and-fro motion into rotation.

LEFT-HAND MECHANISM

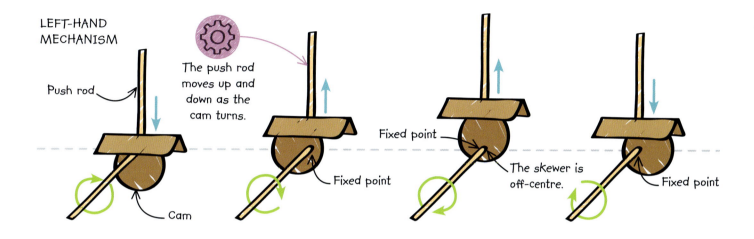

Push rod

The push rod moves up and down as the cam turns.

Fixed point

Cam

Fixed point

Fixed point

The skewer is off-centre.

Fixed point

RIGHT-HAND MECHANISM

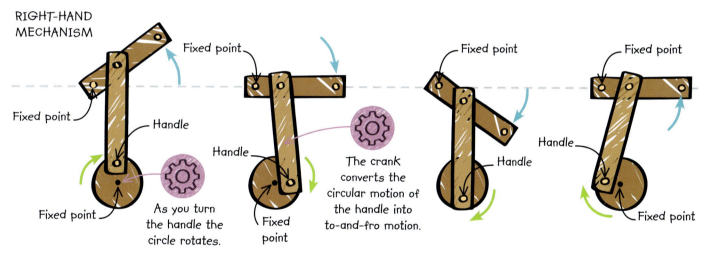

Fixed point

Handle

Fixed point

Fixed point

As you turn the handle the circle rotates.

Handle

Fixed point

The crank converts the circular motion of the handle into to-and-fro motion.

Fixed point

Handle

Fixed point

Handle

Fixed point

REAL WORLD: TECHNOLOGY
CAR ENGINE

Cranks and cams are very important components in most petrol- or diesel-powered car engines. Pistons push up or down, and cranks turn that motion into circular motion that turns the wheels. A set of cams on a shaft open and close valves that allow petrol or diesel vapour into the engine and exhaust gases out at just the right moments.

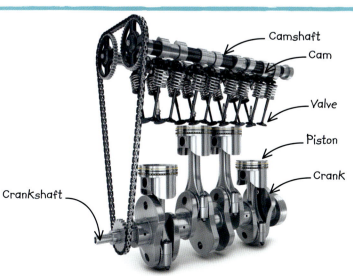

Camshaft

Cam

Valve

Piston

Crank

Crankshaft

SPEED TRIALS

Feel the whoosh as these rubber band racers zoom down the track. With just a few bits and pieces, you can build your own speed buggy and even customize it to boost its performance. Then time how long the racers take to complete a course, work out how fast they're going, calculate their average speeds, and tweak the design to improve your racer's speed.

Decorate your track with sticky white squares.

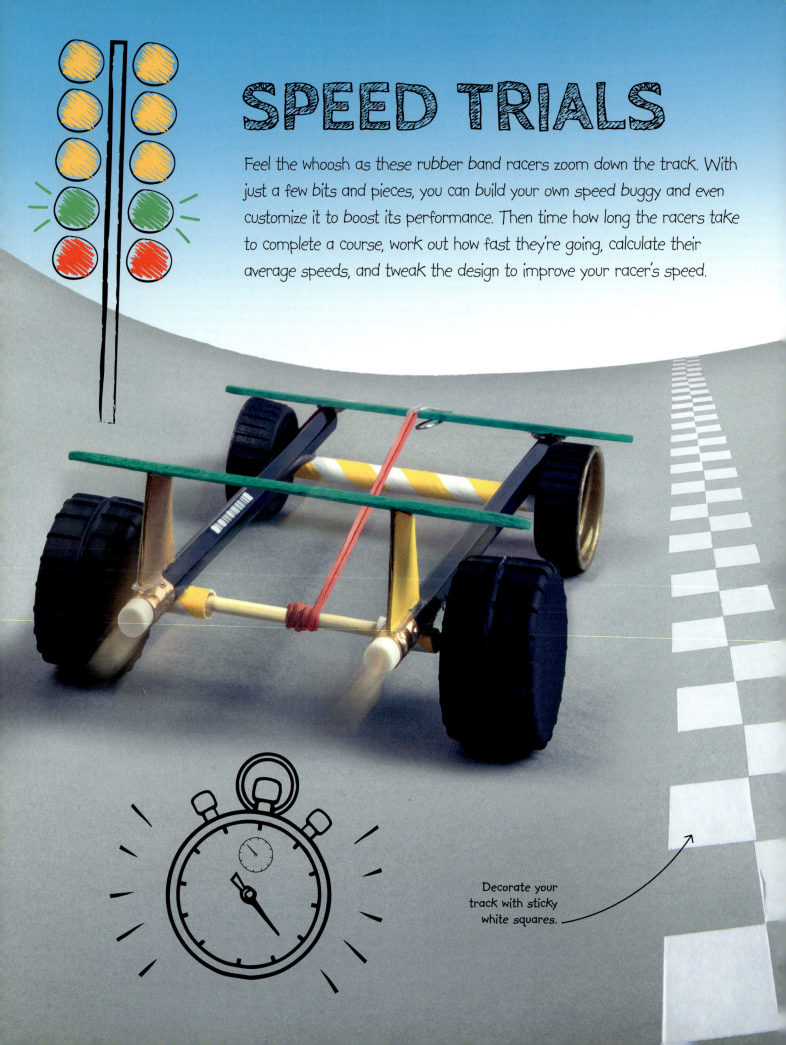

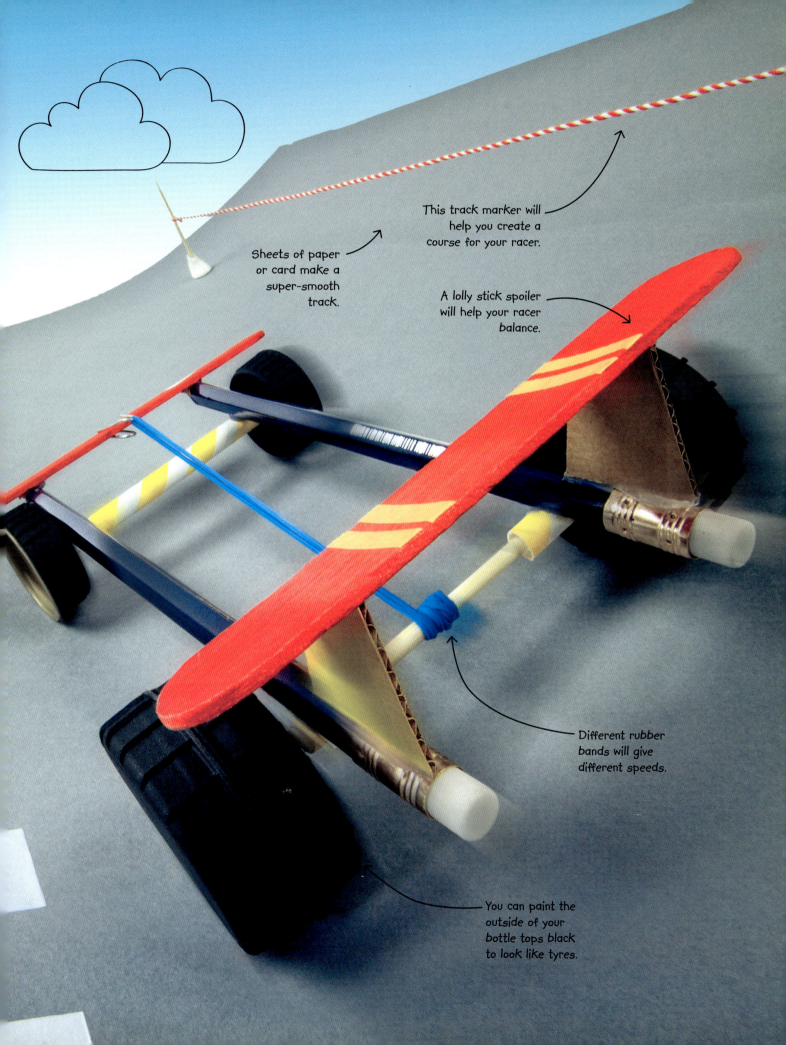

This track marker will help you create a course for your racer.

Sheets of paper or card make a super-smooth track.

A lolly stick spoiler will help your racer balance.

Different rubber bands will give different speeds.

You can paint the outside of your bottle tops black to look like tyres.

HOW TO MAKE A
RUBBER BAND RACER

The tension in a twisted rubber band stores energy that, when released, will speed the racer away. By making a track with a set distance, and timing your racer, you can calculate its average speed.

Time
45 minutes

Difficulty
Medium

STEM YOU WILL USE
• MATHS: An average is a number that represents a collection of numbers, and lies midway between them all.

WHAT YOU NEED

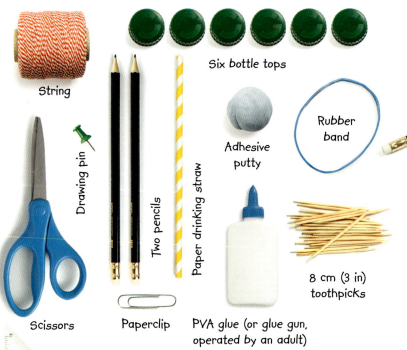

String

Six bottle tops

Drawing pin

Two pencils

Paper drinking straw

Adhesive putty

Rubber band

Scissors

Paperclip

PVA glue (or glue gun, operated by an adult)

8 cm (3 in) toothpicks

Make sure your pencils are parallel.

3 cm (1¼ in)

5 cm (2 in)

1 Place two pencils 5 cm (2 in) apart. Then place a lolly stick (or stiff card cut to size) at the end of the pencils and make two marks 3 cm (1¼ in) inside each end of the lolly stick.

Stiff card

Set square

Notebook

Tape measure

Stopwatch or smartphone

Two extra wide lolly sticks
11.5 x 1.7 cm
(4½ x ⅔ in)
(you can use card cut to size)

Hold the pencils in place until the glue sets.

Keep the pencils parallel.

2 Glue the tips of both pencils to the pencil marks. Keep the pencils parallel to each other.

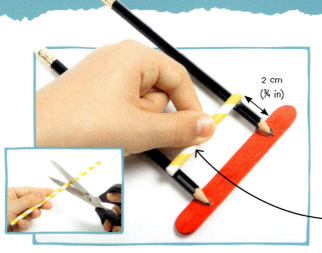

You could use a set square to check that the straw is perpendicular (at a right angle) to the pencils.

3 Cut a piece of straw to 6.5 cm (2½ in). Glue it to the underside of the pencils, 2 cm (¾ in) from the lolly stick. This will be the front of the racer.

2 cm (¾ in)

QUADRILATERALS

A quadrilateral is a four-sided two-dimensional (2D) shape. These shapes are all quadrilaterals.

Square

Kite

Irregular quadrilateral

Rhombus

Parallelogram

Trapezoid

Rectangle

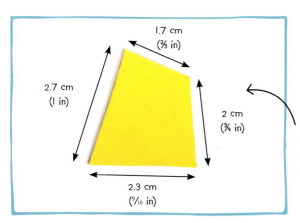

1.7 cm (⅔ in)

2.7 cm (1 in)

2 cm (¾ in)

2.3 cm (⁹⁄₁₀ in)

Don't worry if your measurements aren't precise.

4 To make the spoiler, draw a quadrilateral (a four-sided shape) on a piece of card. The length of the top edge should match the width of the lolly stick.

5 Make a second, identical quadrilateral and then attach one quadrilateral to the end of each pencil. The top of the quadrilateral should slope away from the end of the pencil.

Try to align the lolly stick so there is an equal amount of overhang on both sides.

6 Glue along the top of the two quadrilaterals and attach the second lolly stick to them to form the spoiler that will balance your racer.

The straw will hold a toothpick attached to the wheels.

FIND THE CENTRE OF A CIRCLE

Draw a line across the circle. Halfway along this line, measure a 90° angle and draw another line. The centre is halfway along this second line.

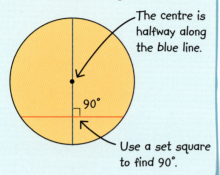

The centre is halfway along the blue line.

90°

Use a set square to find 90°.

7 Find and mark the centre of four bottle tops. Press a drawing pin through these caps to create a hole that will fit a toothpick.

Place a ball of adhesive putty inside the cap to ensure the pin doesn't mark your table when you press it through.

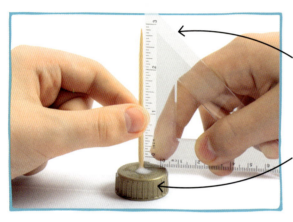

Use a set square to check your axle is perpendicular, otherwise your wheel may wobble!

Add some glue to the inside of the bottle top, too, for added strength.

8 Place glue on top of the hole and push in a toothpick so it is perpendicular to the bottle top. Repeat with another toothpick and bottle top.

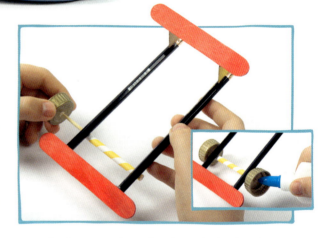

9 Push one of the axles through the length of straw. Use a big dollop of glue to attach a bottle top to the other end of the toothpick.

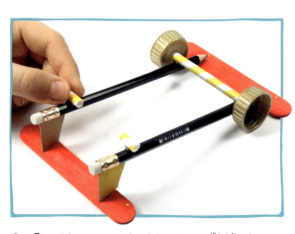

10 Measure and cut two 2 cm (¾ in) pieces of straw to hold the rear axle. Glue them to the rear of each pencil, in line with each other and parallel to the front axle.

The weight of the putty will help the rear wheels grip the track.

11 Place a large piece of adhesive putty inside one of the bottle tops and press another on top of it so they stick together. Next, thread the toothpick through the two pieces of straw.

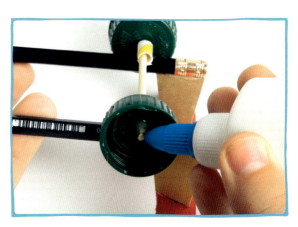

12 Push the second back wheel onto the toothpick and secure well with glue. Fill the cap with adhesive putty and press another top on.

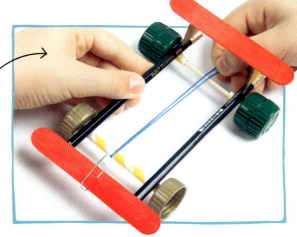

Make sure you hold the racer steady while you pull the band back.

13 Thread a long, thin rubber band onto a paperclip. Attach the paperclip to the front lolly stick, then stretch the rubber band towards the rear axle.

14 Wrap the rubber band over itself multiple times at the rear axle so that it holds itself in place. Don't let go of the wheels as you twist the band!

Decorate your racer with stickers.

You can paint your wheels black to look like rubber.

15 To make your racer go, wind up the rubber band by placing the car on the ground and pulling it backwards. Let go and watch it speed off!

16 To make the track markers, stick a toothpick into a large splodge of adhesive putty. Tie one end of the string to the toothpick.

17 Starting from the toothpick, measure out 1 m (39½ in) of string. Mark it with a pencil or pen, then measure out another 50 cm (20 in), and another. You will use this excess to lengthen the track.

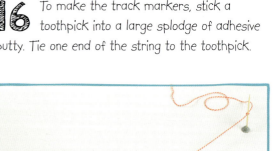

18 Place another toothpick in a blob of adhesive putty and tie the string to it at the first point that you marked. The length of string is your track.

Keep the string taut so you know the length of the track is accurate.

19 Set your racer down just before the start of the track and pull it back to wind it up. Prepare your stopwatch by setting it to zero. You could ask a friend to help by being the timekeeper.

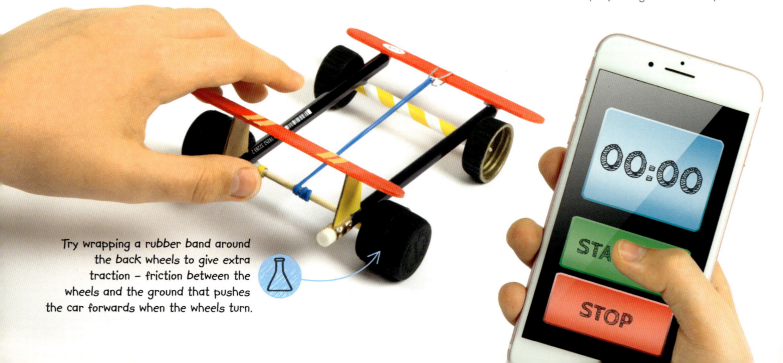

Try wrapping a rubber band around the back wheels to give extra traction – friction between the wheels and the ground that pushes the car forwards when the wheels turn.

20 Release the racer and at the same moment start the stopwatch. Stop the stopwatch as soon as the racer passes the finish.

Distance = Speed x Time

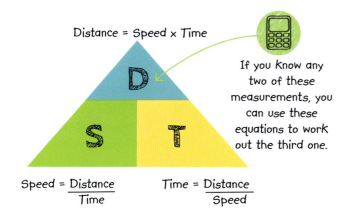

D

S   T

Speed = Distance / Time

Time = Distance / Speed

If you know any two of these measurements, you can use these equations to work out the third one.

21 Calculate your racer's speed by dividing the distance it travelled by the time it took to get there. If your racer completes a 60 cm (23⅓ in) course in 3 seconds, it travels at 20 cm per second (8 in/s).

You can calculate the average by dividing the total of the three tests by the number of tests.

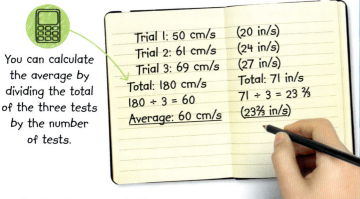

Trial 1: 50 cm/s   (20 in/s)
Trial 2: 61 cm/s   (24 in/s)
Trial 3: 69 cm/s   (27 in/s)
Total: 180 cm/s   Total: 71 in/s
180 ÷ 3 = 60   71 ÷ 3 = 23 ⅔
Average: 60 cm/s   (23⅔ in/s)

22 To get a reliable measure of your racer's speed, you need to take an average of several time trials.

TAKE IT FURTHER

To find out more about your racer's performance, try changing a single element (a variable) of the test while keeping everything else the same. What happens to the results?

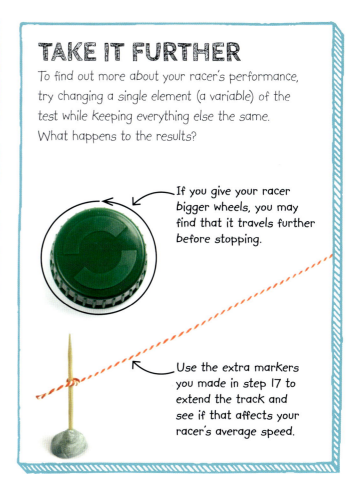

If you give your racer bigger wheels, you may find that it travels further before stopping.

Use the extra markers you made in step 17 to extend the track and see if that affects your racer's average speed.

REAL WORLD: MATHS
USING AVERAGES TO IMPROVE

If you only measure something once, you might get an unexpected or unlikely result. Finding an average means you can be more confident that your measurement is consistent and accurate. Formula One engineers use averages of several time trials to work out how to tweak and improve their team's performance.

LIQUIDS AND REACTIONS

Getting to know the properties of everyday liquids such as water and oils is a great way to learn about science. In this chapter, you'll turn your kitchen, and maybe even your garden, into a chemistry lab. You'll investigate how water wears away soil and sediments in nature, as well as how tornadoes work. Experiment with chemical reactions using a variety of household substances to make an erupting volcano and gooey slime!

STEM YOU WILL USE

- SCIENCE: Plants only need water, air, and light to grow.
- TECHNOLOGY: Hydroponics is the technique of growing plants quickly without needing to use soil.

The leaves reach upwards in search of light, which the plant needs to make food to help it grow.
The roots eventually grow down towards the water.
250 ml
200
150

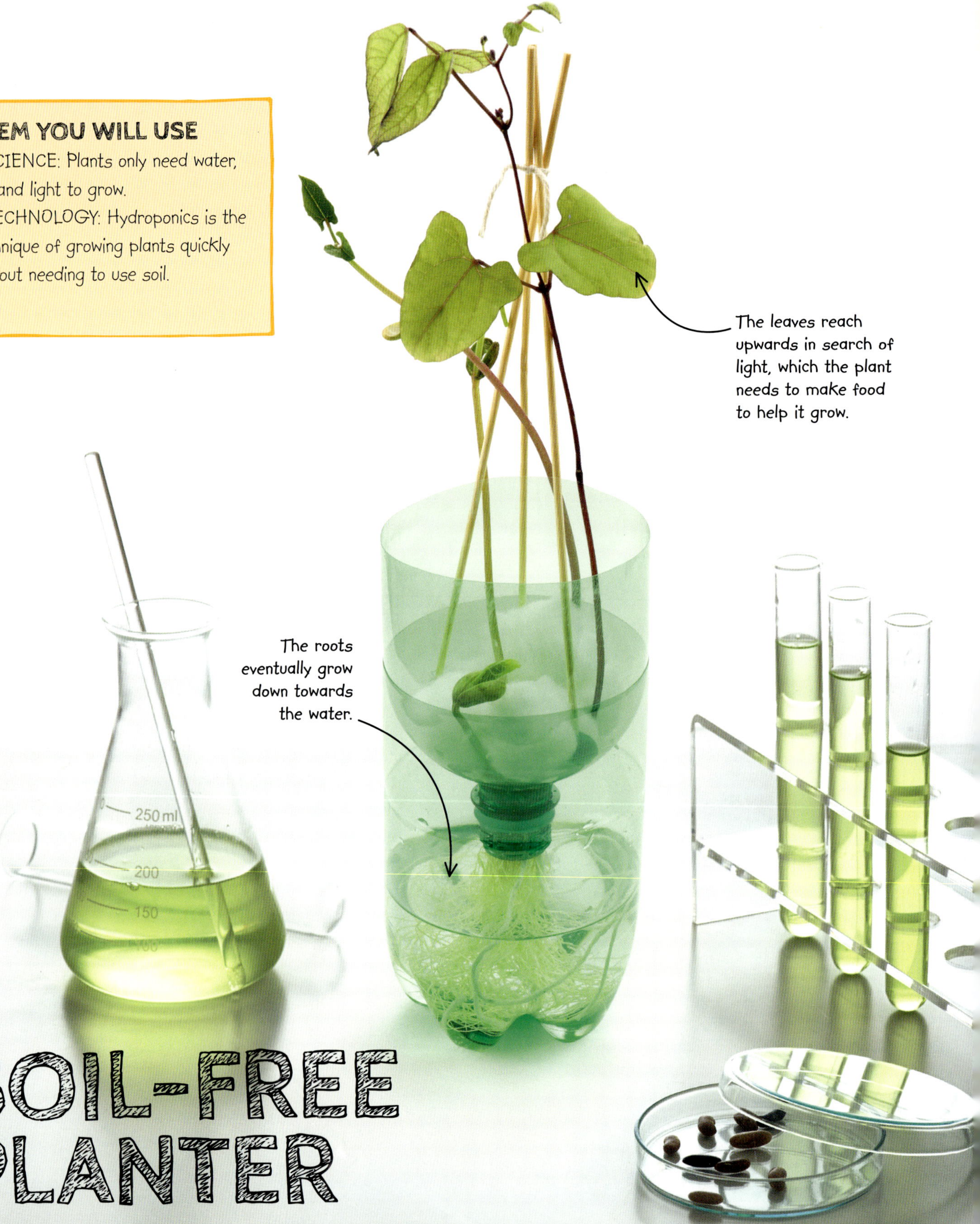

SOIL-FREE PLANTER

How would you grow plants if you were on a long space mission, and your ship had no room for a garden? You'd use a technique called hydroponics, in which plants grow without any soil. Here, you can try it for yourself.

HOW TO MAKE A
SOIL-FREE PLANTER

This planter is easy to make, and it can be constructed mostly from simple household items. The bean seeds you plant will take a few days to germinate (begin sprouting roots and a shoot), and a week or two to grow into small plants.

Time
30 minutes plus growing time

Difficulty
Medium

WHAT YOU NEED

Modelling clay

String

Scissors

Bean seeds

Wooden skewers

Cotton wool balls

Large plastic bottle

Jug of water

1 Cut five pieces of string about as long as the bottle. Four will soak up water to feed the plants and one will tie the wooden skewers together to make a tripod to support the growing plants.

Ask an adult to help if you get stuck.

2 Use the scissors carefully to cut a 5 cm (2 in) section from the middle of the bottle. Keep the top and bottom, and recycle the middle section.

3 Place the top section upside down in the base section. This provides a platform for the seeds, and it stops the water evaporating.

Fill the planter with water up to this point, just below the neck.

The wet string will bring water to the growing seeds.

4 Pour water into the planter so it fills the bottom almost up to the bottle's neck. The water should be about 10 cm (4 in) deep.

5 Feed four of the pieces of string down through the opening of the bottle, but leave a few centimetres of each string in the top section.

6 Put several cotton wool balls into the top of the planter, then drop a few bean seeds onto the cotton wool.

Be careful of the skewer's pointed end.

7 To make a tripod that will support the stems of the plants as they grow, put a blob of modelling clay on the pointed end of each wooden skewer.

8 Stand the three skewers on end and bring the tops together so they cross. Use the final piece of string to tie them together, to make a tripod.

9 Place the tripod on top of the cotton wool, and put the planter in a bright place.

The tripod supports the stems as the plants grow taller.

The cotton wool balls are damp because water has soaked through the string.

The cotton wool absorbs water because it is porous, meaning it contains thousands of tiny air-filled holes.

The roots will grow down into the water within one or two weeks.

10 The seeds should germinate after a few days. After a few weeks, transfer your plants to a pot with soil, or ask an adult to add fertilizer to the water, so the plants can flourish.

HOW IT WORKS

Water from the bottom of the planter soaks up through the strings and wets the cotton wool. The seeds grow roots and a shoot when they absorb water. Water, air, and light are all a plant needs to start growing – that's why this plant can grow without any soil. A special chemical in the roots, called auxin, helps to direct them downwards so that they grow towards the water. Auxin makes a root grow more slowly on one side, causing it to bend in the direction of the force of gravity.

There is more auxin in the underside of the root, because of gravity – so that side grows more slowly.

Bean seed

Root

Auxin

Once the root is pointing straight downwards, the auxin on both sides equalizes, and the root continues growing straight down.

REAL WORLD: SCIENCE
AQUAPONICS

Some plants are grown in hydroponic tanks, where they are fed water containing the nutrients, normally found in soil, that they need to grow quickly and healthily. Aquaponics, a type of hydroponics, feeds plants with nutrients from the waste products of fish kept in tanks. The fish provide food for the plants, and the plants filter the water for the fish.

Stick coloured pencils through a bag full of water without spilling a drop!

STEM YOU WILL USE
- SCIENCE: Salty water is more dense than fresh water.
- TECHNOLOGY: Kitchen bags are made of a strong material called polythene.

WHAT IS WATER?
Water is made of extremely tiny particles called water molecules. These molecules are so small that even a drop of water is made of trillions and trillions of them. In liquid water, the molecules move around each other freely, which is why water flows. But water molecules also cling to each other, which is why you see droplets if you spill some water.

WONDERFUL WATER

We use water every day – to wash, cook, and drink, to water plants, and to swim in. It fills Earth's rivers, lakes, and oceans, and we often see it fall as rain – so we're all familiar with how water feels and behaves. Yet water can still surprise us, as these three activities demonstrate. You'll need to do these experiments outside, or at least over a kitchen sink – you might get wet!

Learn about density with these colourful jars of saltwater.

When these pins are pulled out, what do you think will happen?

HOW TO MAKE A
WATERTIGHT WONDER

Here's an amazing science trick that looks like magic: stick pencils right through a plastic bag filled with water... without any of the water leaking out! But do this activity outside because the water will spill when you pull the pencils out. The tricky part is pouring the water into the kitchen bag, so ask someone if they can hold the bag open for you.

Time
15 minutes

Difficulty
Easy

WHAT YOU NEED

Clear kitchen bag

Several coloured pencils

Jug of water

1 Set the bag on a flat surface, then slowly and carefully fill it nearly to the top with water. Ask someone to hold the bag open for you if you need.

2 Seal the top of the bag tightly and securely, trying not to spill any water.

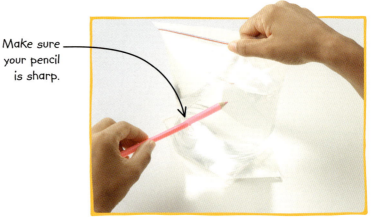

Make sure your pencil is sharp.

3 Holding the bag at the top with one hand, push a pencil, sharpened end first, through the bag in one smooth movement.

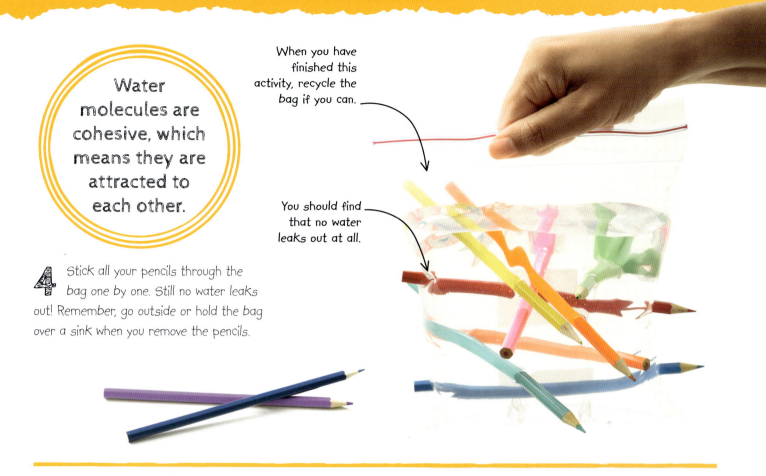

Water molecules are cohesive, which means they are attracted to each other.

When you have finished this activity, recycle the bag if you can.

You should find that no water leaks out at all.

4 Stick all your pencils through the bag one by one. Still no water leaks out! Remember, go outside or hold the bag over a sink when you remove the pencils.

HOW IT WORKS

Kitchen bags are made of polythene, a strong but flexible material. When the pencil makes a hole through it, the polythene wraps tightly around the pencil, but leaves a tiny gap – a hole through which water could escape. Water molecules cling together, so if a hole is small enough, the clinging force between the water molecules near the hole is strong. If it's stronger than the push from the water molecules inside, the water won't escape. Make the hole much bigger and the molecules can't hold back the pressure from inside, and the water leaks out.

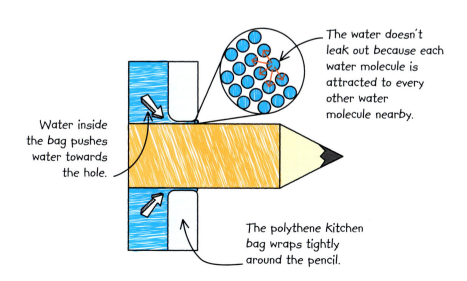

The water doesn't leak out because each water molecule is attracted to every other water molecule nearby.

Water inside the bag pushes water towards the hole.

The polythene kitchen bag wraps tightly around the pencil.

REAL WORLD: SCIENCE
WATER DROPLETS

The way water molecules pull together explains why water forms round droplets whenever it can. Without a strong pull of gravity, water droplets are perfectly round and hang in the air, like this droplet hanging in the air in the International Space Station.

HOW TO MAKE
SALTWATER JARS

In this activity, you will add salt to a cup of water until no more will dissolve. Adding salt increases the density of the water because you've packed more mass (stuff, or "matter") into the same volume (how much space the water takes up). Mixing the salty water with pure water in two different ways will give surprising results.

Time
15 minutes

Difficulty
Easy

WHAT YOU NEED

Two cups of water

Red food colouring

Blue food colouring

1/2 cup of salt

Spoon

Two glass jars

1 Pour *blue* food colouring into one of the plastic cups of water. Stir it with the spoon until the water is completely blue.

2 Pour red food colouring into the other cup of water and use the spoon to stir it.

Add salt until no more dissolves.

3 Add salt to the red water and stir it to help it dissolve. You've added enough salt when no more will dissolve.

4 Pour half the blue non-salty water into one of the glass jars, and half the red salty water into the other.

5 Now it's time to top up the jar containing *blue* water. So you don't disturb it, slowly add the rest of the *red* water into the jar by pouring it over the back of the spoon.

6 Carefully pour the rest of the *blue* water onto the back of the spoon and into the jar containing the *red* water.

7 Let the two jars stand for a while. You should see that in one jar the two colours mix together, but in the other jar the colours remain separate.

HOW IT WORKS

Adding salt to the red water hardly changes its volume, but it does add lots of mass, making it denser than the *blue* non-salty water. When the denser red water is poured on top of the *blue* water, it sinks through it and the two colours mix. When you pour the other way round – the red water before blue – the blue water floats on top because it has been placed on a liquid with a higher density.

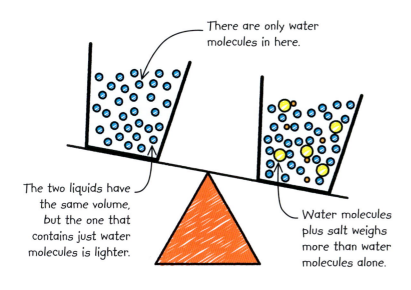

There are only water molecules in here.

The two liquids have the same volume, but the one that contains just water molecules is lighter.

Water molecules plus salt weighs more than water molecules alone.

REAL WORLD: SCIENCE
UNDERWATER LAKES

In this picture, the diver is swimming in a lake of very salty water – but that lake is underwater! Just as happened in the activity, the salty water stays at the bottom *because* it is more dense than the fresh water above it. Salty water is called brine, and underwater lakes of salty water are called brine pools.

HOW TO MAKE A
PIN BOTTLE

Learn how to make water defy gravity! You can make holes in a full bottle of water without the water leaking out, as long as the cap stays firmly closed. This simple but surprising activity lets you explore the forces of water pressure and air pressure. Make sure you recycle the bottle after you finish the experiment.

Time
15 minutes

Difficulty
Easy

WHAT YOU NEED

Bottle full of water

Pins

1 Take your bottle full of water and poke a pin carefully through the bottle near the bottom, leaving the pin in place.

Water can't escape because the pins block the holes they made.

2 Add more pins, pushing them straight in, not at an angle. You can put the pins wherever you like. We put them in a line near the bottom of the bottle.

Does any water leak out?

3 Now for the tricky bit. Carefully remove the pins one by one. Pull them straight out, not at an angle, so that the holes they leave behind are small and round.

Some water may begin to escape, but tiny air bubbles leak in, replacing the water lost.

4 Once all the pins are out, watch the bottle for a few moments. You should find that almost no water escapes, despite the fact that there are holes in the bottle.

Atmospheric pressure stops the water streaming out.

5 Try to do this step over a sink or outside, if you can, as it's messy. Unscrew the bottle's cap. Water will start pouring out through the holes!

What happens when you make the holes vertically above each other instead of horizontally alongside each other?

Water streams out, pushed down by the water above.

HOW IT WORKS

There are two forces acting on the water at the bottom of the bottle, just inside the holes. Firstly, there is atmospheric pressure – the push of the air outside the bottle. Secondly, there is the force of the water at the top of the bottle, which eventually pushes the water at the bottom through the pin holes. Atmospheric pressure is enough to stop the water escaping through the holes... until you unscrew the cap. When the cap is removed, air rushes into the bottle. This air pushes down on the top of the water, which causes it to start leaking out.

CAP ON THE BOTTLE

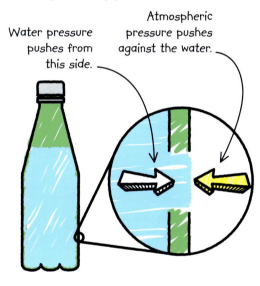

Water pressure pushes from this side.

Atmospheric pressure pushes against the water.

CAP OFF THE BOTTLE

When you unscrew the cap, air rushes into the bottle, pushing down on the water.

Water streams out of the pin holes – that's why it's best to do this outside!

EROSION BOTTLES

Soil is more than a place for plants to grow: it holds the nutrients and water that plants need. We depend on soil, too, because we need the plants that grow in it. Not only do plants produce the oxygen we breathe and the food we eat – we also use them to make shelter, clothes, and medicines. This experiment shows how unprotected soil can be washed away by rain, causing damage to the environment, and it also reveals how the plants dependent on soil to survive can help protect it.

The water has carried particles from the soil.

STEM YOU WILL USE
• SCIENCE: As water flows through the land, it carries soil with it – a natural process known as soil erosion, but plant roots can bind the soil together, preventing water from eroding the land.

Soil is made of tiny pieces of broken rock, plus the remains of long-dead plants and animals.

The grass roots hold on to the soil.

The water is clear because very little soil has been washed away.

HOW TO MAKE
EROSION BOTTLES

This dramatic experiment is easy to do, but you will need to have some patience. Start setting it up at least a week in advance, to give the grass time to grow in one of the bottles. When you actually run the experiment, it's best to do so outside if you can.

Time
30 minutes plus growing time

Difficulty
Medium

WHAT YOU NEED

Three plastic cups

Felt-tip pen

Pencil

String

Adhesive putty

Grass seeds

Scissors

Watering can

Mulch

Three large plastic bottles

Soil

Use a ruler if you find it hard to draw straight lines.

1 Draw a large rectangle on one bottle with the felt-tip pen. You need to make the hole big enough to put soil and then water into the bottle.

2 Cut along your lines and remove the rectangle shape you drew from the bottle. An adult can help you. Recycle the piece of plastic you remove.

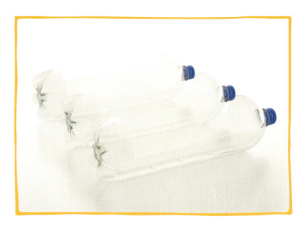

3 Repeat the previous steps for the other two bottles, so you have three bottles just the same. Put two of the bottles to one side for now.

4 Put a layer of soil a few centimetres deep into one of the bottles. The level of the soil should be just below the lid of the bottle.

5 Sprinkle the grass seeds onto the soil, then wash your hands.

Don't add so much water that the soil becomes waterlogged.

6 Using your watering can, pour water over the grass seeds. Use enough to make the soil damp.

7 Leave the bottle in a place where it will get lots of sunlight, and where it won't get too cold. Add a little water each day to stop the soil drying out. After a week or so, your grass should have grown.

8 Once the grass has grown, you can prepare your other two bottles. Add about the same amount of soil to them as you put in the first bottle.

Mulch can include fallen leaves, straw, dried grass, and twigs.

9 Leave one of the bottles with just soil. Into the other bottle, place a layer of mulch on top of the layer of soil. Now wash your hands.

Use a piece of adhesive putty to protect the table.

This bit is fiddly, so you might want to ask an adult for help.

10 Now you need to make three mini buckets. Near the top of each plastic cup, make two small holes opposite each other using the sharp end of the pencil. Put some adhesive putty underneath, before making the hole, to protect the table.

11 Cut three lengths of string, each about 20 cm (8 in) long. Thread one end of a piece of string through one of the holes in the cup and tie a knot in it so it will not come back through. Then do the same in the hole on the other side, to make a handle.

12 Make string handles for your other two cups. You should check that they are strong enough to hold the cups once they are full of water.

13 Hang your buckets from the neck of your bottles. You are now ready to carry out the experiment. It might get messy, so be sure to do this part outside. Remove your bottle lids, then slowly pour water over each of the three bottles. The water will start to trickle through the soil into the buckets.

HOW IT WORKS

Roots are crucial to a plant's survival. The roots grow down into the soil and absorb water into tubes that extend right up into the stem and leaves of the plant, above ground. Each grass plant has roots of many different sizes – from tiny fibrous roots up to bigger ones almost as big as the stem. The fibrous roots push out in all directions in the soil, not just downwards. The result is a complicated web of roots that holds the soil firmly in place. That's why the water runs out almost completely clear from the bottle with the grass growing in it.

When you have finished the experiment, lift the soil out of the grassy bottle by pulling on the grass. You'll see that the roots keep the soil in place.

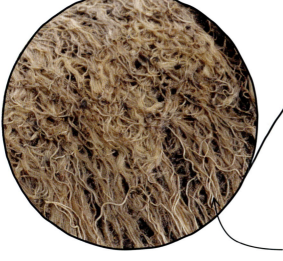

You will be able to see hundreds of tiny roots twisting their way through the soil. It is these roots that prevent the soil from being eroded.

Try squeezing the grassy soil – you'll be surprised how much water is still in it.

REAL WORLD: SCIENCE
SOIL EROSION

If it is left unprotected, soil can be swept away during heavy rains, taking with it the nutrients that plants need to grow. As this image taken from space shows, soil runs off into rivers and can be harmful to fish and other wildlife living there. Planting grass and trees along riverbanks can prevent soil erosion as they hold on to the soil, keeping rivers cleaner. Farmers can protect the soil they need for their crops and animals with a layer of mulch (dead leaves) or the roots of plants.

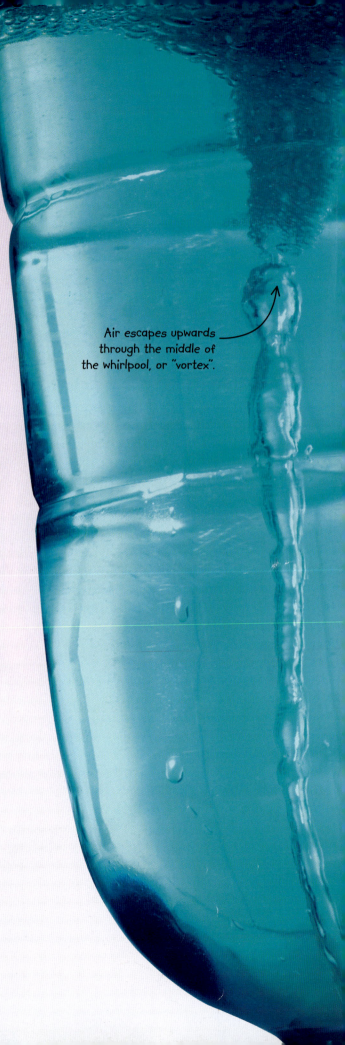

Air escapes upwards through the middle of the whirlpool, or "vortex".

SPINNING WHIRLPOOL

When water empties down a plughole or an oar is pulled through water, you'll see spiralling, funnel-shaped whirlpools, or "vortices". These twisting currents also form in lakes, rivers, and the sea, where waves and tides create streams of water moving in opposite directions. With just two plastic bottles, food colouring, strong tape, and some water, you can make your own mesmerizing whirlpool device.

STEM YOU WILL USE
• SCIENCE: When air is squashed (compressed), it pushes back.
• ENGINEERING: In any device that involves the flow of water, air bubbles can slow that flow.

A force called centripetal force acts on the water, causing it to spin inwards towards the centre.

The water spins fastest at the centre of the vortex.

HOW TO CREATE A
SPINNING WHIRLPOOL

These whirlpool devices are a bit like hourglasses, but with water instead of sand. They are easy to make. You will need two large plastic bottles and some coloured water. You'll need to make sure the point where the bottles join is watertight to avoid any leaks.

Time	**Difficulty**
15 minutes	Medium

WHAT YOU NEED

Strong tape

Adhesive putty

Measuring jug

Food colouring

Two large plastic bottles

Scissors

1 Place a bottle cap upside down on a piece of adhesive putty. Using the scissors, make a neat hole in it about 1 cm (½ in) in diameter with the scissors. Repeat with the other cap.

2 Fill the measuring jug with water and add some food colouring. You'll need enough water to nearly fill a large bottle, so you'll probably have to fill the jug more than once.

This bottle is full of air.

Fill the bottle nearly to the top.

4 Screw on the caps of both bottles tightly enough to make a watertight seal. An adult can help you screw the cap on tightly.

3 Pour coloured water into one of the bottles, almost to the top. Make sure you do this outside or over a sink. Leave the other bottle empty.

It'll be easier to see the whirlpool with coloured water.

5 Place the *bottle* that's filled with just air upside down on top of the bottle containing water. Try to line up the holes in the two caps.

Ask an adult to help you with this step.

6 Wrap strong tape around both bottles' lids. Pull it tight, so it holds the *bottles* firmly together sand won't allow water to leak out.

7 Turn the device upside down. If you don't disturb the water too much, it should stay in the top bottle, even though it's heavier than the air below.

The water is pressing down on the air in the bottom bottle.

If you've taped the bottles securely, they shouldn't leak, but it's a good idea to do this experiment outside, just in case.

The bottom bottle might look empty, but it's not – there is air inside pushing back against the water.

Some water may drip into the bottom bottle as you steady your whirlpool device.

8 Grasp the bottles and twirl them around. Rotating the bottles causes the water to spin, creating a vortex. The water will slowly begin to pour through the connection.

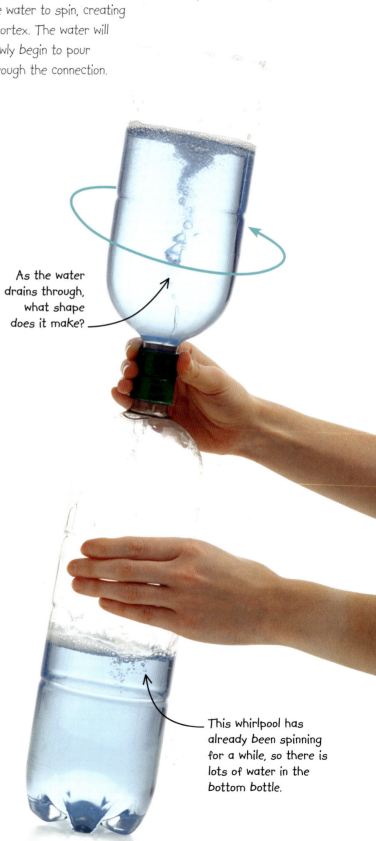

As the water drains through, what shape does it make?

This whirlpool has already been spinning for a while, so there is lots of water in the bottom bottle.

HOW IT WORKS

When you first tip the whirlpool device upside down, the water doesn't drain through, even though it's heavier than the air in the bottle below. This is because the bottom bottle is full of air, which presses against the sides of the bottle and also upwards against the water above. This air pressure holds back the water in the top bottle, but once you spin the bottles, you allow the air a way to escape upwards, so the water can drain through to the bottom.

Air rushes up to fill the space at the top of the bottle.

The pressure of the water pushes against the sides of the bottle.

When the water is still, the pressure from the air in the bottom bottle is strong enough to hold back the water.

The air in this bottle pushes against the sides. This is called "air pressure".

A type of force called "centripetal force" causes the water to spin rapidly inwards as it drains, forming a vortex.

As you spin the bottles, the water in the top bottle starts to drain through.

The air travels up through the centre of the vortex.

As the water drains into the bottle below, it displaces (moves) more air upwards.

REAL WORLD: SCIENCE
TORNADOES

The vortex you've created in your whirlpool bottles looks a lot like another kind of vortex: a tornado. These dangerous and terrifying swirling winds extend down from the base of thunderclouds and can destroy trees, houses, and cars. A tornado forms when a downward current of air from a thundercloud draws in air from all around it, creating a rapidly spinning column with very fast winds.

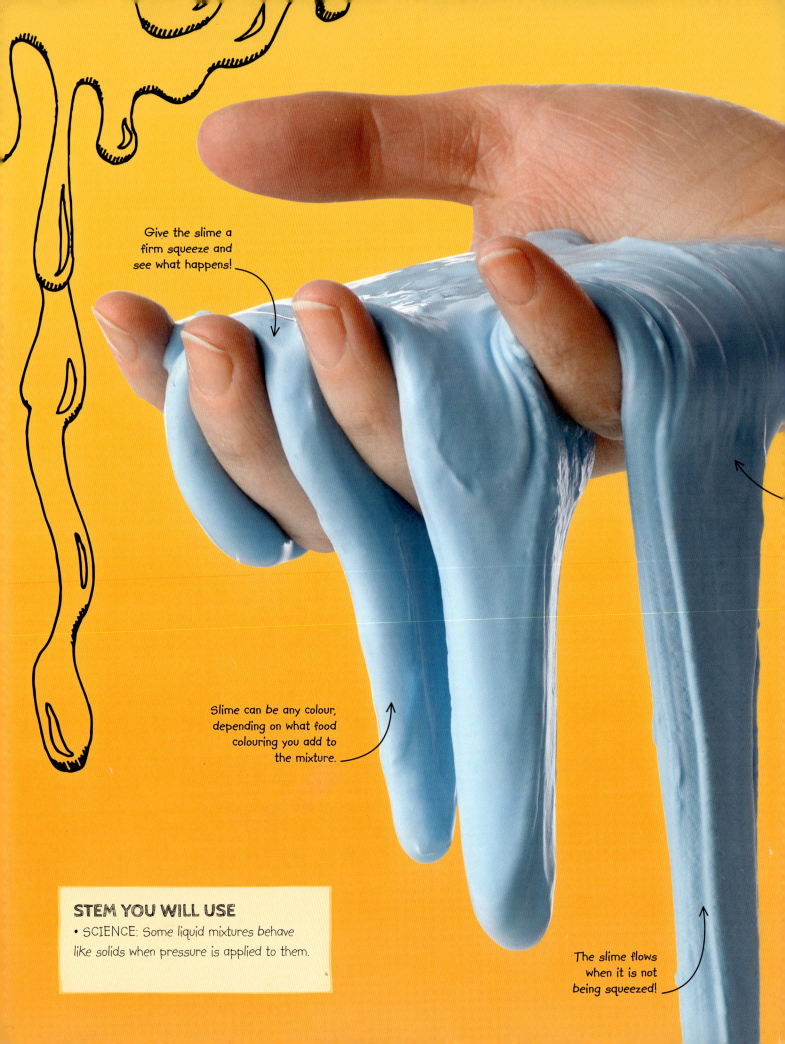

Give the slime a firm squeeze and see what happens!

Slime can be any colour, depending on what food colouring you add to the mixture.

STEM YOU WILL USE
• SCIENCE: Some liquid mixtures behave like solids when pressure is applied to them.

The slime flows when it is not being squeezed!

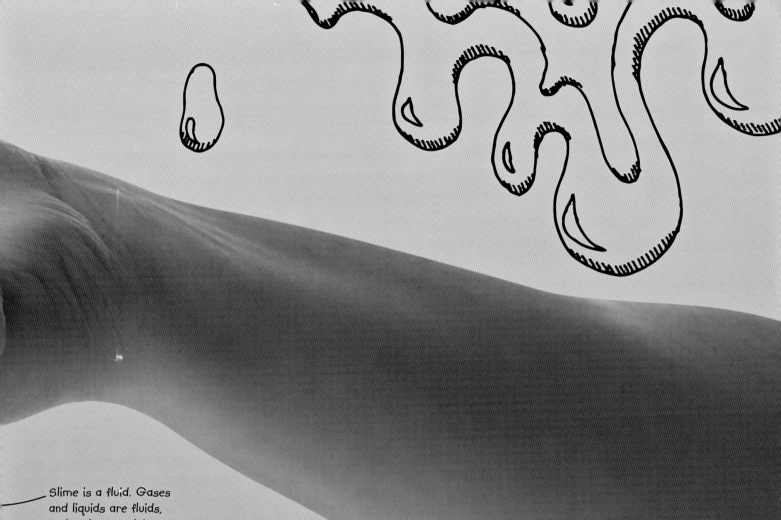

Slime is a fluid. Gases and liquids are fluids, and so is any mixture that can flow.

STICKY SLIME

This sticky substance is easy to make, fun to play with, and behaves very weirdly indeed. Hold it in your hand for just a few seconds and see if you can figure out if it is a solid or a liquid. Not sure? There's no wonder, as this slime will flow through your fingers like a thick liquid, but then, if you give it a squeeze, it will behave like a solid. Believe it or not, gooey mixtures like this are still liquids even when they're behaving like solids. Try not to make too much of a mess!

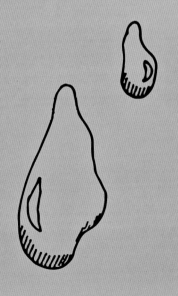

HOW TO MAKE
STICKY SLIME

This experiment can get messy, so put down greaseproof paper to catch any sticky spills. Although there's nothing poisonous in the mixture, don't put the slime in your mouth. If you want slime that is more gloopy, warm water is ideal – but don't use boiling water, which could scald you. It's also a good idea to wash your hands after you've finished playing with the slime, as this avoids getting slime all over the furniture!

Time
20 minutes

Difficulty
Medium

Blue food colouring contains a pigment that absorbs all colours of light except blue.

WHAT YOU NEED

Airtight container

Food colouring

Sticky tape

Greaseproof paper

Tablespoon

Spatula

120 ml (4 fl oz) shampoo

Warm water

Large mixing bowl

500 g (1 lb) cornflour

1 Tape a sheet of greaseproof paper to your work surface. Pour a generous amount of food colouring into the large mixing bowl. Then add the shampoo. Notice how slowly the shampoo flows – the technical term for this gloopy behaviour is "viscosity".

2 Add the cornflour to the mixing bowl and stir the contents with the spatula. This is hard at the start because there's a lot of powder and not much liquid. Don't worry: more liquid is going in.

3 Add a few tablespoonfuls of warm water. Keep stirring with your spatula to mix the water into the cornflour. The water makes starch (a substance in the cornflour) expand, forming a network that holds the water and cornflour together in a slimy mixture.

4 Gradually, your mixture will turn into a thick paste. Pick it up and knead it in your hands – it will get really gloopy! But if you thump or *squeeze* the slime, its viscosity increases enormously and it *becomes* hard, like a solid.

5 Now go for it! Squash, punch, or slam your slime on the table to make it turn solid. Whenever you stop, it will turn into a liquid again. If you want to keep the slime, pour it into an airtight container while it's runny. That way it won't dry out and you can use it for about a month.

HOW IT WORKS

A molecule is the smallest part of a compound. It's the starch molecules reacting with water that are responsible for the slime's viscosity. As long as the molecules can move around, the mixture behaves like a liquid. Sudden pressure, though, makes the molecules jam together, so the mixture can't flow.

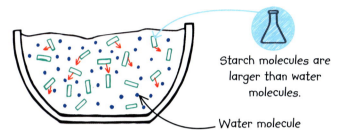

Starch molecules are larger than water molecules.

Water molecule

WITHOUT PRESSURE

As long as you handle the slime gently and don't squish it too hard, the starch molecules can move about, suspended in the water. This behaves like a thick, slow-flowing liquid.

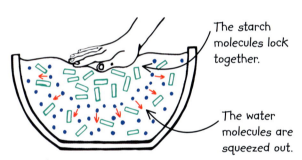

The starch molecules lock together.

The water molecules are squeezed out.

WITH PRESSURE

If you press hard on the slime, you squeeze out the water molecules from *between* the starch molecules, which lock together and make the slime feel more solid.

REAL WORLD: SCIENCE
QUICKSAND

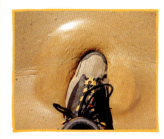

A liquid with a viscosity that changes under pressure is known as a "non-Newtonian fluid". Some of these liquids, such as slime, get thicker and behave like solids. But quicksand – a mixture of sand, clay, and water – is an example of a liquid that gets runnier. If you get stuck in quicksand and struggle to get out, your movements will cause you to sink.

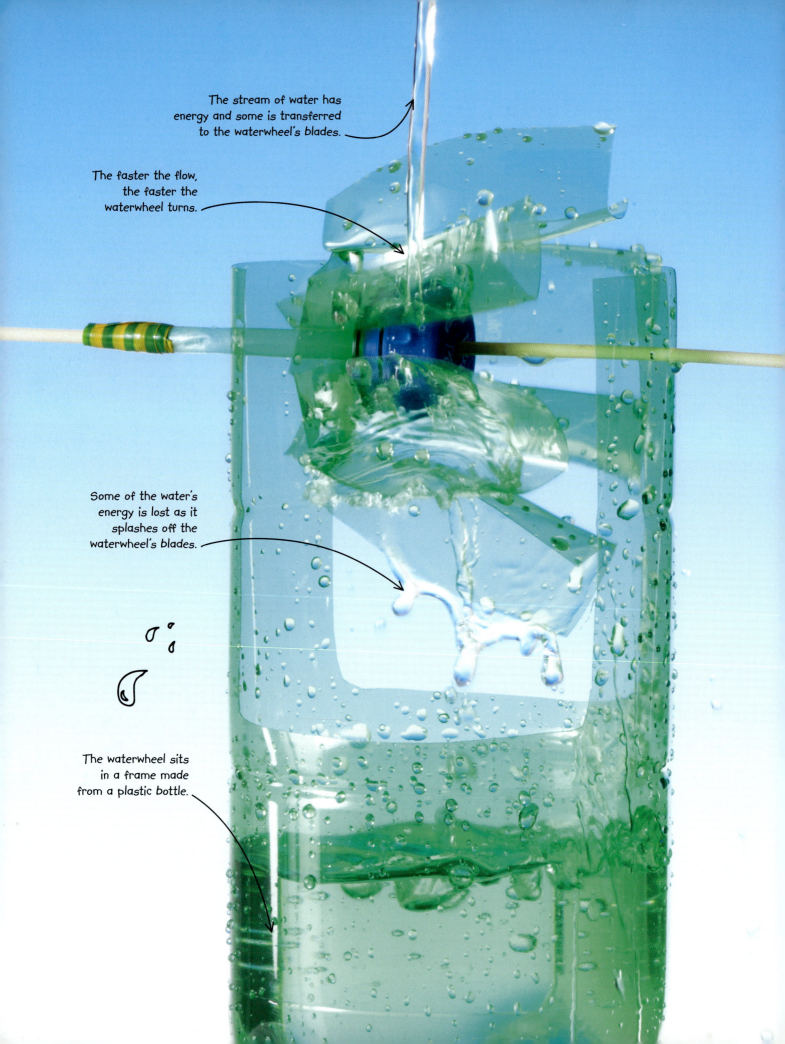

The stream of water has energy and some is transferred to the waterwheel's blades.

The faster the flow, the faster the waterwheel turns.

Some of the water's energy is lost as it splashes off the waterwheel's blades.

The waterwheel sits in a frame made from a plastic bottle.

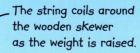

FEEL THE ENERGY
A waterwheel is an "energy-transfer device".
Like anything that moves, flowing water
possesses a form of energy called kinetic energy.
Your waterwheel will capture some of that energy
and begin turning. A string wrapped around the
shaft of your waterwheel can lift a weight. As the
weight lifts higher up, it gains potential energy (it
has the "potential" to fall down again), also called
stored energy.

The string coils around
the wooden skewer
as the weight is raised.

Tension in the
string pulls
upwards against
the weight of the
adhesive putty.

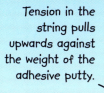

WATERWHEEL

Gravity pulls
the adhesive
putty down.

Question: how can you lift a weight just by turning on a tap or
pouring water from a jug? Answer: with a waterwheel, of course.
Waterwheels have been used to extract energy from flowing water
for many hundreds of years – to grind corn, power machinery, or lift
heavy objects. You can make your own waterwheel from a plastic
bottle, a straw, and a wooden skewer. It'll create quite a splash!

The waterwheel lifts
a weight made of
adhesive putty.

HOW TO MAKE A
WATERWHEEL

To make your waterwheel, you have to cut up a plastic bottle: this can be a little bit tricky, so ask an adult if you need help. The other thing to watch out for is using a wooden skewer to make the shaft of the waterwheel. You might want to cut off any sharp points before you begin. And don't forget that water is wet, so when you're ready to test your waterwheel, take it outside or place it in a large sink.

Time
1 hour

Difficulty
Hard

STEM YOU WILL USE
• ENGINEERING: The energy of falling water can be used to lift heavy loads, and the blades of a turbine shaft need to be angled if the shaft is to turn under falling water.

WHAT YOU NEED

Electrical tape

Adhesive putty

String

Plastic bottle

Jug of water (or just use a tap)

Scissors

Biodegradable straw

Wooden skewer

Ask an adult for help if you find this step difficult.

Leave enough of the bottle's sides to make a sturdy frame.

1 Cut right around the bottle, about two thirds of the way up. Keep the top part, including the cap, as you'll need it later to make the wheel itself.

2 Next, cut out two U-shaped pieces from the sides of the bottle, as shown. What you have now is the frame that will support the waterwheel.

3 With the point of the scissors, carefully make a small hole in one side of the frame. Then cut a notch in the opposite side, level with the hole.

4 Now get the top part of the bottle, and make six evenly spaced cuts that end level with each other at the neck. These flaps will actually be the blades.

5 Fold each of the six blades back on itself and crease the fold. Try to keep all the folds level, cutting a little deeper if you need to.

Don't make the cuts too long, or the blades may tear off.

If you crease the folds well, each blade should have an angle of about 90°.

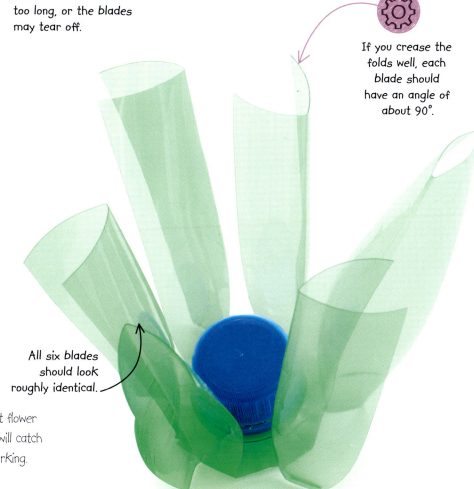

6 Cut halfway along the base of each blade, where it joins the bottle neck. Then fold each blade in half along its length and crease it.

All six blades should look roughly identical.

7 Bend the splayed wheel into a compact flower shape. This makes the surfaces that will catch the falling water once you get your wheel working.

8 The blades of the waterwheel have to fit inside the frame and be able to turn around easily. To achieve this, hold the waterwheel next to the frame and trim the blades to the right length.

9 Remove the bottle cap and pierce a hole through it. You have to push hard, so secure the cap in some adhesive putty – and mind your fingers! Screw the cap back onto the wheel.

10 Cut the straw so you have a straight part, about 5 cm (2 in) long. Carefully snip one end into four sections. Fold the sections down at right angles to the straw.

You can snip the sharp end of the skewer once it's through the bottle cap.

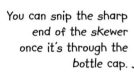

Electrical tape is made of a plastic called polyvinyl chloride (PVC) with a pressure-sensitive adhesive.

Check that the wheel turns freely.

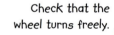

11 Slide the skewer through the straw and tape the straw onto it, about 3 cm (1¼ in) from the end. Then push the wooden skewer through the hole in the bottle cap.

12 Pack adhesive putty into the bottle cap to secure the cut sections at the end of the straw. Now try turning the skewer with your fingers. The waterwheel should turn, too!

13 Push one side of the skewer through the hole in the base of the bottle, resting the other side in the open notch. The bottle cap should not touch the side of the frame.

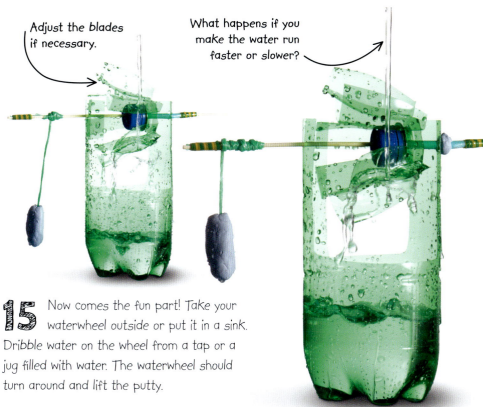

Adjust the blades if necessary.

What happens if you make the water run faster or slower?

14 Tape a piece of string near the end of the skewer without the straw. Then press a lump of adhesive putty around the other end of the string – this will act as a weight.

15 Now comes the fun part! Take your waterwheel outside or put it in a sink. Dribble water on the wheel from a tap or a jug filled with water. The waterwheel should turn around and lift the putty.

HOW IT WORKS

When you pour the water, it exerts a force on the blades of the waterwheel, making them turn. The blades turn the wooden skewer, which acts as a shaft. As the shaft turns, it also applies a force on the attached string, which pulls up the adhesive putty weight.

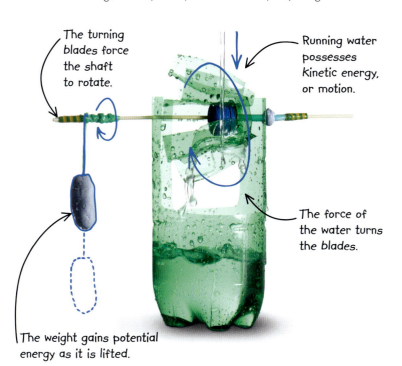

The turning blades force the shaft to rotate.

Running water possesses kinetic energy, or motion.

The force of the water turns the blades.

The weight gains potential energy as it is lifted.

REAL WORLD: ENGINEERING
HYDROELECTRICITY

Flowing water can be used to generate electricity. In a hydroelectric power station, river water is held back by a dam, so that it builds up huge pressure and lots of potential energy. It flows under pressure through pipes, turning specially designed waterwheels called turbines. These, then, turn electric generators that supply many homes and businesses with electricity. This picture shows the tops of the shafts of several turbines that spin horizontally. The generators are inside the round parts near the tops of each turbine.

SOAP-POWERED BOAT

Get ready to set sail on the soapy seven seas! Make a little boat, float it on some water, and then – using nothing but a dab of washing-up liquid – send it whizzing across the surface. The soap doesn't really power the boat but it releases hidden energy in the water. Hoist anchor and have a go!

This cut-out area is where the washing-up liquid goes, acting as a kind of "fuel" for the boat.

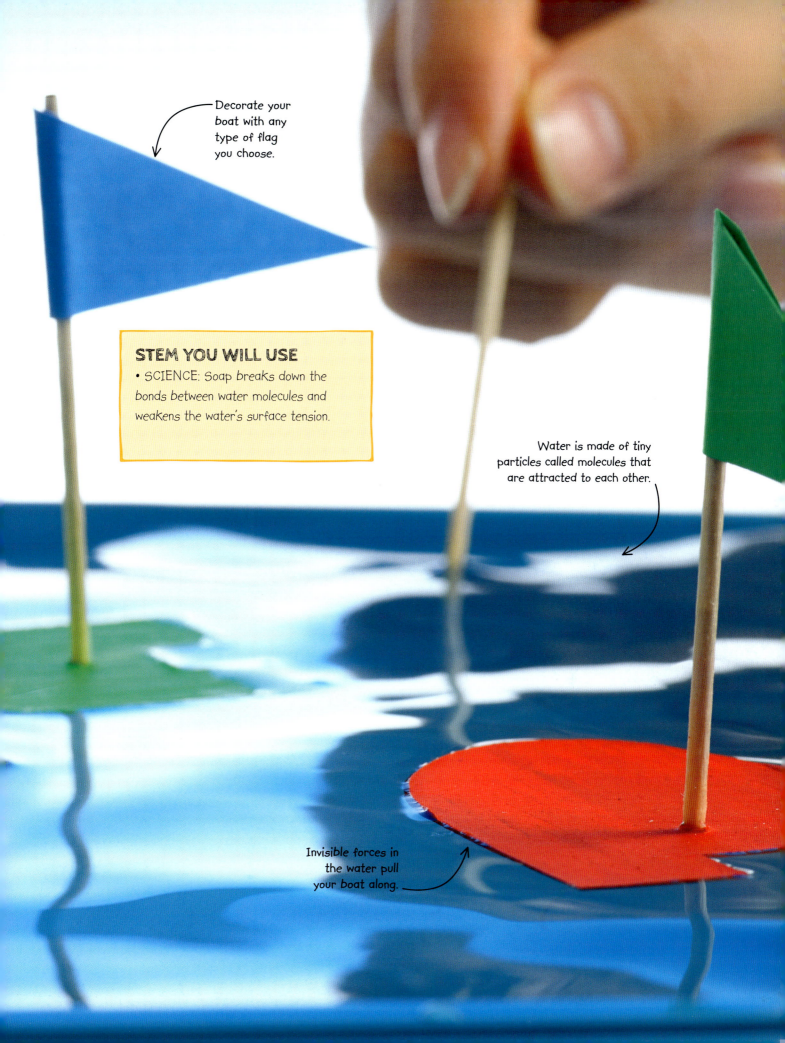

Decorate your boat with any type of flag you choose.

STEM YOU WILL USE
• SCIENCE: Soap breaks down the bonds between water molecules and weakens the water's surface tension.

Water is made of tiny particles called molecules that are attracted to each other.

Invisible forces in the water pull your boat along.

HOW TO MAKE A
SOAP-POWERED BOAT

This boat has to be light to zoom along propelled only by tiny forces in the water. The materials you use weigh almost nothing and are easy to cut into the right shapes. But if you don't want to do the cutting out yourself, ask an adult to help you. The boat shown here has a very simple design, so you can make it very quickly and get sailing straight away. Paint your boat in any colour you like.

Time
10 minutes

Difficulty
Easy

WHAT YOU NEED

Coloured card

Paintbrush

Two toothpicks

Paint

Scissors

Washing-up liquid

White card

Tray with water inside it

1 Start by making the hull, or base, of the boat. Use your scissors to cut out a small square of white card, with each side of the square measuring about 4 cm (1½ in). Cut a point at one end to make the bow, or front, of the boat.

Card is made of plant fibres, just as paper is, and it is thicker and more rigid.

2 Cut out a 0.5 cm (¼ in) square notch at the back, or stern, of your boat. This is the end where you'll put the washing-up liquid. If you like, you can try out other sizes and shapes for the notch.

Sails are used to propel boats forward – but this sail is only for show!

3 For the sail, cut out a piece of coloured card and put a toothpick through it. The sail won't move your boat, but it looks good. Then paint your boat with any colours that you like.

The paint acts as a partial seal, preventing the card from absorbing too much water.

4 When the paint dries completely, it's time to secure the toothpick sail to the boat. Your boat is ready to set sail!

5 Float your boat on the water-filled tray – keep it close to one corner and point it towards the middle. Dip a toothpick in washing-up liquid and touch the water's surface, in the notch at the boat's stern.

6 Watch your boat go! Just keep dipping the toothpick in the washing-up liquid and touching it to the notch. But if the water gets too soapy, you'll need to change it or the experiment won't work.

HOW IT WORKS

This soapy experiment makes use of something called surface tension – because water molecules cling together, they pull each other in all directions. This motion pulls tight the surface of the water, like the skin of a balloon. But when you drop washing-up liquid into the water, the molecular bonds behind the boat weaken, reducing surface tension. The rest of the water surface pulls away, dragging the boat along with it.

As soon as you apply the washing-up liquid, it quickly spreads in all directions.

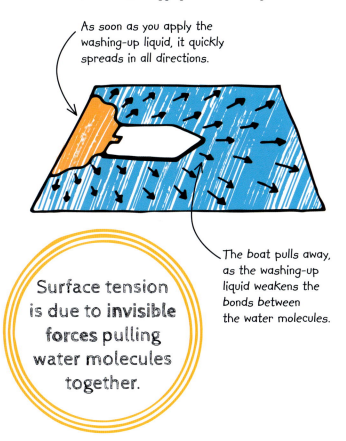

The boat pulls away, as the washing-up liquid weakens the bonds between the water molecules.

Surface tension is due to **invisible forces** pulling water molecules together.

REAL WORLD: SCIENCE
BLOWING BUBBLES

Have you ever wondered why you can't blow bubbles with just water? It's because the surface tension is so strong you can't make the water stretch into a different shape. Mixing in soap reduces the surface tension enough for you to blow air inside the water without the bubble collapsing immediately.

ERUPTING VOLCANO

Volcanoes are huge, cone-shaped mountains formed over thousands or millions of years. Every so often, they erupt, sending hot, molten (liquid) rock out from the top of the cone, called the crater. Now you can make your own volcano on a dramatic landscape, using a plastic bottle for the crater and papier mâché for the cone. Your molten rock may not be as hot as the real thing, but you will have a lot of fun creating a foamy liquid produced by a chemical reaction using basic household ingredients. Remember to stand back before the volcano lets rip!

The lava produced by the chemical reaction races down the side of your volcano.

The land around a real volcano sometimes floods with molten lava.

STEM YOU WILL USE
• SCIENCE: Vinegar and bicarbonate of soda react rapidly, producing carbon dioxide gas.
• ENGINEERING: Flour mixed with water makes a useful glue.

A chemical reaction inside your volcano produces the bubbling lava.

The cone of your volcano is made of papier mâché.

HOW TO MAKE AN
ERUPTING VOLCANO

This gets messy, so work outdoors if you can. Your volcano is built from papier mâché, made from newspaper dunked in a runny paste. The spectacular eruption is produced by two very ordinary household products: vinegar and bicarbonate of soda. If you clean and dry the volcano with kitchen paper or tissues after an eruption, you can use it again and again.

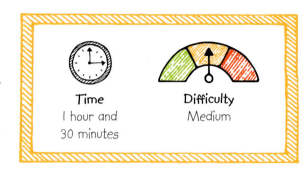

Time
1 hour and
30 minutes

Difficulty
Medium

WHAT YOU NEED

Bicarbonate of soda

Vinegar

Warm water

Washing-up liquid

400 g (14 oz) flour

Bowl of water

Large piece of cardboard

Newspaper

Small plastic bottle

Paintbrush

Packing tape

Spoon

Paints

Scissors

Food colouring

1 Using your scissors, carefully cut off the top of the bottle. This is so you can easily add the ingredients later on – and for it to come out again in the form of an eruption. This will be the centre of the volcano, with the bottle's mouth as the crater.

2 Using several pieces of packing tape, stick the bottle to the middle of your large piece of cardboard. When everything is secure, you're ready to start building up the volcano's cone around the bottle.

Pull the tape tight so that the paper balls can't move.

3 Tear off several pieces of newspaper and scrunch them into tight balls. Arrange the paper balls around the bottle. Make the stack wider at the bottom than at the top. Tape the balls securely to the cardboard base and to the bottle.

4 Now you can shape the volcano's cone using papier mâché. To begin with, tear or cut 50 or more strips of newspaper, about 2–3 cm (¾–1¼ in) wide. These will be dunked in a watery glue, which you make from flour and water in step 5.

Starch grains from the flour dissolving in the water make this mixture sticky.

Overlap the strips in a way to create your desired shape.

5 To make the glue, add flour to the bowl of water and mix it in with a spoon. Keep on adding flour and mixing until you have a runny paste about as thick as pancake batter. Note, you might not need all the flour.

6 Saturate the newspaper strips in the paste. Run the strips through your fingers to remove excess paste, then lay them over the paper cone. Smooth out the strips, sticking some to the cardboard base and over the mouth of the bottle.

7 You've now built your volcano's cone. The papier mâché must dry and harden before you go on to the next stage. So leave it in a warm place overnight.

When the papier mâché is dry, it's time to paint it.

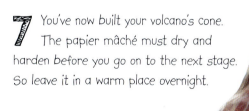

When the glue dries, the starch from the flour clings to the cellulose molecules in the paper.

The cone of a real volcano is made of old lava that has **cooled** and **turned solid.**

Stand your volcano somewhere warm, so the paint dries quickly.

8 Paint the cone dark brown, but leave an unpainted strip at the bottom. If you don't have brown paint, mix together red, green, and blue. If you can get it, add a little sand for a gritty texture.

9 Paint the bottom of the cone and the cardboard base in shades of green to represent the grass or jungle below. If you like, paint the top of the cone red, to look like fiery lava.

10 Here comes the really messy bit! Pour the ingredients shown below into the volcano's opening. Once you have added them all, mix them with a spoon.

11 Get your camera out if you have one because your volcano is about to explode! Add two or three teaspoons of bicarbonate of soda into the volcano's cone and wait for a few seconds.

Pour in about 40 ml (1½ fl oz) of washing-up liquid.

Pour in about 40 ml (1½ fl oz) of warm water.

Pour in about 50 ml (1¾ fl oz) of vinegar.

Finally, add a few drops of red food colouring.

A foam – a mixture of liquid filled with bubbles of gas – spills over and pours down the slopes.

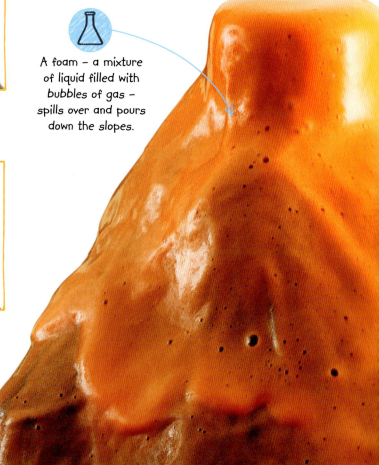

TAKE IT FURTHER

Instead of using papier mâché on a cardboard base, you could use mud to build up a volcano cone on a wooden base. In this version, just leave a hole in the top of the soil cone and press a plastic cup into it. This makes the crater where you will mix up the lava. If you're allowed to use lots of vinegar and bicarbonate of soda, stir up a really large cupful of ingredients and create a truly gigantic eruption. Or you could see what happens if you replace the vinegar with cola, which contains phosphoric acid.

When the flow starts to slow, keep the fun going by adding more bicarbonate of soda and vinegar.

Red food colouring makes your foamy mixture actually look like lava.

The lava is easy to wipe up when the eruption is finally over.

HOW IT WORKS

Mixing bicarbonate of soda (a base) with vinegar (which contains acetic acid) causes a rapid chemical reaction that produces lots of carbon dioxide gas. Tiny bubbles of this gas become trapped in your soapy lava mixture. This creates a foam that takes up much more space than the liquid ingredients – so it all comes frothing out of the mouth of the volcano and trickles down the sides. Real lava has tiny bubbles of carbon dioxide in it, too. When it cools and sets hard, the bubbles are trapped.

REAL WORLD: SCIENCE
TUNGURAHUA VOLCANO

Your volcano is the shape of what is known as a cinder cone volcano. Tungurahua, shown in the picture, is an active volcano of this type in Ecuador, South America. When it erupts, lava and ash run down and solidify, forming another layer of rock to build up the growing cone.

INSIDE A VOLCANO

There are several types of volcano, but deep inside each one there is a large pool of molten rock, called the magma chamber. When underground pressures increase, the magma is pushed into a central tube and out through the crater as lava.

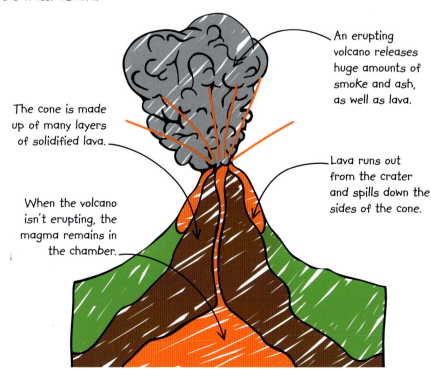

The cone is made up of many layers of solidified lava.

When the volcano isn't erupting, the magma remains in the chamber.

An erupting volcano releases huge amounts of smoke and ash, as well as lava.

Lava runs out from the crater and spills down the sides of the cone.

SHAPES AND STRUCTURES

A building or a bridge needs to be strong enough to stay standing, and it also needs to hold up anything placed in or on top of it. But what makes a structure strong enough to support loads? It's all down to what it is made from, what shape it is, and how it's built. In this chapter, you'll be building some surprisingly strong structures using paper, sand, and drinking straws. You'll even build tall towers from spaghetti and marshmallows!

SPAGHETTI TOWER

For a tower to stay standing, it must be strong enough not to buckle under its own weight, and it must have a stable base. This tower is strong because of the shapes used in its construction: triangles. And its wide base stops it toppling over.

The tower must stand straight or the force of gravity will tip it over.

Triangles are strong because they can't twist out of shape.

The main part of the tower is made of two large cubes stacked together.

The base carries all the tower's weight.

HOW TO MAKE A
SPAGHETTI TOWER

All you need to build this tower is spaghetti, marshmallows, and willpower! The sticky marshmallows hold the ends of the spaghetti in place, and the spaghetti forms a sturdy framework. If you like marshmallows, you'll need willpower to stop yourself eating your building materials!

Time
20 minutes

Difficulty
Medium

STEM YOU WILL USE
• ENGINEERING: A structure will topple over if the centre of gravity is not supported.
• MATHS: A pyramid is a 3D shape with triangular sides and a pointed top.

WHAT YOU NEED

Spaghetti

Marshmallows

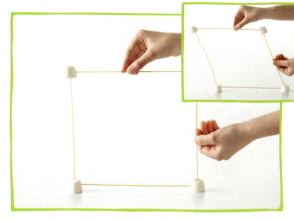

1 Begin by making a square. To see why a square isn't a strong shape, push it gently from one side. It leans easily, becoming a parallelogram.

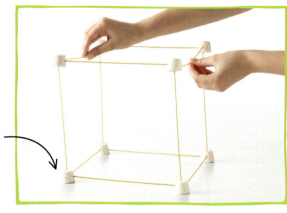

Make sure the bottom marshmallows sit on their flat bases.

2 Make a cube. Try twisting it gently. Because it's made of squares, you'll find it leans very easily and isn't stable.

Sliding the marshmallows inwards helps to make the cube stronger.

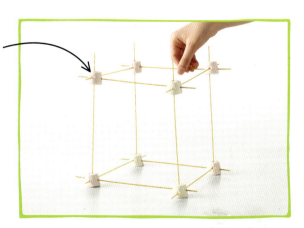

3 To make the cube stronger, you'll need to add diagonal pieces. To fit them, first make the cube smaller by sliding the marshmallows inwards so the spaghetti strands poke out the other side.

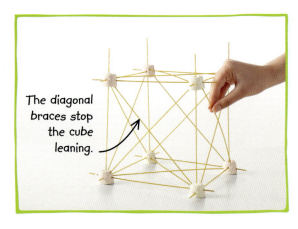

The diagonal braces stop the cube leaning.

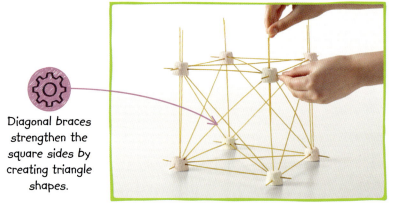

Diagonal braces strengthen the square sides by creating triangle shapes.

4 Add the diagonal pieces, called braces, across each face from corner to corner.

5 Strengthen the vertical edges by feeding a second piece of spaghetti down through the marshmallows at the top corners.

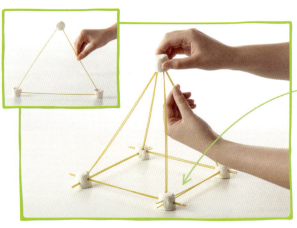

Make sure the square base of the roof is the same size as the top of your cube.

6 Make the roof, starting with a triangle. You'll notice this is stronger than a square as it doesn't lean. Add more spaghetti and marshmallows to form a pyramid with a square base.

7 Build a second braced cube and fix it very carefully on top of the first one. Then, just as carefully, fix the pyramid on top. Your tower is now complete!

Push the base of the top cube onto the bits of spaghetti sticking up from the first one.

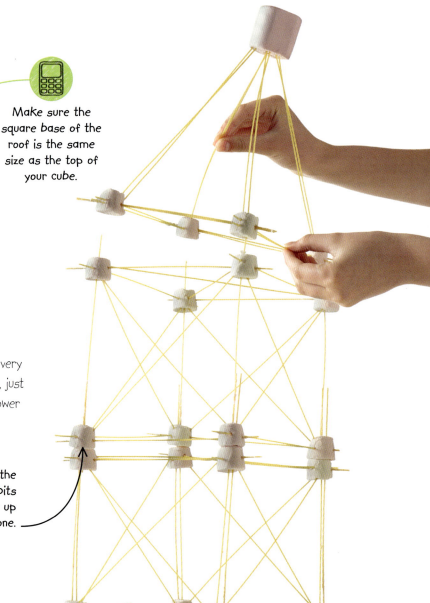

TAKE IT FURTHER

Now you've mastered the art of building spaghetti towers, why not try different designs? You could try building a tower that is one big pyramid. You'll need to plan the shapes carefully to make sure they all fit together. You might want to try to make your tower much taller. Can you make a tower that stands taller than you? The spaghetti pieces bend less if they're shorter – can you make a taller tower by using shorter pieces of spaghetti? If you want your tower to be stable, you'll need to make the base wide and the top the same width or narrower.

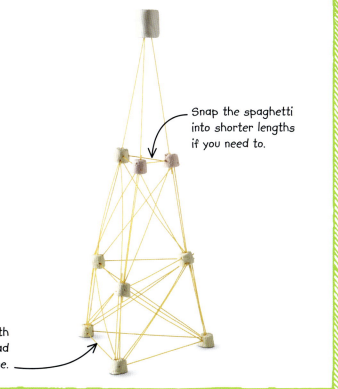

Snap the spaghetti into shorter lengths if you need to.

Try building a tower with a triangular base instead of a square base.

HOW IT WORKS

Triangles are the key to the strength of your tower. Unlike a square, which can lean over and turn into a parallelogram when pushed, a triangle can't change shape and so remains upright and rigid. The base of your tower must also be wide. For every object, there is an imaginary point called the centre of gravity. Its position is determined by the distribution of mass within the object. For the tower, it is closer to the base. Objects are stable if the centre of gravity is above the base. If an object leans, so that its centre of gravity is not above the base, it will topple.

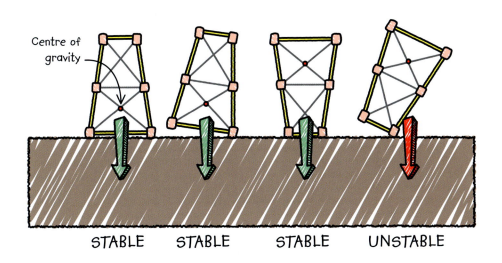

Centre of gravity

STABLE   STABLE   STABLE   UNSTABLE

REAL WORLD: ENGINEERING
TOKYO SKYTREE

With a height of 634 m (2,080 ft), the Tokyo Skytree in Japan is the tallest tower in the world. It's made of steel tubes arranged as strong triangles, and its base is much wider than its top.

NEWSPAPER STOOL

A single sheet of newspaper is very flimsy. It crumples and folds easily, and you would probably never think of using it to make anything really strong. But use lots of sheets of newspaper together, in just the right way, and you can make a stool so strong that it can support your weight!

Duct tape holds all the rolls together to make the stool.

Individual sheets of newspaper are not very strong at all.

Each roll of newspaper is held together by sticky tape.

HOW TO MAKE A
NEWSPAPER STOOL

You'll have to collect lots of newspaper to do this activity. If you want to make your stool really strong, you'll need to roll the newspaper very tightly. You might want to ask a friend to help, so that one of you can roll, and the other can stick. If you ever want to dismantle your stool, remove the tape first – then you can recycle the newspaper.

Time 45 minutes

Difficulty Easy

WHAT YOU NEED

Sticky tape

Duct tape

Scissors

Lots of newspapers

1 Roll up about 20 sheets of newspaper together lengthways. Roll it as tightly as you can. The roll should feel strong and rigid.

Try to keep the newspaper rolled as tightly as possible.

2 Wrap sticky tape around the roll, close to each end. You might want to ask someone to help you, as you need at least one hand to hold the roll. Repeat until you have 25 rolls.

3 Take another pile of about 20 sheets and cut it in half. You will use the two halves to make two short rolls.

4 Roll up and tape each half at the ends as before, so you finish with two rolls half the length of the others.

This duct tape is formed of three layers made from glue, fabric mesh, and plastic to make it water-resistant.

5 Line up eight long rolls with one short roll in the middle. Wrap duct tape around them, to secure them all together. Repeat this step with another eight long rolls and one short roll.

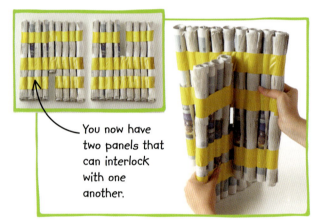

You now have two panels that can interlock with one another.

6 Slot one set of paper rolls into the other, using the gaps left by the short rolls in the middle of each. You should now have an X-shape that stands up on its own.

Make sure the seat is securely attached to the X-shape with lots of tape, to stop it falling off!

7 To make your seat, line up the remaining nine long rolls of newspaper and secure them together with duct tape. Stand your X-shape on top of your joined rolls and use duct tape to attach it.

The rolls of paper compress when you sit on the stool.

The paper rolls are arranged as a cross, giving the stool stability.

8 Stand your stool the right way up, so that the row of nine rolls is on top. Your stool is finished. Now, go ahead and sit on it!

HOW IT WORKS

The rolls of paper you used to make the stool are strong in two ways. Firstly, a cylinder has no corners, and so no point is weaker than any other, making it a very strong shape. Secondly, by rolling the paper rolls very tightly, you are increasing the density of the cylinders – packing more matter (stuff) into the same volume (space). If you made the rolls looser so they were much less dense, they wouldn't be as strong.

The force to support your weight comes from the molecules that make up the paper. When you sit on the stool, you squash, or compress, the paper slightly. The molecules of which the paper is made are pushed a tiny bit closer together, and that produces an equal force that pushes in the opposite direction – as if there are springs between them.

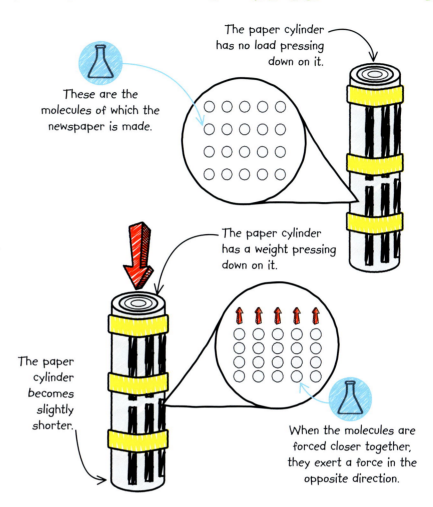

These are the molecules of which the newspaper is made.

The paper cylinder has no load pressing down on it.

The paper cylinder has a weight pressing down on it.

The paper cylinder becomes slightly shorter.

When the molecules are forced closer together, they exert a force in the opposite direction.

REAL WORLD: ENGINEERING
COMPRESSED COLUMNS

You can see cylindrical shapes like the paper rolls you used to make your stool in the columns that support big buildings. Just like your paper rolls, these columns are very strong in compression – even stronger than the paper, as they are made of dense stone.

REAL WORLD: SCIENCE
HOLLOW BONES

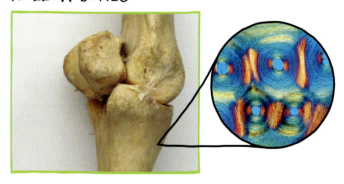

The long bones in your legs that support your weight work in a similar way to the paper rolls in your stool. They are hollow in the middle (to allow for the marrow, where blood cells are made), but very dense and strong around the outside. The dense part of the bone is made up of many small tubes (osteons), each one very weak. Just as several rolls of paper bound together can support a weight, so the clusters of osteons make the bone very strong.

SUSPENSION BRIDGE

Engineers build huge suspension bridges from concrete and steel cables. The concrete towers support the cables, and the cables support the road, which can carry hundreds of cars and lorries at a time. The best way to understand how these forces work together to make a strong and stable structure is to build your own model suspension bridge. In this activity, you can do just that by using bundles of drinking straws instead of concrete, and string instead of steel cables.

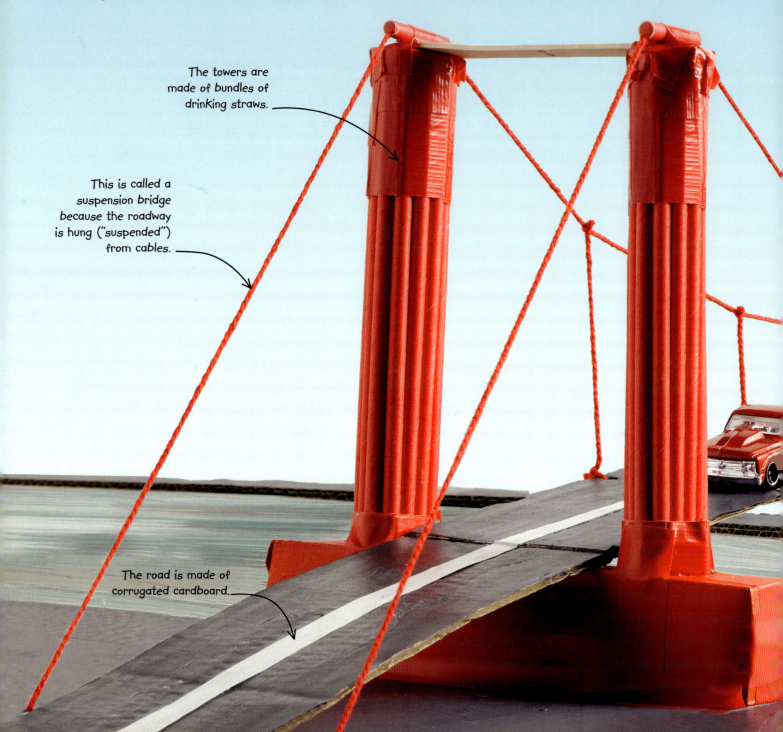

The towers are made of bundles of drinking straws.

This is called a suspension bridge because the roadway is hung ("suspended") from cables.

The road is made of corrugated cardboard.

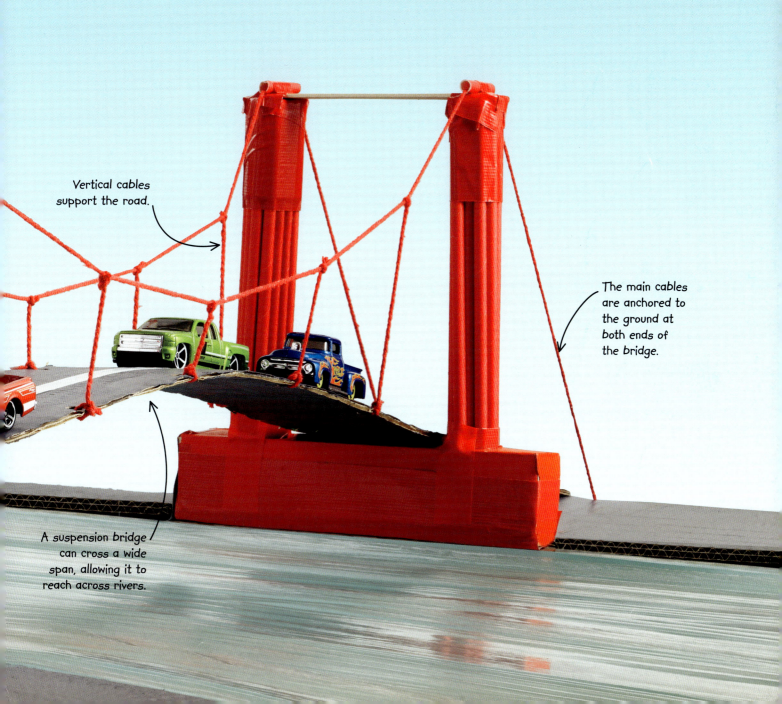

Vertical cables support the road.

The main cables are anchored to the ground at both ends of the bridge.

A suspension bridge can cross a wide span, allowing it to reach across rivers.

HOW TO MAKE A
SUSPENSION BRIDGE

The bases of the bridge's towers are made from toothpaste tube boxes. If you can't find any, you can make boxes the right size from cardboard. The towers are made from bundles of drinking straws. We used 15 in each bundle – if your straws are wider or narrower than ours, use fewer or more straws.

Time	Difficulty
1 hour	Hard

WHAT YOU NEED

Double-sided tape

Strong tape

String

Rubber band

Hole punch

Scissors

Grey paint

Four lollipop sticks

Pencil

Black felt-tip pen

White paint

Paintbrush

Small pebbles

Ruler

Lots of corrugated cardboard

Two toothpaste boxes, each 5 cm x 5 cm x 20 cm (2 in x 2 in x 8 in)

61 paper straws

Use a rubber band to hold the bundle temporarily before wrapping the tape around.

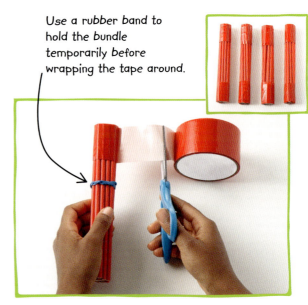

1 Make a bundle of fifteen straws. Now wrap a piece of wide, strong tape around each end. Repeat three times, to make a total of four towers.

2 Firmly tape two lollipop sticks side-by-side across the tops of two of your towers. Repeat with the other two towers.

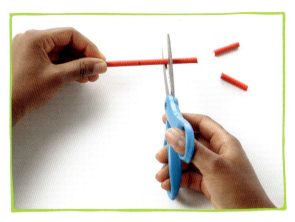

3 Cut four 2½ cm (1 in) pieces from the last straw. These will hold the bridge's two main cables in place.

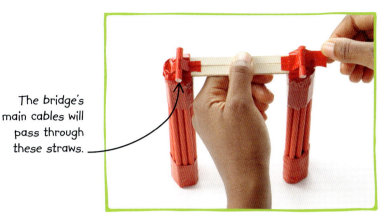

The bridge's main cables will pass through these straws.

4 Tape each piece of straw to the top of a tower at a 90° angle to the lollipop sticks.

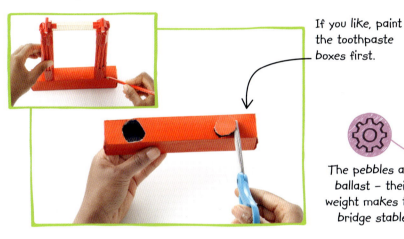

If you like, paint the toothpaste boxes first.

5 Draw around the bases of your towers on one side of each toothpaste box. Cut around the lines and push the towers into the holes.

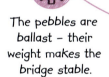

The pebbles are ballast – their weight makes the bridge stable.

6 Fill both boxes with the pebbles. You may need to adjust the position of the towers to fit the pebbles around them. Close the boxes and secure them with strong tape.

7 Cut out two 20 cm (8 in) wide cardboard squares and, if you want, paint the tops grey. These will form the base your bridge stands on.

Make sure the painted side of the base faces upwards.

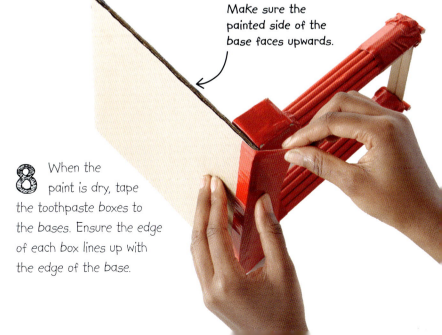

8 When the paint is dry, tape the toothpaste boxes to the bases. Ensure the edge of each box lines up with the edge of the base.

If you like, paint a white line in the centre of the road.

9 To make the road, take a piece of cardboard 1 m (3¼ ft) long and as wide as the gap between the towers. Then paint it grey.

10 Add a piece of double-sided tape between the two towers on each base. Remove the protective strip so the tape is sticky.

Tape the road down here.

11 Press the road onto the double-sided tape at both ends, as shown here, and then tape the end of the road to the edge of the base.

A real bridge's roadway might crack rather than sag, if it was made of concrete, which can be brittle.

12 If you put objects on the bridge now, it will sag. That's because the bridge still needs cables to support heavy weights.

13 Make pen marks 10 cm (4 in) apart along both sides of the road to mark the points where cables will attach.

Take care not to punch holes through the edge of the road.

14 Use a hole punch to make a hole at each mark. Make sure you push the hole punch well onto the road so that the hole isn't too near the edge.

15 Now make your cables. Cut two long pieces of string, each 1½ m (5 ft) in length. Then cut 10 short pieces of string, each 15 cm (6 in) long.

16 Thread the long pieces of string through the short straws on top of both ends of the bridge. You should then have two parallel "cables".

The long pieces of string will be the bridge's main cables. In a real bridge, the cables are made from steel.

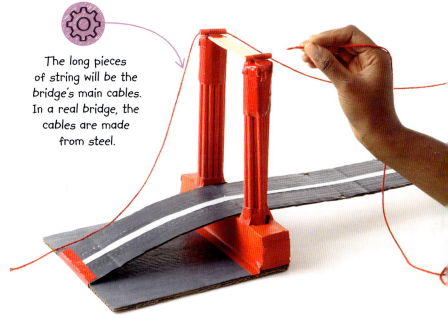

17 Cut short slits in the base at both ends of the bridge, and wedge the ends of the main cables into the slits. Don't pull the string tight – it should hang in the middle of the bridge.

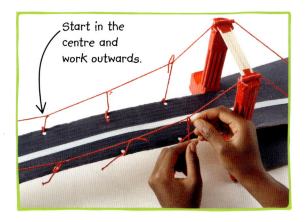

Start in the centre and work outwards.

18 Tie the short pieces of string between the holes in the road and the main cables. Starting from the middle, they should be about 3 cm (1¼ in), 5 cm (2 in), and 7 cm (2¾ in) long.

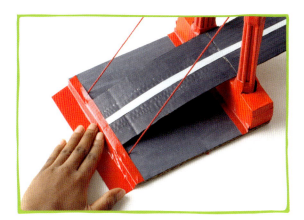

19 Pull the main cables through the slits in the bases so that they're taut. Then secure the ends of the bridge to a table or board with tape. Your suspension bridge is now complete!

GEODESIC DOME

This impressive structure is known as a geodesic dome. It's easy to make, and though it is quite light and looks fragile, it is actually extremely sturdy because of its shape. Once you've made your dome, you can cover it with clear cellophane to make a small greenhouse.

Triangles make the structure sturdy and stable.

Cellophane traps heat from the Sun inside the greenhouse, making it warmer.

The straws are the struts.

Succulent plants can survive in hot environments with little rain, such as the inside of a greenhouse.

Pipe cleaners, hidden by the tape, connect the struts.

HOW TO MAKE A
GEODESIC DOME

This geodesic dome is made of 65 struts, of two different lengths, joined together by connectors made from pipe cleaners. We've used two kinds of paper straw, to distinguish the long struts from the short struts, and two kinds of pipe cleaner: one for the feet connectors at the base of the dome, and one for the regular connectors. You don't have to use the same colours as we have.

Time
I hour

Difficulty
Hard

WHAT YOU NEED

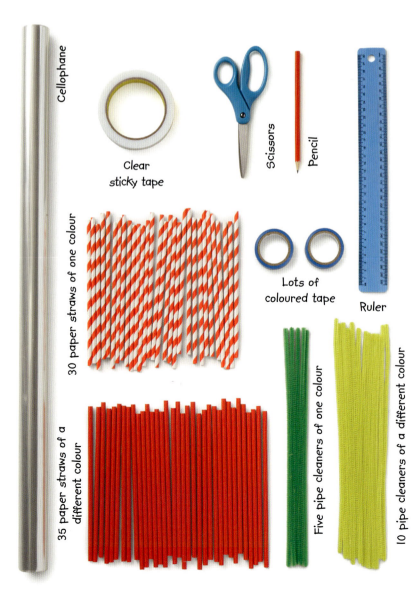

Cellophane

Clear sticky tape

Scissors

Pencil

Ruler

Lots of coloured tape

30 paper straws of one colour

35 paper straws of a different colour

Five pipe cleaners of one colour

10 pipe cleaners of a different colour

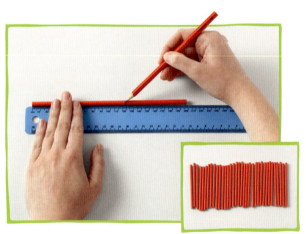

1 First, make the 35 long struts from straws. They should be 12 cm (5 in) long. For each one, draw a line first, then cut the straw at the line.

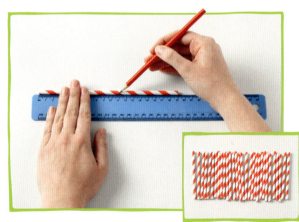

2 Now make 30 short struts from the other straws. These should be 11 cm (4½ in) long. Make sure you recycle the bits of straw you don't need from steps 1 and 2.

You should end up with 20 of one colour and 40 of the other.

3 Gather together five pipe cleaners of one colour and 10 of the other. Fold each one in half and cut, and then cut each half in half again.

4 Twist together pairs of pipe cleaners from the pile of 20, just like in the picture here, to make 10 "feet" for your dome.

5 To make the connectors, twist together three lengths of the other pipe cleaner. You'll need 12 of these connectors altogether.

A flat 10-sided shape is called a decagon.

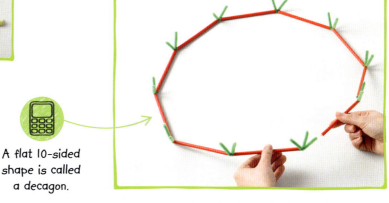

6 Connect 10 of the long struts by using the pipe-cleaner feet. You'll end up with a 10-sided shape.

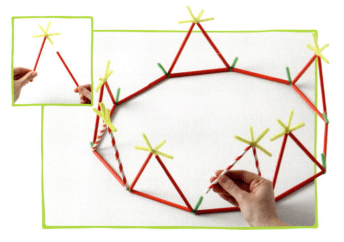

7 Use the connectors to begin building up the dome, forming the bottom layer of triangles. Alternate the long and the short struts, as shown.

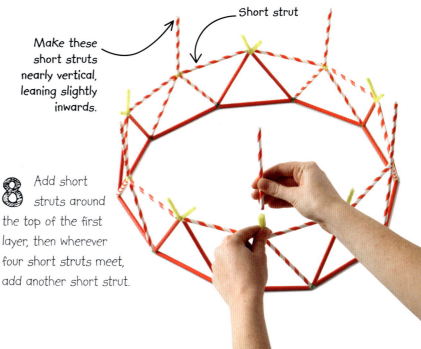

Make these short struts nearly vertical, leaning slightly inwards.

Short strut

8 Add short struts around the top of the first layer, then wherever four short struts meet, add another short strut.

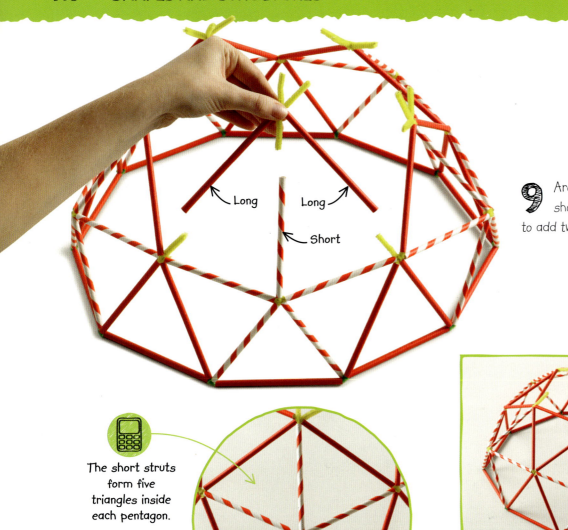

Long   Long

Short

9 Around each near-vertical short strut, use a connector to add two long struts, as shown.

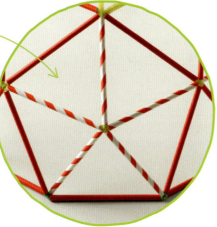

The short struts form five triangles inside each pentagon.

10 Connect five more of the long struts around the top of the middle layer. These will form a pentagon on top of the dome.

One strut will have two pipe cleaner legs tucked into it.

11 To complete the top of the dome, join five short struts with a connector. Tuck the spare sixth leg of the connector into one of the struts.

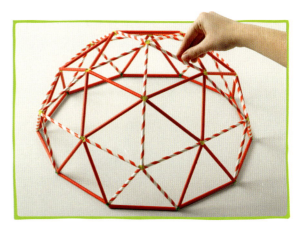

12 Join the five remaining short struts to the spare connectors at the top of the dome.

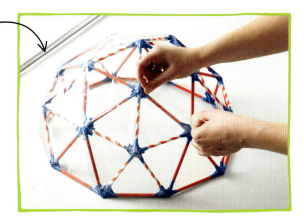

The cellophane covering will turn your geodesic dome into a small greenhouse ready for plants.

13 Wrap short lengths of coloured tape around all the joints to strengthen the structure.

14 Now cover your dome in cellophane and secure the pieces in place with clear sticky tape. Your geodesic dome is complete!

HOW IT WORKS

The geodesic design is very sturdy because it has the stability of the triangle shape as its building block. Triangles are strong because they don't distort when put under pressure. If pressure is put on one corner of a triangle, the other two corners distribute the force evenly. In your geodesic dome, the triangles are repeated, so any force on the building divides repeatedly at each intersection and spreads efficiently through the structure.

In a geodesic dome, the weight of the building is distributed efficiently across the whole structure.

The triangle shape divides the forces evenly at every intersection.

The forces are reduced at each level of the dome.

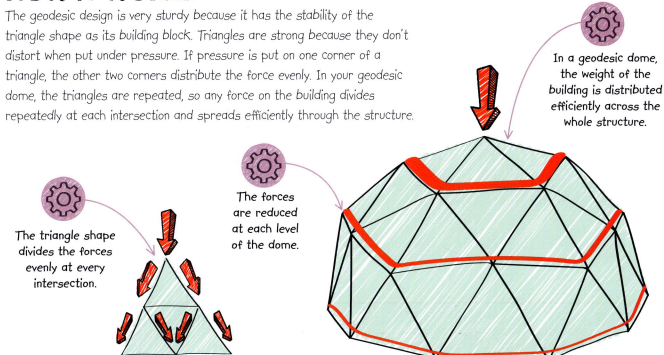

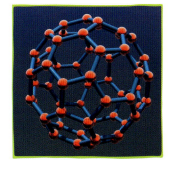

REAL WORLD: SCIENCE
BUCKMINSTERFULLERENE

In 1986, scientists discovered a form of the element carbon whose atoms are arranged in a geodesic shape of pentagons and hexagons. This form of carbon was named buckminsterfullerene, after one of the most important designers of geodesic domes, the American architect Richard Buckminster Fuller.

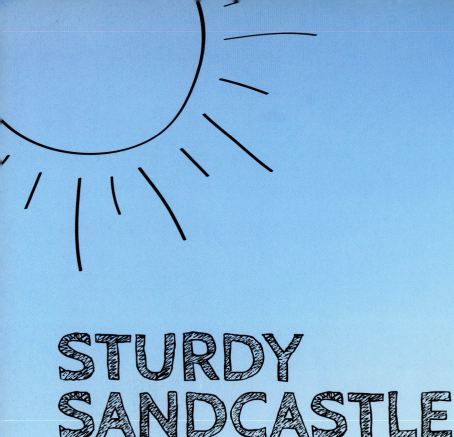

STURDY SANDCASTLE

If you've ever made a sandcastle, you'll know you have to use a bit of water to make the sand damp in order to bind the grains together. Try it with dry sand and you'll end up with a heap *because there's nothing to stick the grains together. But even a castle made with damp sand will collapse under a little weight. With the help of a little science and engineering, however, this project reveals how you can make a super-strong sandcastle – one that might even *be able* to support your weight!

STEM YOU WILL USE
• SCIENCE: Water molecules are attracted to sand molecules, that's what makes them clump together easily.
• ENGINEERING: Reinforcing materials, such as bandages, can make a structure stable and support much heavier loads.

In wet sand, the water binds the sand grains, helping to hold the structure together.

There is a force caused by the books pressing downwards on the sandcastle.

The sandcastle is "reinforced", which means it has been strengthened with extra material.

Layers of bandages give this castle extra strength.

HOW TO BUILD A
STURDY SANDCASTLE

There is a special ingredient that makes this sandcastle strong: strips of bandage. Apart from that, it's just like most sandcastles: you fill a bucket with damp sand, then turn it over. If you do this activity on a beach, make sure you take the bandages with you afterwards and dispose of them carefully. You can leave the sand behind, though!

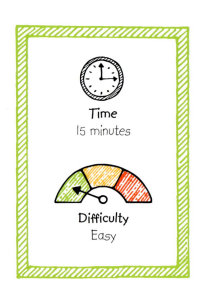

Time
15 minutes

Difficulty
Easy

WHAT YOU NEED

Water

Trowel

Bandages

Bucket

Scissors

Sand

Heavy books

1 Pour enough water into the sand to make the sand slightly damp. Stir the mixture thoroughly, so that there is no dry sand and no excess water.

2 Use the trowel to make a layer of sand about 5 cm (2 in) deep in the bottom of the bucket. Spread the sand evenly across the bucket's base.

3 Press down firmly on the damp sand with your hand, to compact it. Make sure the layer is flat.

As you start to build your sandcastle and press down, you force the sand grains together.

4 Carefully cut several strips of bandage that are about as long as your bucket is wide. You can always cut more if you run out of pieces.

The number of layers depends on the size of your bucket.

Bandages are made of a thin but strong mesh of woven fabric.

5 Put a few strips of bandage on top of the layer of sand. Place them so that they overlap slightly, in order to cover the sand completely.

6 Keep adding layers of damp sand 5 cm (2 in) deep, with strips of bandage between them. Press down each layer firmly.

7 Don't worry too much if your bucket is an odd shape, like this one. Just cover as much of each sand layer as possible.

8 Fill the bucket to the top with sand. Cover this final layer with strips of bandage that extend slightly over the edge of the bucket.

Lift up your
bucket slowly!

9 With one hand over the bandages to stop them falling off, carefully turn the bucket upside down and place it on the ground or a table.

10 Gently tap the sides of the bucket, and then lift it away, just as you would if you were making an ordinary sandcastle.

12 Load more books on top of your sandcastle. See how heavy a load your sandcastle can support before it collapses!

11 Your sandcastle is ready to test! To see how sturdy it is, gently place one of the heavy books on top.

Place the books carefully on top of your sandcastle!

Engineers use the word "loading" to describe the forces a structure has to withstand.

This is what happens to a normal sandcastle when you put books on it!

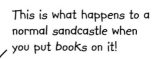

TAKE IT FURTHER

Your sandcastle should be able to support quite a heavy load, but can you make it even stronger? What happens if you replace the strips of bandage with paper, plastic bags, or bits of an old T-shirt? Does coarse or gritty sand make a better sandcastle than fine sand? Could you make a castle from gravel instead of sand?

HOW IT WORKS

Sand grains are made of rock and shells that have been broken down into tiny pieces by the action of moving water in the sea or in rivers. An ordinary sandcastle would collapse if you placed a load on top of it, because the sand grains can easily slip sideways over each other. But your sandcastle can support a load because the bandages increase the friction between the grains as they slip sideways. Friction is the resistance created when two or more objects are pushing past each other. Increasing the friction between the bandage strips and the grains prevents the grains from slipping sideways.

The heavy load pushes the sand grains together.

With reinforcement, the sandcastle is able to support a heavy load.

Without reinforcement, there is little friction, or resistance. The sand grains slip sideways, collapsing into a pile.

ORDINARY SANDCASTLE

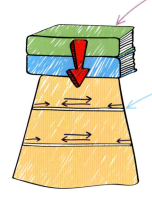

REINFORCED SANDCASTLE

The strips of bandage increase the amount of friction in the structure, so the sand grains can't slide sideways as easily.

REAL WORLD: ENGINEERING
STABILIZING SLOPES

The combination of sand and strips of bandages used to build your sandcastle is similar to a technique used by engineers to create reinforced structures. They use grainy materials like soil or sand and pack them between strips of mesh. Where a motorway carves through the land, engineers use this technique to reinforce unstable slopes beside the road. Seawalls protecting coastal areas are also built in this way, as they are able to absorb the impact of waves and prevent coastal erosion.

SYMMETRICAL PICTURES

We find images that are symmetrical – with two halves that reflect each other – appealing and attractive, and in this project you're going to make two symmetrical pictures two different ways. You'll also learn how to use coordinates on a grid to structure your art.

This central line is the key to making a symmetrical painting.

You can use coordinates to make the reflection super precise.

PROJECT 2 – ARCHITECTURAL ART

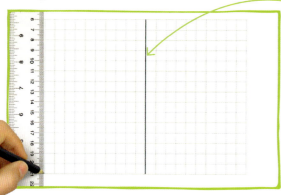

This vertical line is the y-axis of your grid and will be the line of symmetry.

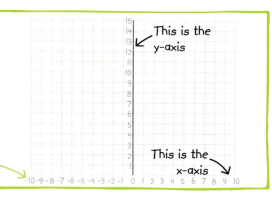

1 With a pencil, draw a rectangle 20 x 15 cm (8 x 6 in) on a piece of paper. Mark every 1 cm (½ in) along each side and connect the lines to make a grid. Draw a thicker line down the centre of your grid.

Numbers to the left of the zero are negative.

2 Starting from the left and working your way to the right, begin numbering grid lines along the x-axis, starting from -10, until your reach 10. Then number the y-axis up to number 15.

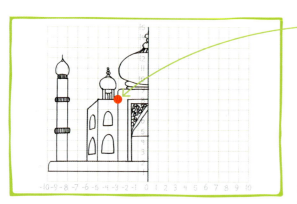

The coordinates of this vertex are (-3,8).

A coordinate with a negative number of -3 becomes 3 when it is plotted on the other side of the mirror line.

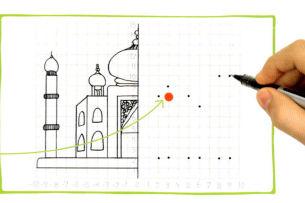

3 On one side of the y-axis, draw one half of a building. Follow the grid where you can. You will use grid numbers to work out coordinates for each point where the lines meet. This is called a vertex.

4 To work out where to draw the reflection of each vertex, convert the first part of each coordinate from a negative to a positive number. Plot these coordinates on the other side of the y-axis.

COORDINATES

The numbers that are used to identify the exact position of something on a grid or map are called coordinates. They are written in brackets, with the first number referring to the x-axis and the second, to the y-axis. A comma always separates the two numbers.

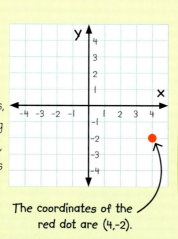

The coordinates of the red dot are (4,-2).

5 Use a pencil to draw lines connecting the vertices and then fill in any additional detail. Once you are happy with your picture, go over the pencil lines in black marker pen.

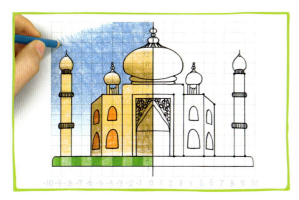

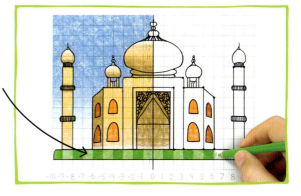

This square is light green on the left of the y-axis so it has to be light green on the right of it, too.

6 Colour in the left-hand side of the picture using different coloured pencils or pens. You can create interesting patterns by using two tones of the same colour, such as light and dark green.

7 Next, carefully repeat the pattern to the right of the line of symmetry by colouring in the opposite squares. Use the coordinates to help you work out what colour should fill each square.

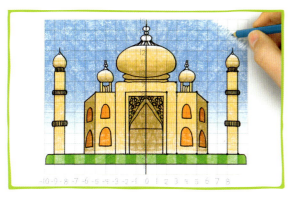

8 Repeat the process until you have coloured in the whole drawing. What other images do you think would make a good symmetrical picture?

REAL WORLD: MATHS SYMMETRY IN ARCHITECTURE

Symmetry is used in the design of buildings, not just to make them strong structures but because our brains find symmetrical things attractive. The structure of the Eiffel Tower in Paris, France, and the patterns of the metal crosses up its sides are both symmetrical.

ROTATIONAL SYMMETRY

An object has rotational symmetry if it can be turned around a point called the centre of rotation and look exactly the same. The number of times an object can do this is called the order of rotational symmetry.

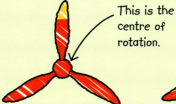

This is the centre of rotation.

1 To help show this propeller's order of rotational symmetry, we have marked the blade at the top of one of the propellers yellow.

2 Rotate the propeller until it matches the position in step 1. You'll see the yellow tip has moved around the central point.

3 Rotate the shape until the yellow tip is back at the top. To do this, it will have repeated the position in step 1 three times, meaning it has a rotational symmetry of 3.

The beauty of tessellating patterns is that the picture will look good whichever way up you hang it!

TESSELLATING PATTERNS

A tessellating pattern is made up of identical shapes that fit together without any gaps or overlap. Have you ever noticed that honeycomb built by bees is made up of tessellated hexagons, fitting neatly together with spectacular effect? Have a go at making your own eye-catching masterpiece using tessellating patterns – what shape will you choose?

We've chosen a smiley face for our tessellating pattern. Even simple designs can create detailed tessellations.

HOW TO MAKE
TESSELLATING PATTERNS

This art project creates an impressive end result. To get started, decide on the shape you want to tessellate and make a template. We'll show you how to create a template that will match our smiley face pattern, but you could use this technique to make an artwork of your own by tweaking the template in step 2.

TESSELLATING SHAPES

Shapes tessellate if they fit together perfectly with no gaps or overlapping. How many tessellating shapes can you think of?

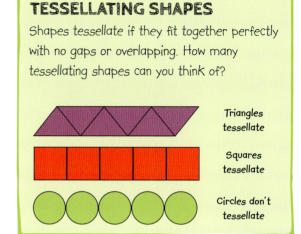

Triangles tessellate

Squares tessellate

Circles don't tessellate

Time
2 hours

Difficulty
Medium

Make sure you measure your square accurately, so all the sides are equal.

WHAT YOU NEED

Ruler

Black felt-tip pen

Scissors

Pencil

Coloured pencils of your choice

Rubber

Coloured paper

A3 paper

Adhesive tape

5 cm (2 in)

5 cm (2 in)

1 Use a ruler to measure out a 5 x 5 cm (2 x 2 in) square on your card and then carefully cut it out with a pair of scissors.

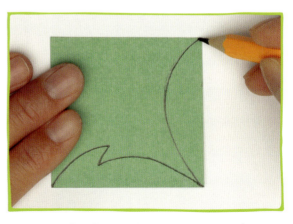

2 Copy the shapes shown here, drawing lines between the corners on two edges of the square. If you are designing your own pattern, make your line wavy or jagged, but not too detailed as this will make it difficult to cut out.

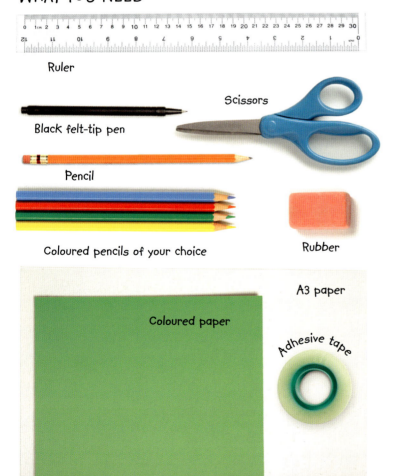

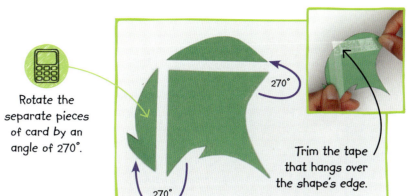

Rotate the separate pieces of card by an angle of 270°.

270°

270°

Trim the tape that hangs over the shape's edge.

3 Using a pair of scissors, carefully cut along the lines you have drawn. You will be left with three separate pieces.

4 Rotate the pieces you have cut out and place them on the outside of the adjacent sides of the shape. Use tape to stick the shapes together.

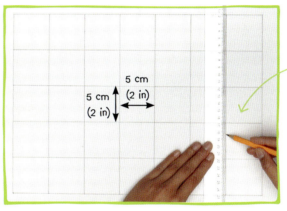

5 cm (2 in)
5 cm (2 in)

The grid will be made up of squares measuring 5 x 5 cm (2 x 2 in).

5 On an A3 sheet of paper, use a pencil and ruler to mark out 5 cm (2 in) intervals along all four sides. Then draw horizontal and vertical lines connecting the marks to create a grid.

Align the shape's vertical and horizontal lines with those on the grid.

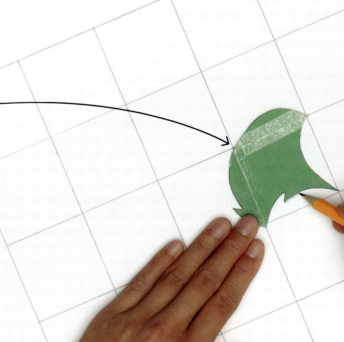

6 Place your shape in one of the squares in the centre of the grid. Use one hand to keep the shape in position while you carefully trace around it in pencil to give the outline of the shape.

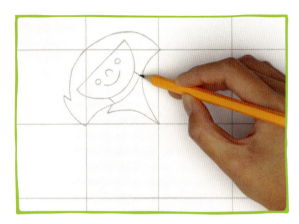

7 Consider what you could draw in your shape to bring it to life. We have gone for a happy face. Draw these details on your pencil outline.

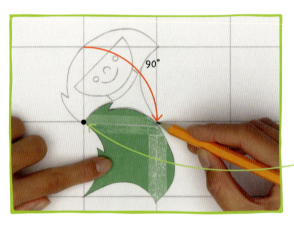

90°

8 Rotate the card by 90° onto an adjacent square and trace around it again. See how the shapes interact with each other like puzzle pieces.

The centre of rotation should stay fixed as you turn your shape.

ROTATION

When an object moves around a centre point it rotates. The distance we move the shape is called the angle of rotation.

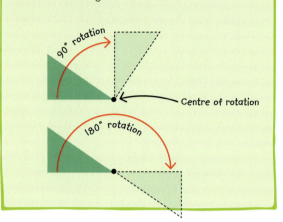

90° rotation

Centre of rotation

180° rotation

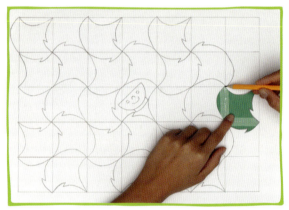

9 Continue drawing around your card template, turning it 90° each time until you have filled the entire grid with tessellating shapes.

10 Now draw a face or repeat your pattern on all the shapes, until each one has the same design as your very first one.

You may find it easier to rotate your paper as you add detail to the shapes.

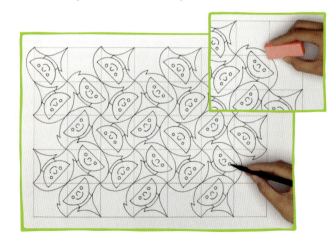

11 Using a black felt-tip pen, carefully go over your pencil lines to make your tessellation more defined and then rub out all the pencil grid lines.

12 Now colour in your tessellating pattern using coloured pencils or felt-tips.

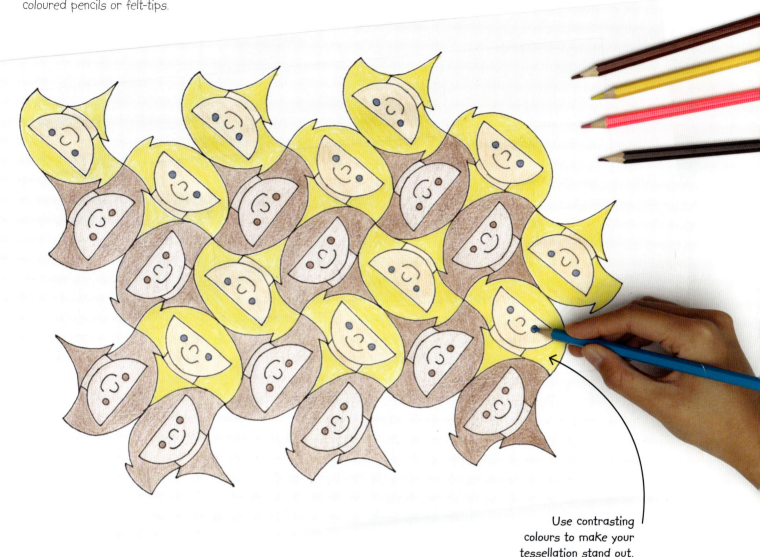

Use contrasting colours to make your tessellation stand out.

MORE COMPLEX TESSELLATIONS

Once you've mastered the basics of creating tessellations, why not have a go at more complex patterns. These use the same technique that you've just learned but start with more complex versions of the template you drew in step 2. You can also experiment with colour to make your pattern look even deeper and more detailed.

Friendship bracelets
are meant to be worn
until they fall apart.

FRIENDSHIP BRACELETS

Show your *best* friends how much they mean to you by making them friendship
bracelets. You can go for a two-tone or multicoloured bracelet – the choice is
yours. To make one, you can either put your maths skills to good use by dividing
a cardboard circle into eight equal parts to make a loom, or just weave a pattern
freehand. Whatever you choose, your friends will be queuing up wanting more.

Why not make a two-tone bracelet and double its length so the two strands overlap?

Wool and other threads are called "yarn".

Make bracelets for your friends in their favourite colours.

HOW TO MAKE
FRIENDSHIP BRACELETS

Have a go at making two different types of friendship bracelet. The first uses a cardboard loom to help you weave your band, while the Candy Stripe bracelet is woven using forward knots. The loom lets you weave different patterns, but the stripe method is simpler.

STEM YOU WILL USE

• MATHS: The circumference helps you to work out the minimum length the bracelet needs to be. Then use angles to divide a circle into equal parts to create your loom, and mark it with vertical, horizontal, and diagonal lines to make slits.

Time
2 hours per bracelet

Difficulty
Medium

WHAT YOU NEED

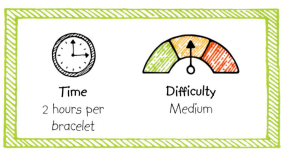

Ruler

Protractor

Compass and pencil

Scissors

Tape measure

Adhesive putty

Different-coloured wool or embroidery thread

Adhesive tape

Stiff cardboard

1. USING A CARDBOARD LOOM

The circumference is the perimeter of a circle or ellipse.

1 Start by measuring the circumference of your friend's wrist with a tape measure. The friendship bracelet will need to be longer than this so you can tie the ends together.

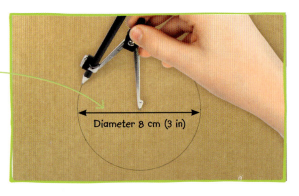

The diameter is a straight line that goes from one side of a circle to the other, passing through the centre.

Diameter 8 cm (3 in)

2 Set your compass to 4 cm (1½ in), insert a pencil, and then draw a circle with a diameter of 8 cm (3 in) on a piece of stiff cardboard.

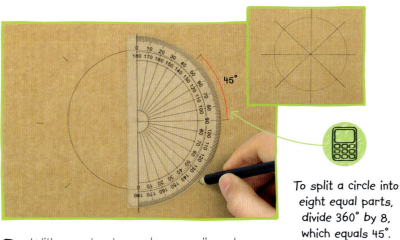

3 With a protractor, make a pencil mark every 45°. Then use a ruler to draw lines from the marks into the centre of the circle. You will now have a circle with eight equal-sized segments.

To split a circle into eight equal parts, divide 360° by 8, which equals 45°.

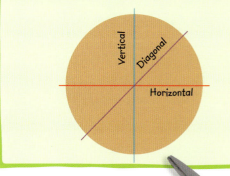

TYPES OF STRAIGHT LINES

In maths there are different types of straight lines. A vertical line goes straight up and down, while a horizontal line is level and goes from side to side. A diagonal line is a line that slants.

Vertical

Diagonal

Horizontal

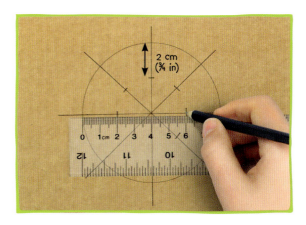

2 cm (¾ in)

4 Along each vertical, horizontal, and diagonal line, use a ruler to measure 2 cm (¾ in) in from the edge of the circle and mark these points with a pencil.

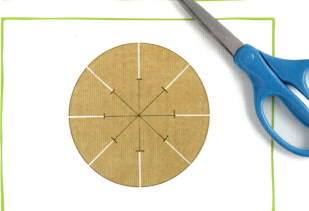

5 Cut out the cardboard circle using scissors. Then carefully cut slits along each line up to the 2 cm (¾ in) mark. This circle will act as your loom.

We've chosen to use seven different colours of wool, but you can use any colours you like.

6 Gently punch a hole in the centre of the cardboard loom using the tip of a pencil and adhesive putty. The hole needs to be big enough to feed the wool or embroidery threads through it.

7 Choose the colours of wool or embroidery thread you want to use. Measure seven lengths of thread each approximately 90 cm (35½ in) long using a tape measure and then cut with scissors.

8 Bring all the strands of wool together and tie a knot in one end. Then thread the loose ends through the hole in the middle of the cardboard loom.

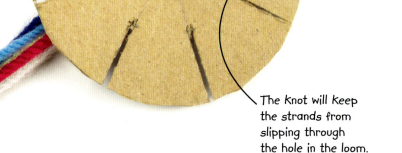

Using different coloured wool will help you remember which strand to use next when you start weaving.

The knot will keep the strands from slipping through the hole in the loom.

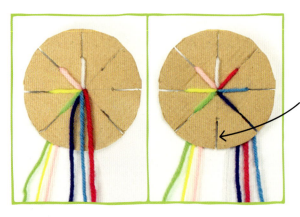

Leave the bottom slit empty.

9 Turn the cardboard loom over so the knot is on the underside and then fold one strand of wool over each slit. Leave the bottom slit empty. You are now ready to start weaving your bracelet.

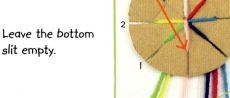

Rotate the loom anticlockwise by 135°.

10 Count clockwise from the empty slit and take the third strand of wool and pull it across to fill the empty slit. Turn the loom anticlockwise so the new empty slit is at the bottom.

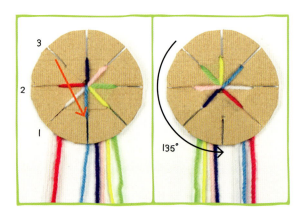

11 Repeat step 10: count three up from the bottom slit and take the wool and thread it over the empty slit. Turn the loom anticlockwise again, so that the new empty slit is pointing downwards.

12 Keep repeating this process, turning the loom anticlockwise each time. You will see the bracelet start to form on the underside of the loom.

13 Keep going until you have a length of woven strands long enough to go around your friend's wrist with about 2 cm (¾ in) of extra length for tying it together.

Leave about 2 cm (¾ in) of wool after the knot to stop the bracelet coming apart.

14 Take the threads off the cardboard loom and pull the bracelet through the hole. Knot the end to stop the weave unravelling and cut off any extra thread, leaving a short tassel after the knot.

15 Tie the finished bracelet around your friend's wrist with a knot as a symbol of your friendship.

TAKE IT FURTHER

Once you get good at making a friendship bracelet, why not take your skills further by creating friendship bracelets with geometrical patterns or complex colour sequences? Look for books in your local library, or search online, for instructions on how to make them.

Why not make a bracelet using dark and light tones of the same colour, like this one?

2. CANDY STRIPE BRACELET

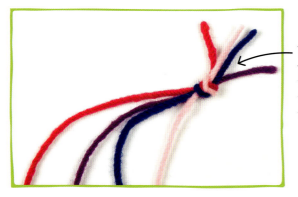

The more threads you use, the wider the bracelet but the longer it will take to make.

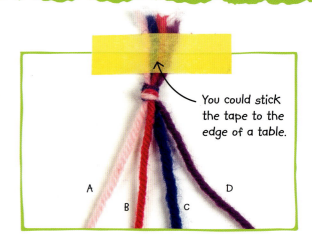

You could stick the tape to the edge of a table.

A   B   C   D

1 Choose the colours and number of threads you want to weave. We have used four threads of different colours. Cut each thread to about 90 cm (35½ in), then line them up and tie the ends together.

2 Use adhesive tape to attach the threads above the knot to a suitable surface. Separate the strands below the knot and arrange them in the order you'd like the colours to appear in the bracelet.

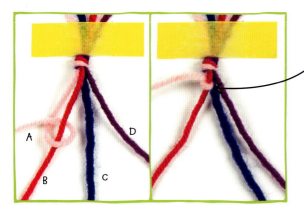

A   B   C   D

The colour of the first diagonal stripe in the bracelet will be light pink, or strand A.

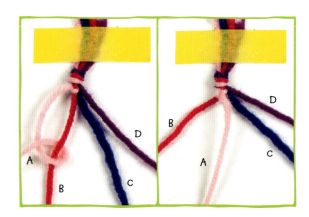

A   B   C   D

3 Pick up the far left-hand thread (A) and loop it over and under and then through thread B. Holding onto B, push the knot up to the top of the strands and pull it tight.

4 Repeat step 3 using thread A again. This type of knot is called a forward knot. When you have tied the double knot, swap threads A and B, so the order is now B, A, C, D.

TYING A FORWARD KNOT

To tie a forward knot, take thread A and first cross it over and then under thread B. Then loop A through thread B. Hold thread B and pull the knot tight. Repeat to form a double knot.

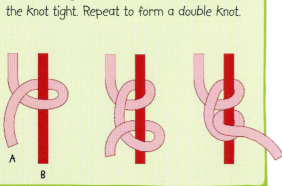

A
B

Each time you create a forward knot, you will change the order of the threads.

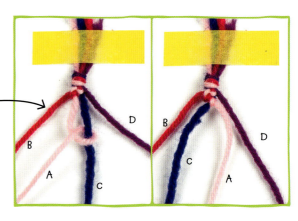

B   A   C   D

5 Repeat steps 3 and 4, but this time knot thread A twice around thread C. The order of threads will swap to B, C, A, D.

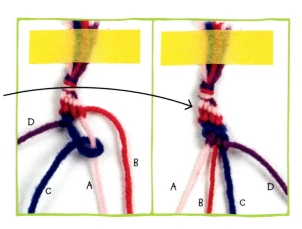

Each time you weave a row of coloured thread, you will create a pattern of diagonal stripes.

6 Follow steps 3 and 4 again, but this time knot thread A twice around D. The order of threads will then become B, C, D, A and you will have completed one row. Do the process again, starting with thread B.

7 When you have finished weaving a row using thread B, repeat with strand C and then D. Continue braiding until the coloured thread is back to A, B, C, D, which is the order you started with.

8 Repeat steps 3–7, weaving your bracelet row by row. Stop when your bracelet is the right length to fit around your friend's wrist.

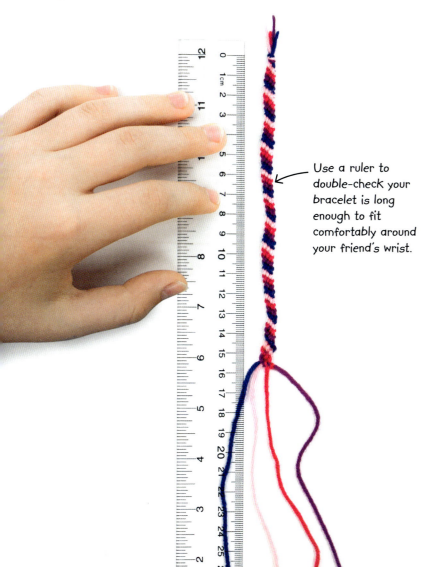

Use a ruler to double-check your bracelet is long enough to fit comfortably around your friend's wrist.

9 Tie the end to stop it coming loose and cut any extra thread, leaving 2 cm (¾ in) of wool after the knot. Then fasten it around your friend's wrist.

REAL WORLD: MATHS
WEAVING ON A LOOM

Weaving is a technique in which two sets of thread are interlaced at right angles to make cloth. Looms such as the one pictured here hold hundreds of threads in place, making it possible to weave on a large scale.

Silver paint makes the runners look like shiny steel.

These towers have been painted to look like rusty old pipes.

MARBLE RUN

Budding engineers will love the thrill of this challenge. With just a few cardboard tubes, PVA glue, and a little bit of patience you can build your own marble race track. Use angles to add a few twists and turns, then watch as the marbles whizz down the run at top speed!

The steeper the slope, the faster the marble will zoom down the track.

STEM YOU WILL USE

• SCIENCE: Gravity makes balls roll down.
• ENGINEERING: Planning is crucial in a complicated build.
• MATHS: Accurate measurements help you figure out the height of the towers, the length of the runners, and the time it takes to complete the run.

It is the force of gravity that makes the marbles accelerate down the slopes of your marble run.

HOW TO MAKE A
MARBLE RUN

The secret to making this marble run is to take your time: plan out your design first, then work on the construction, just like an engineer would. The more securely you slot the cardboard tubes together, the sturdier the marble run and the better the end result.

Time
3 hours, plus time for paint and glue to dry

Difficulty
Hard

WHAT YOU NEED

Ruler

Paint brush

Pencil

Adhesive putty

Marbles

Piece of old sponge (optional)

PVA glue (or a glue gun, operated by an adult)

Paints of your choice

Cardboard tubes of different lengths

White paper

Large piece of flat, stiff card

Scissors

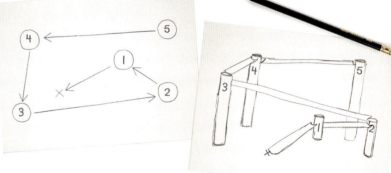

Our marble run has five towers, but you can use more if you like.

30 cm (12 in)

40 cm (15¾ in)

50 cm (20 in)

10 cm (4 in)

20 cm (8 in)

1 Plan your marble run by stacking cardboard tubes on top of each other to create towers of different heights. Then position the towers in decreasing height order, with varying distances between them to create a set of angled slopes.

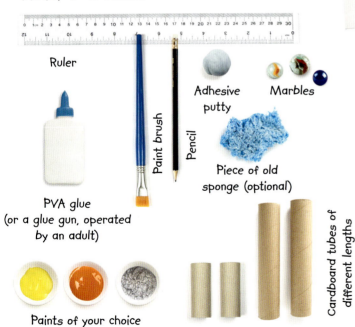

2 Sketch out the design from a bird's-eye and side-on view, remembering to mark with a cross where you would like the marble run to finish. Number each tower from 5 to 1, with 5 being the tallest tower.

3 Use PVA glue to stick the cardboard tubes together to form towers. Leave them to dry overnight standing upright so they don't separate. You should now have five towers of different heights.

4 Paint the towers and leave them to dry. You could add stripes or other details. We painted ours yellow, then dabbed rust-coloured paint using a sponge to make them look like rusty old pillars.

Draw a line with a ruler first to guide you with the cut.

5 To make the runners, glue two long kitchen roll tubes together to create an extra long one. Repeat twice. Leave upright to dry overnight, then cut them lengthways to create six long runners.

6 Trim 1 cm (½ in) off the width of each runner to make them slightly narrower. Paint all six and leave to dry. We used silver paint to make them look like steel, but you can use any colour you like.

A 3D shape with a circular face is called a cylinder.

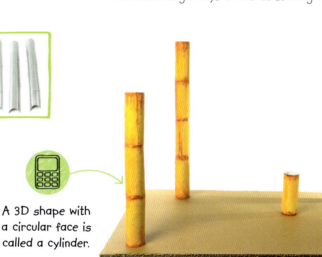

7 Refer back to your sketch and place the painted towers vertically on a large piece of flat cardboard in the positions according to your plan. Draw a circle around the base of each tower.

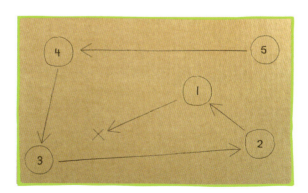

8 Number the circles as you did in your plan. Mark where the end of the marble run will be with a cross. In pencil, lightly draw arrows so you remember where the runners will be placed.

The distance between towers might be more than one ruler length. You'll need to add together the two measurements.

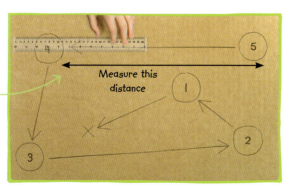

Measure this distance

9 Measure and note the distance between the furthest edge of circle 5 and the nearest edge of circle 4. Repeat this to work out the length of each runner in the marble run.

10 With a ruler and pencil, measure out the equivalent lengths on your painted runners and cut them to length. Number each section so you remember which runner will link which two towers.

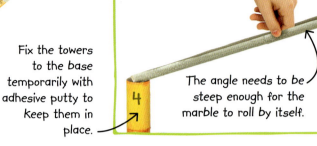

Fix the towers to the base temporarily with adhesive putty to keep them in place.

The angle needs to be steep enough for the marble to roll by itself.

11 With towers 5 and 4 on the cardboard base, rest one end of runner 5 on top of tower 4 and adjust its angle so that it reaches near the top of tower 5. Mark the meeting point on tower 5 in pencil.

12 Use the runner as a template to draw a curve on the side of tower 5, above the mark you made. Draw two vertical lines at each end and a horizontal one joining them to make a "shield" shape.

13 To make it easier to cut out the "shield", press the tip of a pencil through the card to make a hole, then use scissors. Use the offcut as a template in the next step.

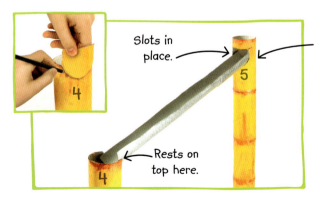

Slots in place.

Make sure the runner fits snugly inside tower 5 so that the marbles don't drop down inside.

Rests on top here.

14 Use the template to draw a curve at the top of tower 4, and cut it out with scissors. Insert the first runner between towers 5 and 4, but don't glue it in place just yet.

The vertical towers are connected by diagonal runners.

15 Repeat steps 11 to 14 until all the towers are connected. Make sure the slots and runner cuts are made on the correct side of each tower so they follow the direction of travel.

16 When you are happy with your construction, test the run with a marble and adjust the lengths of the runners if needed. Then secure the marble run. Glue the bottom of each tower to the base first, then put the runners in place and glue securely.

A marble is a 3D shape called a sphere.

17 Once the glue has dried, drop a marble into your run and watch it speed down the track. Have fun!

HOW FAR WILL THEY GO?

Can you guess how far a marble will roll once it reaches the end of the track? Test it out and record your results. Measure the distance with a ruler – did you guess correctly? You can also have fun predicting how long it will take different-sized marbles to whizz down the track and come to a stop. Use a stopwatch to time the marbles and then measure the distance they travel. The length and angle of the runners will impact on the marble's speed. The shorter the distance between the towers, the steeper the angle and the faster the marble will roll. Does the size of the marble change your results?

How far will your marble travel before stopping?

PANTOGRAPH

Invented in 1603, the pantograph is a device that was once used to copy drawings and enlarge them at the same time. It's made of four rigid pieces that pivot around joints. When you move the pencil in the middle, the end of the right arm copies the movement of your hand but covers greater distances. The effect is quite spooky, as though an invisible hand is holding the second pen and copying you. Why not try this spooky drawing machine for yourself?

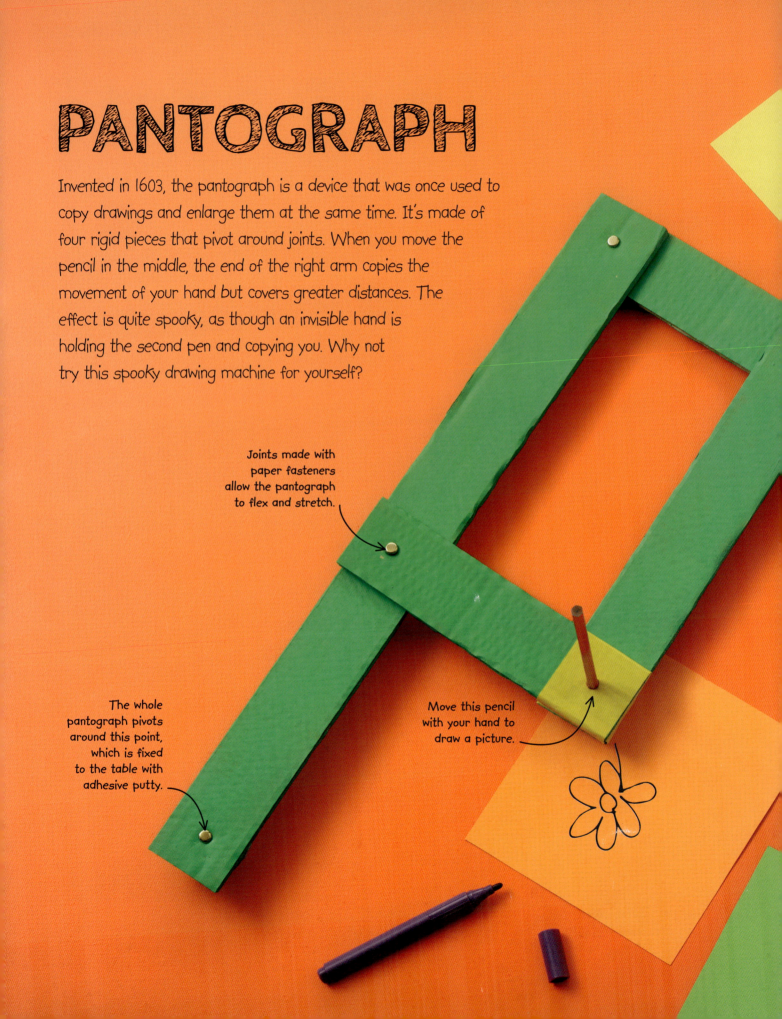

Joints made with paper fasteners allow the pantograph to flex and stretch.

The whole pantograph pivots around this point, which is fixed to the table with adhesive putty.

Move this pencil with your hand to draw a picture.

This pen draws an enlarged copy of your picture.

HOW TO MAKE A
PANTOGRAPH

Your pantograph is made of four rectangles of cardboard joined by paper fasteners. It's important that the cardboard can move freely at the joints. The pantograph works best if you draw a simple picture in a single, continuous line without lifting the pencil.

Time
30 minutes

Difficulty
Medium

WHAT YOU NEED

Felt-tip pens

Adhesive putty

Sticky tape

Pencil

Paintbrush

Two bottle caps

Scissors

Paint

Paper fasteners

Ruler

Paper

Corrugated cardboard

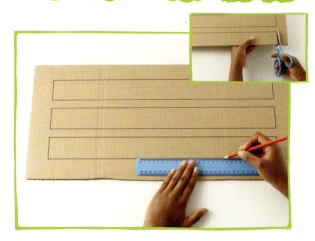

1 Use the pencil to draw three rectangles on the cardboard, each 50 cm (20 in) long by 5 cm (2 in) wide. Cut them out.

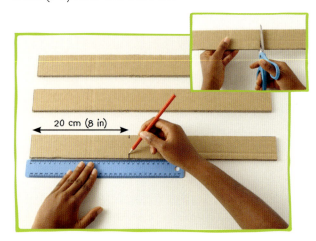

20 cm (8 in)

2 Use a pencil to mark a line on one of the rectangles, 20 cm (8 in) from the end. Cut across this line to make two rectangles, one 20 cm (8 in) long and the other 30 cm (12 in).

3 You now have all four pieces for your pantograph. If you like, paint them and allow the paint to dry.

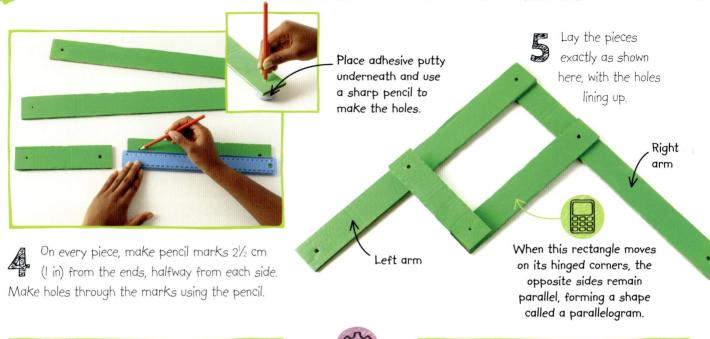

Place adhesive putty underneath and use a sharp pencil to make the holes.

4 On every piece, make pencil marks 2½ cm (1 in) from the ends, halfway from each side. Make holes through the marks using the pencil.

5 Lay the pieces exactly as shown here, with the holes lining up.

Right arm

Left arm

When this rectangle moves on its hinged corners, the opposite sides remain parallel, forming a shape called a parallelogram.

Joints are connections between moving parts in a machine.

Don't fasten this joint yet.

6 Poke paper fasteners through the two holes shown and fold the metal wings back. Don't put a fastener in the other holes yet.

7 Place a bottle cap on a lump of adhesive putty and use a sharp pencil to make a hole in it. Do the same to the other bottle cap.

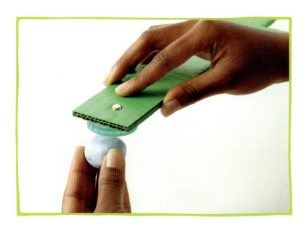

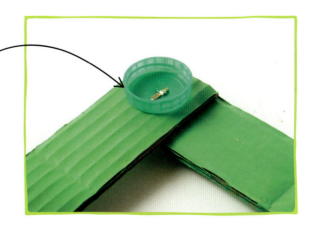

Use a paper fastener to secure the bottle cap.

8 Use a paper fastener to fix a bottle cap to the end of the left arm. Push in a lump of adhesive putty. This will secure the arm to the table.

9 Fix the other bottle cap underneath the joint between the two arms. This will keep the cardboard parts raised above the table.

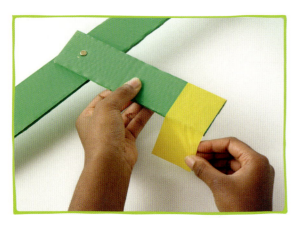

10 Wrap tape around the ends of the two short bits of cardboard and the free end of the right arm. This will stop the cardboard splitting when you push the pencil and pen through.

11 Push the pencil through the taped ends of the short bits of cardboard and leave it in place. Then make a hole through the end of the long arm and push the felt-tip pen through it.

12 To use the pantograph, draw a picture with the pencil and watch the felt-tip pen as it makes a larger copy. Try to do this in one continuous movement, without lifting the pencil or repeating lines. You can also use the pantograph to trace existing pictures and enlarge them.

The pantograph acts as a lever that magnifies movement rather than forces.

If the pantograph won't stay in place as you use it, hold the fixed end down with one hand.

HOW IT WORKS

The pantograph is an example of a mechanical linkage – a machine made of rigid pieces that are joined but can still move. A mechanical linkage changes one kind of movement into another. In this case, the movement you put in is magnified. In the centre of the pantograph is a parallelogram – a shape whose opposite sides are parallel (lined up in the same direction). The pencil and pen are mounted on parallel parts, so they trace out the same shape as they move. However, because the pen is on a longer arm, the shape it draws is magnified. The magnification equals the length of the pen's arm divided by the length of the pencil's arm (A ÷ B in the diagram).

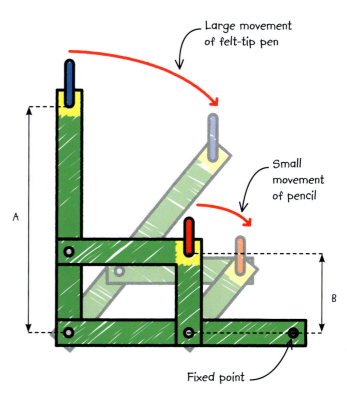

Large movement of felt-tip pen

Small movement of pencil

A

B

Fixed point

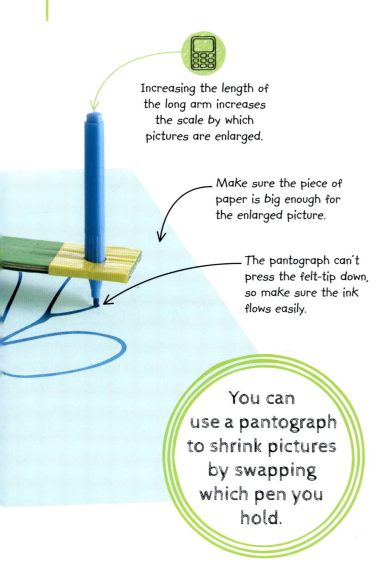

Increasing the length of the long arm increases the scale by which pictures are enlarged.

Make sure the piece of paper is big enough for the enlarged picture.

The pantograph can't press the felt-tip down, so make sure the ink flows easily.

You can use a pantograph to shrink pictures by swapping which pen you hold.

REAL WORLD: SCIENCE
UMBRELLA

Mechanical linkages are found in many different machines and devices, including something you probably have at home: an umbrella. When you push up on the sliding part inside an umbrella (the rider), the rods and pivots inside the umbrella magnify the movement of your hand to lift up the entire canopy, giving you shelter from the rain.

Push down on the back of your frog to send it leaping through the air!

Give your frog some extra camouflage by drawing dots on its back.

Add googly eyes so your frog can be on the watch for flies.

ORIGAMI JUMPING FROG

Use origami – the ancient Japanese art of paper folding – to make your own jumping frog. The length of its leap could put any self-respecting amphibian to shame, so set up a track to measure how far you can get your frog to jump. Now hop to it!

Using brightly coloured paper will give your frog an exotic look.

HOW TO MAKE AN
ORIGAMI JUMPING FROG

To make this frog, you'll need to start with square paper, and step 1 shows you how to make that from an ordinary A4 sheet. You can also buy thin, square paper designed for origami at craft shops. As you fold, make sure your creases are precise so that the frog looks just right.

1 With a pencil, mark 15 cm (6 in) along the top and left edges of the A4 paper. Draw straight lines along the marks to make a square, then cut it out.

Time
20 minutes

Difficulty
Medium

WHAT YOU NEED

Pencil

Googly eyes

Scissors

PVA glue

Ruler

Thin A4 green and blue paper

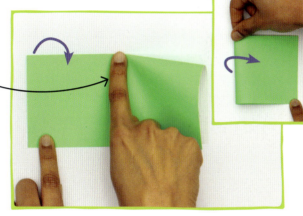

Run your finger along the crease to create a neat, sharp fold.

2 Fold the square in half so you have a green rectangle. Fold it again to create a small square, then unfold it so you have two squares.

Here, you are folding a right angle in half, or bisecting it.

3 Fold the top corner of each square to the opposite corner, then unfold and do the same with the bottom corners. When you unfold the bottom corners, you will have crossed folds in both squares.

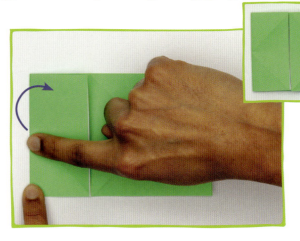

Looking closely at the creases, how many shapes can you see within your piece of paper?

4 Flip the paper over and fold each square in half lengthwise through the centre of each cross to make a square that is open in the middle.

5 Flip the paper over again and repeat the same folds as in step 4. Once opened out, the triangles at the top and bottom of the paper should pop up.

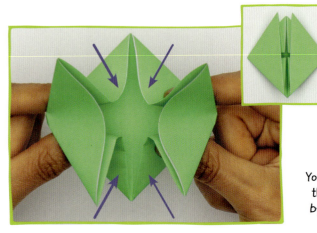

You are bisecting these triangles by folding them in half.

6 Push the outer four triangles on both sides together. As your paper collapses inwards, it will form a diamond shape.

7 Taking the tip of the top-right triangle, fold downwards to the centre of the diamond. Then fold it upwards on itself to create a smaller triangle. Repeat on the left-hand top triangle.

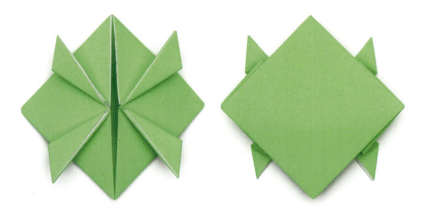

8 Repeat step 7 for the bottom two triangles, but first fold upwards and then downwards to create a mirror image of the folds you just did. Turn the frog over so the flat side is facing upwards.

BISECTION
Bisecting means to cut or divide something into two equal parts. This 40° angle has been bisected, giving two equal 20° angles.

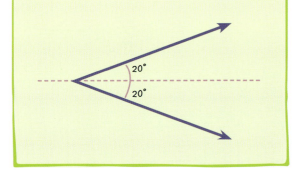

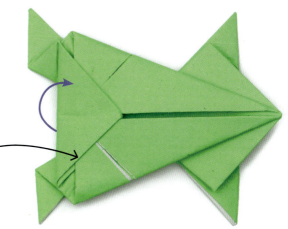

Make sure the tips are tucked into the pockets of the triangle.

9 Fold the bottom edge of the diamond along the centre line of the frog. Repeat on the other side to create a Kite shape.

10 Fold the left edge of the diamond to form a triangle. Tuck the inner tips of the kite into the pockets of the triangle you just made.

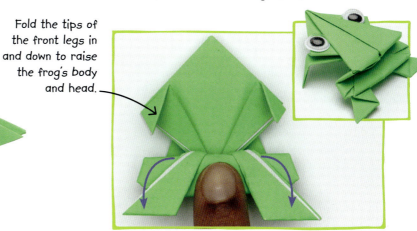

Fold the tips of the front legs in and down to raise the frog's body and head.

11 Turn your frog over and rotate it 90° so the point is at the top. Then fold the frog in half through the middle so that the back feet touch the front feet.

12 Fold the back legs in half towards you to make the spring. Then make small folds in the front feet to raise the head, before turning your frog over and adding googly eyes with PVA glue.

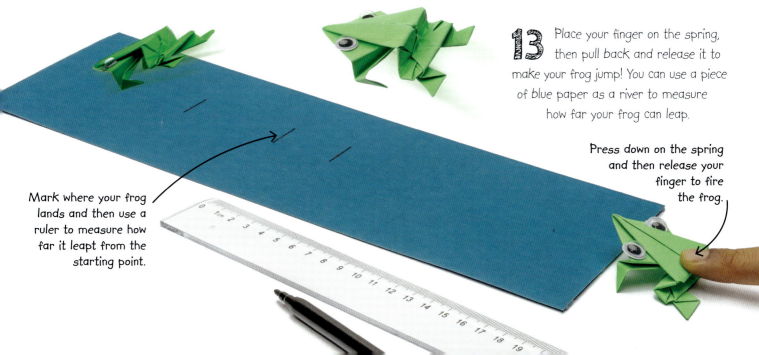

13 Place your finger on the spring, then pull back and release it to make your frog jump! You can use a piece of blue paper as a river to measure how far your frog can leap.

Press down on the spring and then release your finger to fire the frog.

Mark where your frog lands and then use a ruler to measure how far it leapt from the starting point.

LIGHT AND SOUND

Waves are associated with water, but light and sound also travel in waves. The sounds we hear are caused by vibrations that disturb the air, and the vibrations travel through the air as waves. In this chapter, you'll study light with a scientific device called a spectroscope and investigate how electric currents flow to illuminate a lamp. You'll make musical sounds, by creating your own harmonica and guitar, and hear the sound of bells – with spoons!

BEAUTIFUL SUN PRINTS

Discover your inner artist by making these intriguing and beautiful Sun prints. You need some special light-sensitive paper, which you can get from most craft shops or online. For best results, do this experiment on a bright sunny day, although it will also work on a cloudy day – it just takes a little longer. You can use any flat or nearly flat objects, such as leaves and feathers, to create a stunning gallery.

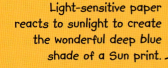

Think about what shape of frame works best with your Sun print – square, rectangle, or something else entirely.

Light-sensitive paper reacts to sunlight to create the wonderful deep blue shade of a Sun print.

A circular card mount gives a "designer touch" to the Sun print of this fern.

HOW TO MAKE
BEAUTIFUL SUN PRINTS

This experiment uses light-sensitive paper, which is coated with chemicals that react to sunlight. For best results, pick a sunny day and work outside. Remember, this is a fast-paced project, so have a tray of water ready to immerse the paper when the exposure time is up. Once exposed to light, you can't use this paper again.

Time
10 minutes plus a few hours waiting time

Difficulty
Easy

WHAT YOU NEED

Light-sensitive paper
(shown in wrapper)

Pins

Feathers

Tea towel

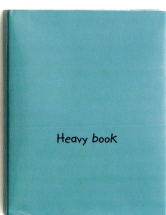

Sheet of
corrugated
cardboard

Heavy book

Tray with water inside

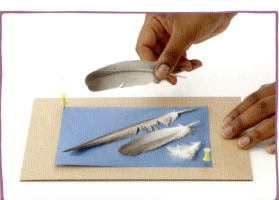

1 Go outside and take one sheet of the light-sensitive paper out of its pack. Then, pin it to the cardboard sheet and, as fast as possible, arrange the feathers on the paper. Wait for a few minutes and try not to move anything.

2 The paper will turn from deep blue to pale blue. Then, remove the feathers and unpin the paper from the card. You'll see shadows where the feathers stopped the sunlight from reaching the paper.

Use a tea towel to soak up water from the wet paper.

3 As quickly as you can, immerse the paper in the tray of water. You'll notice that the deep *blue* colour of the feathers washes right off, and the pale *blue* areas turn darker *blue*. Leave the paper in the water for a few minutes.

4 To dry the paper, place it carefully in a clean, folded tea towel. Then put a heavy *book* on top of the tea towel, as this will help press out the water and *keep* the paper flat. Leave the paper pressed inside the towel for at least a few hours.

5 Unfold the tea towel to check the paper. If it's dry, your Sun print is ready! You will *see* how the paper has changed colour yet again. The *blue* areas are much darker now, so the white feather prints really stand out.

Ultraviolet light from the Sun causes the paper to turn blue.

Marvel at the stunning detail of the feather prints.

TAKE IT FURTHER

Why not show off your *beautiful* Sun prints to your friends and family in a sophisticated frame? All you need is a ruler, pencil, piece of card, glue, and scissors.

1 Using a ruler and sharp pencil, draw a rectangle on a thick piece of card. Make the rectangle slightly smaller than the Sun print paper. Cut it out carefully.

2 Spread a generous amount of glue around the back of the frame, then stick on the Sun print paper. Make sure you place it the right way up!

HOW IT WORKS

Light-sensitive paper is coated in chemicals that react together when they are exposed to a type of light called ultraviolet. This reaction causes a deep-blue compound, known as Prussian blue, to form on the paper. When the paper is put in water, the original chemicals – which remain in areas that sunlight hasn't reached – wash away, but Prussian *blue* stays on the paper.

REAL WORLD: SCIENCE
FRAGILE FLAG

If some materials are left in sunlight for a long time, ultraviolet light can damage them. So important museum objects, like this 200-year-old American flag, are often kept in dimly lit areas.

SINGING SPOONS

In this activity, you'll use metal spoons to create amazing noises that sound like bells or gongs chiming – but you'll only hear these incredible sounds if you put your fingers in your ears! When the spoons swing and bang together, the metal flexes a tiny amount, and then flexes back again repeatedly. These movements, known as vibrations, are too fast and small to see, but they cause the string attached to the spoon to vibrate as well. The vibrations pass along the string and ultimately into your ears!

You'll need to place your fingers gently into your ears to hear the sounds!

Vibrations pass along the string and through your fingers.

Hanging the spoons from a string means they are able to vibrate freely.

The spoons clink as they knock together, but when you put your fingers in your ears, they sound different.

HOW TO MAKE
SINGING SPOONS

To hear the amazing sounds that spoons can produce, all you need to do is secure three metal spoons to string, wrap the string around your fingers, put your fingers in your ears, and knock the spoons together. This activity is super simple and quick to do, but you'll be surprised by the results!

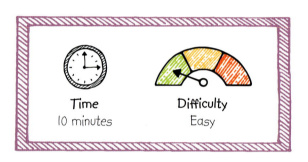

Time
10 minutes

Difficulty
Easy

WHAT YOU NEED

String

Sticky tape

Scissors

Three metal spoons

This string will carry the vibrations made by the spoons as they knock together.

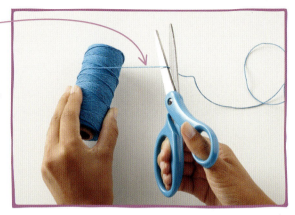

1 Cut a piece of string that is about twice the length of your arm. Lay it flat on a table.

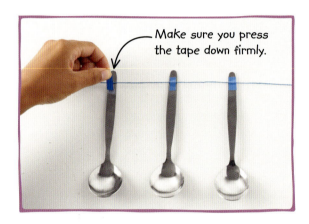
Make sure you press the tape down firmly.

2 At the string's middle point, place the ends of the spoons a few centimetres apart. Secure each spoon to the string with a piece of tape.

Metal spoons are sonorous, which means they make a ringing sound, like a bell.

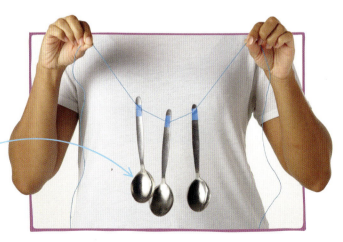

3 Dangle the spoons in front of you and wrap the string around one finger of each hand. Shake the spoons so they knock each other – they'll make a sharp, tinny sound.

Putting your fingers in your ears blocks out other noises, so the sound of the spoons seems even louder.

4 Put the fingers with string around them in your ears. Knock the spoons together – the spoons will sound louder and richer, like bells chiming.

TAKE IT FURTHER

If you switch the metal spoons for other metal objects, such as keys, or nuts and bolts, how does the sound change? Does the experiment still work if you use wooden or plastic spoons instead?

HOW IT WORKS

When metal spoons knock together, they vibrate (move rapidly to and fro). This makes sound because the vibrations make air molecules vibrate too, creating invisible waves that travel through the air to your ears. Sound waves spread out as they travel through air, so the sound you hear is quiet. But the vibrations also pass through solid materials (the string, your fingers, and your skull, which houses your inner ears). Since these vibrations do not spread out, the sound is louder when it reaches your ears. Sound waves travel more effectively through solids than air because the molecules are more tightly packed together. As a result, you hear a richer, more complex pattern of sound waves.

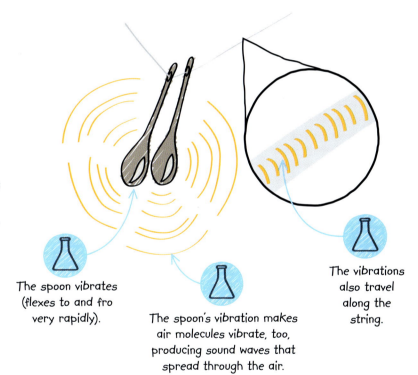

The spoon vibrates (flexes to and fro very rapidly).

The spoon's vibration makes air molecules vibrate, too, producing sound waves that spread through the air.

The vibrations also travel along the string.

REAL WORLD: TECHNOLOGY
STETHOSCOPE

You can't normally hear your heartbeat as it's too quiet. However, a doctor can hear it with a device called a stethoscope. At one end is a cup that the doctor presses on your chest to collect the faint sound of the heart beating. A hollow tube channels this sound to the doctor's ears, preventing the sound waves from spreading out in all directions and becoming too faint to hear.

Light from a torch appears white, but it is a mix of many different colours. It enters through a slit at the top of the spectroscope.

Daylight is a good source of white light if you don't have a torch available.

When white light hits the shiny side of the CD, it bounces off and separates into different colours.

A viewing window lets you see and study the spectrum, or range, of colours present in the torchlight.

SPECTROSCOPE

It might look white, but light is actually a mix of different colours. Scientists use a device known as a spectroscope to study the range of colours (the spectrum) in different kinds of light. In this activity, you can make your own spectroscope.

STEM YOU WILL USE
- SCIENCE: Colour spectrums vary depending on the source.
- TECHNOLOGY: Spectroscopes analyse light by separating it into the colours it's made of.

HOW TO BUILD A
SPECTROSCOPE

In order to clearly *see* the spectrum of colours that make up white light, you'll need a shiny CD for the light to bounce off. A slit at the top of a dark tube lets a small amount of light into the tube and onto the CD. You'll need to use a protractor to measure the angle at which you place the CD. You'll also need black electrical tape to block out unwanted light.

Time
30 minutes

Difficulty
Medium

WHAT YOU NEED

Protractor

Paint

Black electrical tape

Scissors

Torch

Paintbrush

Pencil

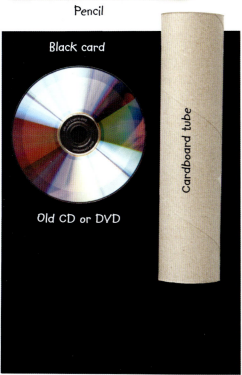

Black card

Old CD or DVD

Cardboard tube

Ruler

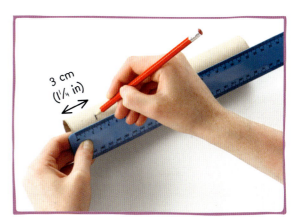

3 cm (1¼ in)

1 Using the pencil, make a mark 3 cm (1¼ in) from one end of the cardboard tube.

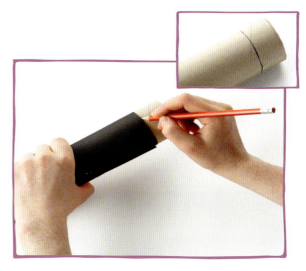

2 Wrap the black card around the cardboard tube at the mark. Use it as a guide to draw a line around the tube.

Check the straight edge of your protractor is still lined up with the pencil line you drew.

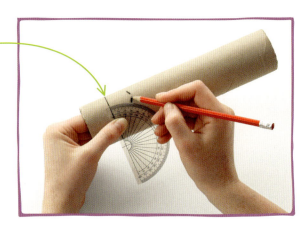

3 Hold the protractor on the tube so the protractor's zero line runs along the pencil line. Draw a short line angled at 30°.

4 Move the protractor and draw another line, angled at 30° in the other direction, so the two slanted lines almost meet.

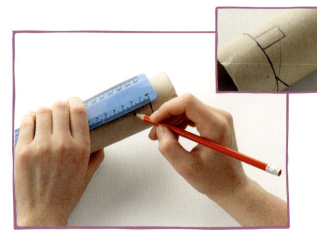

5 Using the ruler, extend both slanted lines so they meet the line that goes around the cardboard tube, forming a triangle.

6 On the opposite side of the tube from the triangle, draw a rectangle 2 cm (¾ in) high and 1 cm (½ in) wide above the pencil line.

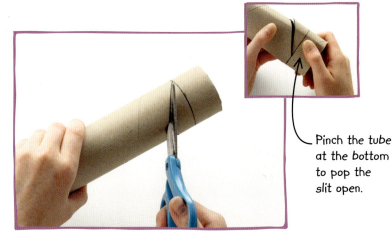

Pinch the tube at the bottom to pop the slit open.

7 Cut along the two slanted lines so that you end up with an angled slot. This is where you'll slide in your old CD.

8 Now carefully cut out the small rectangle you drew, to make a viewing window for your spectroscope. Ask an adult to help if you get stuck.

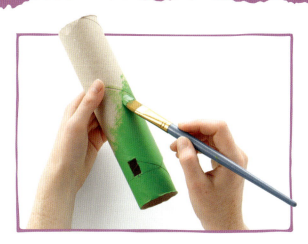

9 Paint the cardboard tube in any colour or design you like, then leave the paint to dry.

10 Push the CD into the angled slot, with the shiny, bottom surface facing upwards.

It's crucial to get the angle of the CD just right so you can see the spectrum clearly.

11 Secure the CD in place inside the slot using black electrical tape.

12 Use strips of electrical tape to close off the end of the cardboard tube closest to the CD. Make sure no light can get into the tube.

The end closest to the CD should be completely covered with black electrical tape.

13 Draw around the open end of the cardboard tube onto the black piece of card, using a pencil. Carefully cut out the circle.

14. The circle of card will cover the open end of the tube, but it needs a slit to let in light. To make the slit, first fold the circle in half.

Light from the torch enters the slit in the top of the spectroscope.

Most modern torches use LEDs (light emitting diodes) as their light source, which is made up of fewer colours than those found in sunlight.

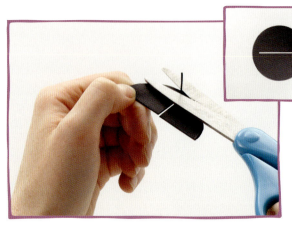

15. Carefully cut two lines close together at right angles from the middle of the fold. Then snip off the thin piece between the lines.

The light hits the shiny CD and bounces off, splitting into different colours.

Carefully tape around the circle of black card to hold it in place.

16. Unfold the circle and tape it over the open end of the tube. The slit should run from side to side, not front to back, so that it aligns with the slot holding the CD.

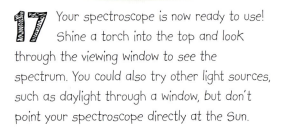

17. Your spectroscope is now ready to use! Shine a torch into the top and look through the viewing window to see the spectrum. You could also try other light sources, such as daylight through a window, but don't point your spectroscope directly at the Sun.

HOW IT WORKS

White light is a mixture of all the colours of the rainbow. When it hits a reflective object, all these colours bounce off, or reflect. Light hitting the shiny underside of a CD reflects in a different way. All the colours reflect, but each one bounces off in a different direction. The different colours spread out to form a spectrum.

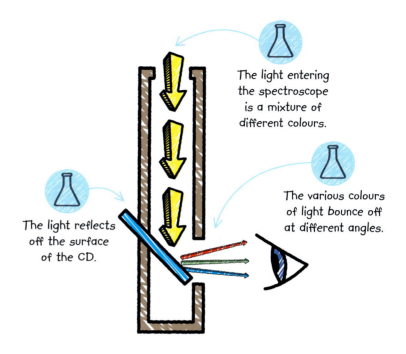

The light entering the spectroscope is a mixture of different colours.

The various colours of light bounce off at different angles.

The light reflects off the surface of the CD.

COMPARING DIFFERENT LIGHT SOURCES

If you compare different light sources, such as daylight or the screen of a mobile phone, you'll find that each one produces a distinctive spectrum. Daylight produces a continuous spectrum, with every colour of the rainbow and no gaps. In contrast, an artificial light source typically produces only certain colours, and so its spectrum has coloured lines with black gaps between them.

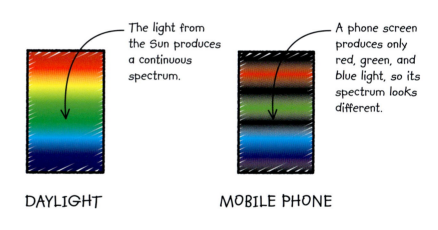

The light from the Sun produces a continuous spectrum.

A phone screen produces only red, green, and blue light, so its spectrum looks different.

DAYLIGHT

MOBILE PHONE

REAL WORLD: SCIENCE
THE LIGHT OF STARS

Each of the chemical elements of which matter is made produces light with a different spectrum when it burns. Chemists in laboratories can identify which elements are present in different substances by using spectroscopes to study the light they give off when burned. Astronomers also use spectroscopes to study light from stars; from lines in the spectrum, they can tell which elements are present.

As the buzzer flies, the rubber band makes a sound like a bee.

Swing the string around to make the buzzer fly.

BUZZER

When you whirl this buzzer around, it'll make a sound like a bumblebee. A bee makes a buzz by flapping its wings more than 200 times a second when it flies. Instead of wings or muscles, your buzzer will use a simple rubber band to mimic a flying bee. The rubber band twists back and forth rapidly as you whirl it through the air, and this fluttering movement creates sound waves.

HOW TO MAKE A
BUZZER

The buzzer is made from a lollipop stick, a rubber band, some card and string, and some adhesive putty. It's quick and easy to make – but you may have to adjust certain things to make your buzzer work well. In particular, you might have to try a few different sizes of rubber band.

Time
15 minutes

Warning
Take care not to hit yourself or anyone else.

Difficulty
Easy

STEM YOU WILL USE
• SCIENCE: The force needed to keep something moving in a circle is known as centripetal force. Also, air flow over a flexible object can cause it to vibrate – a phenomenon known as aeroelastic flutter.

WHAT YOU NEED

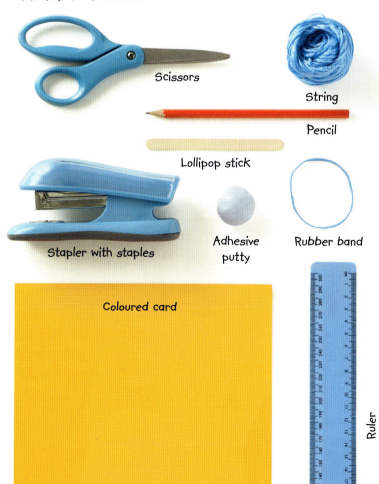

Scissors

String

Pencil

Lollipop stick

Stapler with staples

Adhesive putty

Rubber band

Coloured card

Ruler

1 Fold the card in half. Make a tight crease by pressing down firmly along the fold.

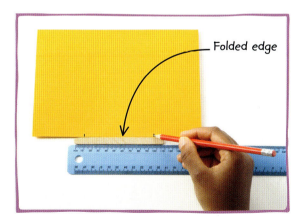

Folded edge

2 Lay the lollipop stick next to the folded edge. Make two pencil marks on the fold, each about 1 cm (½ in) from the end of the stick.

The strings are held in tension.

You can adjust how tightly the strings are held by turning the hooks at the head.

STEM YOU WILL USE
• SCIENCE: A vibrating string produces a note of a particular pitch. The note's pitch depends on the string's tension, thickness and length.
• TECHNOLOGY: A soundboard amplifies the sound the strings produce.
• ENGINEERING: Layering a material, such as cardboard, can give it stiffness and strength.

GUITAR

Making music can be a great way to explore the science of sound – and this guitar can help you do both. With fishing line for strings and an ice cream tub for a body, it's easy to make. And if you set it up right, it will make a surprisingly tuneful sound. In fact, you'll find this project really hits the right notes!

The vibrations of the strings are passed on to the body of the guitar.

The vibrating body of the guitar disturbs the air, sending out sound waves into the air around it.

HOW TO MAKE A
GUITAR

The two most important features of your guitar are the strings and the body. In this project, the strings are made of fishing line. The body of your guitar is made of a plastic ice cream tub. The neck is made of corrugated cardboard.

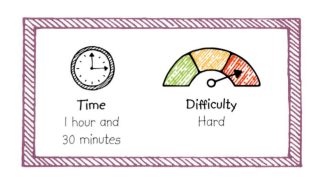

Time
1 hour and
30 minutes

Difficulty
Hard

WHAT YOU NEED

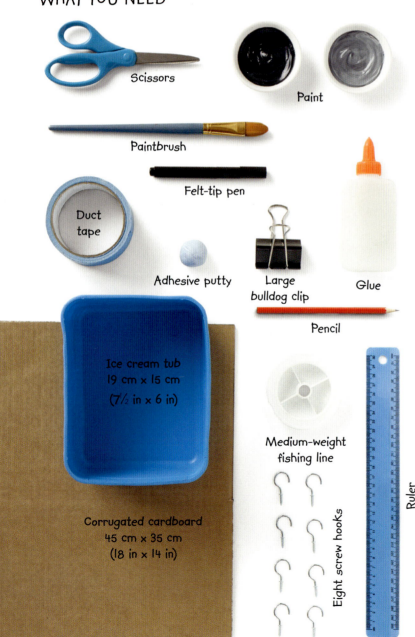

Scissors

Paint

Paintbrush

Felt-tip pen

Duct tape

Adhesive putty

Large bulldog clip

Glue

Pencil

Ice cream tub
19 cm x 15 cm
(7½ in x 6 in)

Medium-weight fishing line

Eight screw hooks

Ruler

Corrugated cardboard
45 cm x 35 cm
(18 in x 14 in)

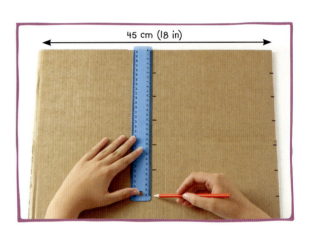

45 cm (18 in)

1 Make pencil marks every 5 cm (2 in) down the shorter side of the cardboard. Repeat the marks in the middle.

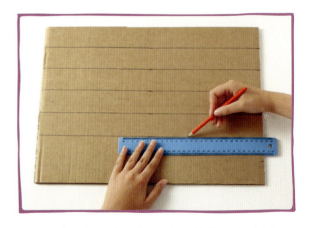

2 Using the ruler, draw straight lines that join the marks you made and extend them across the whole width of the cardboard.

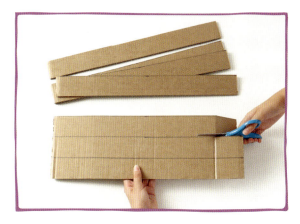

3 Cut along the lines, so that you end up with seven long rectangles of cardboard, each 45 cm (18 in) long and 5 cm (2 in) wide.

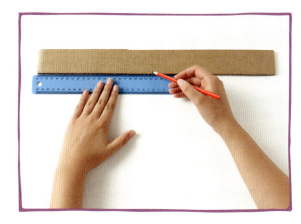

4 On one of the long rectangles, make a pencil mark 22½ cm (9 in) from one end – halfway along its length.

5 Divide the long rectangle into two equal pieces, by cutting where you made the pencil mark.

Stacking and gluing the pieces together like this increases the strength of the neck.

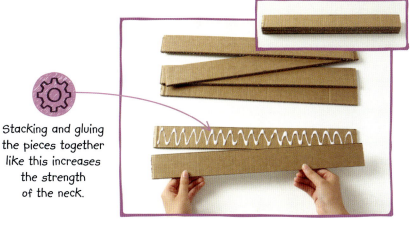

6 Stick the other six long rectangles together by applying glue between them and putting them together into a stack.

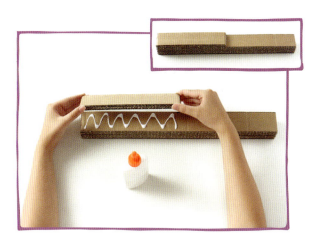

7 Now glue the two shorter pieces on top of one end of the stack, so that the stack is thicker at one end. This is the neck of the guitar.

8 Mix some glue into the paint. This will thicken it and add strength to the neck when applied to it.

The neck of a guitar has to be strong enough to withstand the stress of the tight strings against it.

9 Apply the glue-and-paint mixture all over your guitar's neck, and leave it for half an hour or so to dry and set.

To make it look like a real guitar, we've decorated ours with painted frets. Frets are metal strips on the neck that help the player find the notes.

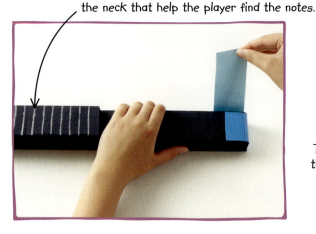

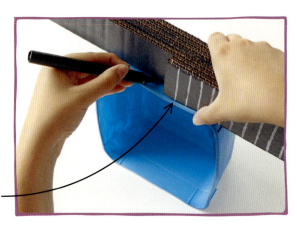

This is to ensure that the neck will line up with the side of the tub.

10 Apply a few pieces of duct tape around both ends of the guitar's neck, to strengthen them further.

11 Stand the tub on one of its shorter sides. Hold the thick end of the neck against the rim of the tub. Make a mark on the tub next to the thinner part of the neck.

Try to position the neck in the middle of the tub's side.

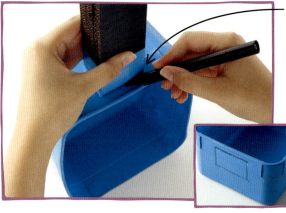

Put adhesive putty under the tub to protect the table.

12 Hold the thin end of the neck against the end of the tub, and line up the top of it with the mark you made. Draw around the neck.

13 Repeat steps 11 and 12 at the other end of the tub. Now carefully use the scissors to make a hole in the middle of each rectangle, from the inside of the box outwards.

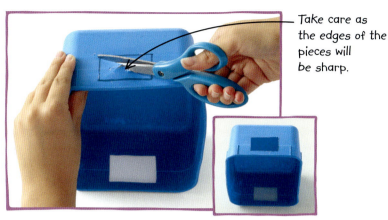

Take care as the edges of the pieces will be sharp.

14 Neatly cut out each rectangle, starting at the hole you made. Cut straight lines out to the corners first, then along the rectangle's sides.

If the neck doesn't fit, you might need to make the hole a bit bigger.

15 Push the thin end of the neck through the two holes, until the thick part of the neck juts up against the side of the tub.

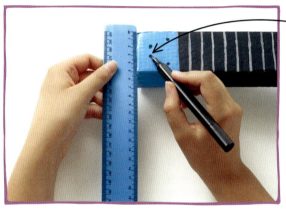

Make two of the holes closer to the end than the other two.

16 Line up a ruler at the thick end of the neck. Mark dots at 1 cm (½ in) intervals, making two of them closer to the end, as shown.

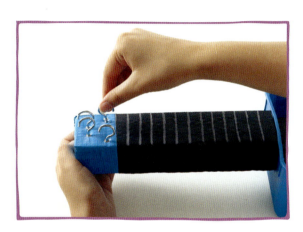

17 Screw the four hooks into each of the holes. These will hold the guitar's strings.

19 Screw a hook into each of the four dots you drew. In each case, make sure the open part of the hook faces away from the body of the guitar.

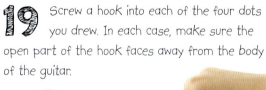

The box will act as a soundboard, or soundbox, amplifying the sound made by the strings.

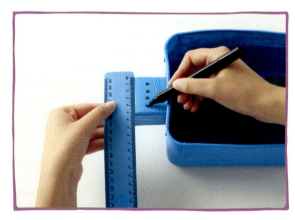

18 Draw four more dots on the tape at the thin end of the neck. Make these 1 cm (½ in) apart, too, but all in a line this time.

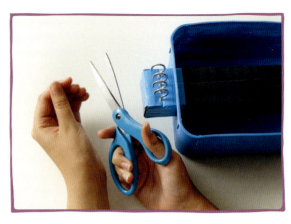

Make sure the strings don't cross or touch one another.

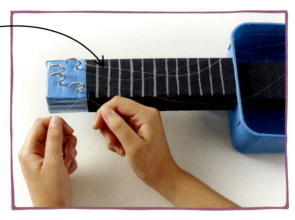

20 Cut four pieces of fishing line, 10 cm (4 in) longer than the distance from one set of hooks to the other set of hooks.

21 At the thick end of the neck, attach each length of fishing line to a hook. Tie a double knot as tightly as you can.

23 Pull the ends of the four lengths of fishing line together, keeping them taut, and then secure them with the bulldog clip. See what happens when you move your fingers up and down the guitar neck while plucking the strings at the same time.

22 Pull the free end of each length taut and wrap it once or twice around a hook at the other end. Do not tie the line at this end.

Pluck one or more strings with the thumb or fingers of your other hand.

The body of the guitar is what amplifies the sound.

Press down on one or more strings with the fingers of one hand.

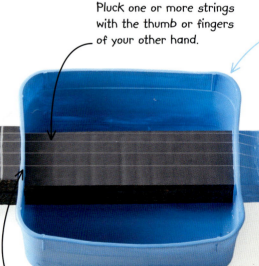

Tighten the strings by turning the hooks at this end until they are taut.

There should be a gap between the strings and the rim of the tub.

You can trim the ends of the strings, but don't make them too short.

HOW IT WORKS

Plucking a string on your guitar causes the string to vibrate many times per second. The more tension there is in the string (the more tightly it's pulled), the more rapidly it vibrates – and the higher the pitch. Pressing a string also raises the pitch. When you press a string, it touches the guitar body in the middle and only its lower half vibrates. This produces a note one octave higher. The strings cause the body of the guitar to vibrate, which disturbs much more air, because it has a larger surface area. This amplifies the vibration of the strings, making it louder.

Plucking the string causes it to vibrate.

Pressing the strings down with your fingers on the cardboard changes the length of the string, which changes the note.

As the body of the guitar vibrates, it amplifies the sound of the strings.

The length, tension, and thickness of the string all affect the note produced.

Without the body of the guitar, the sound waves created by the string's vibrations would barely be audible.

REAL WORLD: TECHNOLOGY
ACOUSTIC GUITAR

Most acoustic guitars have six strings, with each one being a different thickness. The thicker the string, the lower the note it makes. This allows a guitar to produce a great range of notes and sound. Also, unlike your ice-cream-tub guitar, acoustic guitars have a closed front part, with a sound hole, which helps to amplify deeper sounds, as the air inside the guitar is compressed and expands. Finally, the material the guitar is made from greatly affects the sound, as certain materials produce different kinds of sound. Though wood is the most common material, acoustic guitars can also be made from metal or plastic.

LEMON BATTERY

Did you know that you can make a battery using lemons? With just five lemons, some coins, screws, and leads, you can make an electric current flow around a circuit with enough energy to illuminate a small lamp called a light emitting diode (LED). Now just imagine what you could power with one hundred lemons!

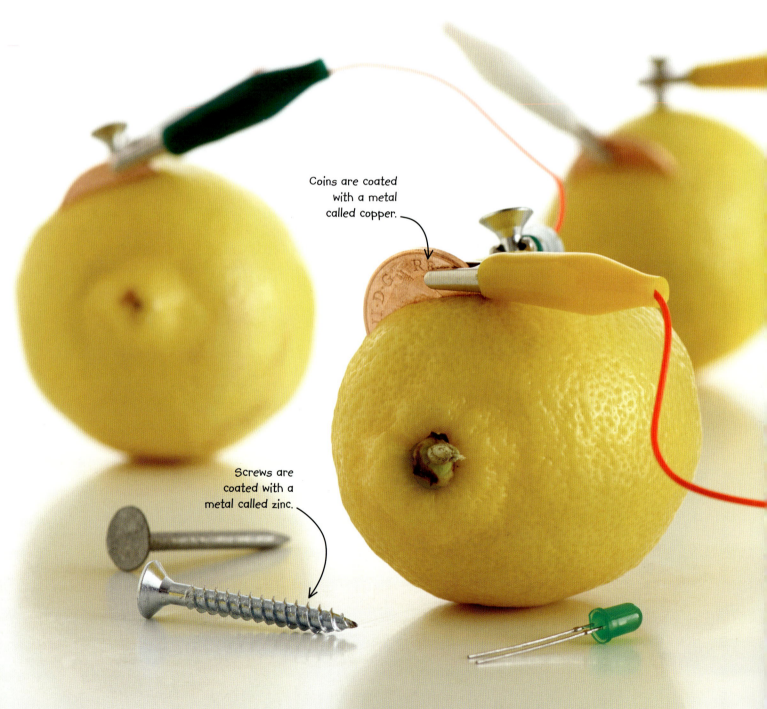

Coins are coated with a metal called copper.

Screws are coated with a metal called zinc.

Leads have metal wires inside and connect the coins with the screws.

LEDs are found in many kinds of electronic equipment.

HOW TO MAKE A
LEMON BATTERY

Ask an adult to help you get hold of what you need. The screws must be galvanized, which means coated with zinc. LEDs and leads with crocodile clips can be found in craft or electronics shops. While this experiment is safe, do remember that electricity can be dangerous. And discard the lemons when you have finished the experiment – don't use them for food.

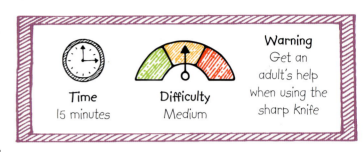

Time 15 minutes

Difficulty Medium

Warning Get an adult's help when using the sharp knife

WHAT YOU NEED

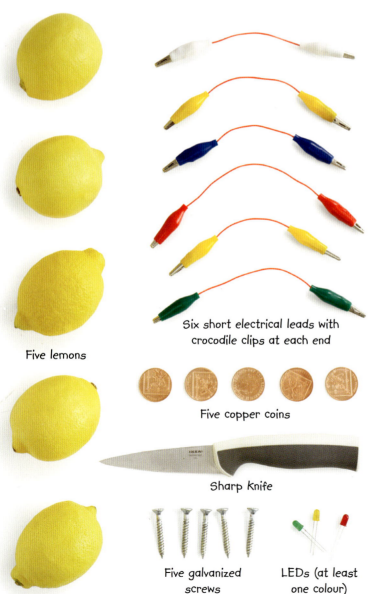

Five lemons

Six short electrical leads with crocodile clips at each end

Five copper coins

Sharp knife

Five galvanized screws

LEDs (at least one colour)

1 With an adult's help, use the knife to make a cut in a lemon, about 1 cm (½ in) from the centre, and roughly 2 cm (¾ in) deep. Now push a coin firmly into the slit you have created. Do the same with the other four lemons.

2 About 1 cm (½ in) from the centre of the first lemon – on the other side to the coin – insert a galvanized screw. Twist it in, clockwise, to secure it in the lemon's flesh. Now repeat with the other four lemons, then arrange the lemons in a circle.

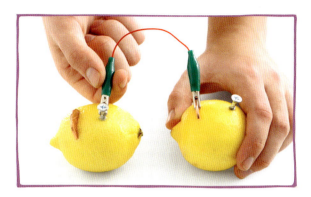

3 Squeeze the crocodile clip on one lead so that it opens, like a crocodile's jaws. Place it around the screw in one lemon, so it grips it. Connect the other clip to the coin in another lemon.

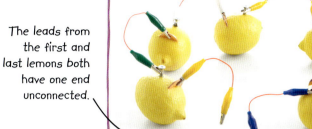

The leads from the first and last lemons both have one end unconnected.

4 Connect all the lemons – coin to screw – as in step 3. For the last lemon, attach a lead to its coin, but don't connect it to the screw in your first lemon. Instead, attach another lead to that screw.

5 Each LED has two legs, which are slightly different lengths. With the free end of the lead that is attached to the coin, fix the crocodile clip to the slightly longer leg of the LED.

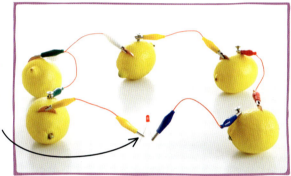

If the light from the LED is weak, try pushing in or wiggling the screws and coins.

6 Now connect the crocodile clip of the other free lead that is connected to the screw to the other, shorter leg of the LED. This now completes the circuit to make the LED light up.

HOW IT WORKS

The electric current that lights your LED is actually caused by countless tiny particles called electrons moving around the circuit. Electrons are present inside every atom. As the zinc dissolves in the lemon juice, two electrons are released from each atom of zinc (from the screw). All electrons are negatively charged, and they push apart as they move inside the wire. When they reach the copper coin, they take part in another chemical reaction, allowing electrons to continue flowing around the circuit.

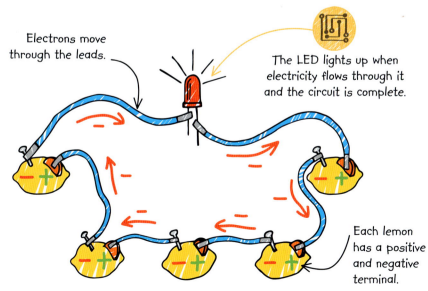

Electrons move through the leads.

The LED lights up when electricity flows through it and the circuit is complete.

Each lemon has a positive and negative terminal.

SENSATIONAL SPEAKERS

Do you love listening to music on a phone but find it doesn't sound as good as you'd like it to? Maybe your family grumbles every time you play your favourite songs really loud? These terrific smartphone speakers could be the answer to both problems. They not only help to get rid of that "tinny" effect, but also direct most of the sound straight to your ears. So your music sounds bigger and better without annoying everyone else in the room.

You can change the colours of your speakers as often as you like.

These brilliant speakers are made from everyday household items.

A smartphone is a mobile phone that is also a mobile computer.

Built-in mini loudspeakers are usually located at the bottom of a phone.

HARMONICA

Here's a fun and simple way to make some musical notes, and to learn a bit about the science of sound. Just like a real harmonica, this one has a part that vibrates when you direct air past it with your breath. In this homemade version, it's a piece of paper held between two pieces of cocktail stick sandwiched between two lollipop sticks. Go on – see what weird and wonderful sounds you can make!

The pitch of the note your harmonica produces – how high or low it is – depends on how fast the paper vibrates. The faster it vibrates, the higher the pitch.

STEM YOU WILL USE
• SCIENCE: Sound is produced by vibrating objects. Musical instruments produce notes that vibrate at either a high or low pitch. By stretching a vibrating rubber band you can produce a higher-pitched sound.

Making harmonicas is a good way to recycle your lollipop sticks, but make sure they are dry first.

As you play the harmonica, you'll be able to feel the tickle of the vibrations that create the sound.

HOW TO MAKE A
HARMONICA

This harmonica is made with lollipop sticks. As you are going to be touching these with your mouth, make sure they are clean. The only other things you need are rubber bands, toothpicks, and a strip of paper. You'll be making music in just a few minutes!

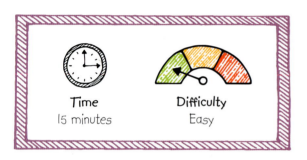

Time
15 minutes

Difficulty
Easy

WHAT YOU NEED

Two rubber bands

Two toothpicks

Pencil

Scissors

Coloured paper

Two lollipop sticks

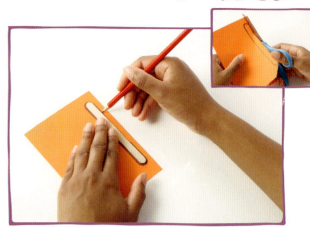

1 On the paper, draw around a lollipop stick with the pencil, then carefully cut around the shape with the scissors.

In your harmonica, the paper vibrates, disturbing the air around it to produce sound.

2 Place the piece of paper you cut out on top of one of the lollipop sticks, then place the other lollipop stick on top.

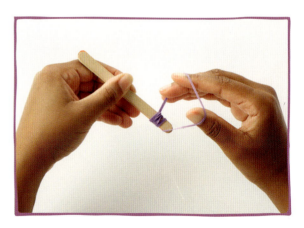

3 Wrap a rubber band several times around one end of the two lollipop sticks, so that it holds them together.

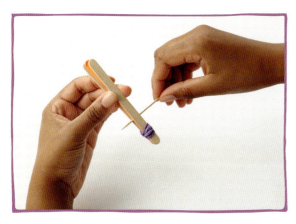

4 Wedge a toothpick between the lollipop sticks, and slide it as far towards the end with the rubber band as you can.

You should end up with a toothpick wedged in at both ends of the harmonica.

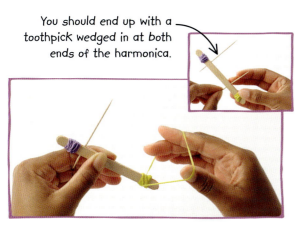

5 Wrap another rubber band around the other end of the lollipop sticks, then wedge another toothpick in at that end.

6 Using scissors, carefully trim the toothpicks and discard the extra pieces. Make sure the paper is flat, not crumpled, then hold the harmonica firmly between your lips and blow. Try sucking, too.

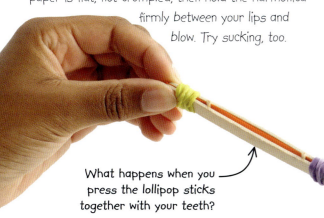

What happens when you press the lollipop sticks together with your teeth?

HOW IT WORKS

The pieces of toothpick hold the paper firmly at each end. When you blow or suck, air rushing past the paper makes it vibrate, and the vibrations create disturbances in the air that travel outwards in all directions as sound waves. If you blow harder or pinch the sticks as you blow, the paper vibrates faster. This creates a higher-pitched sound.

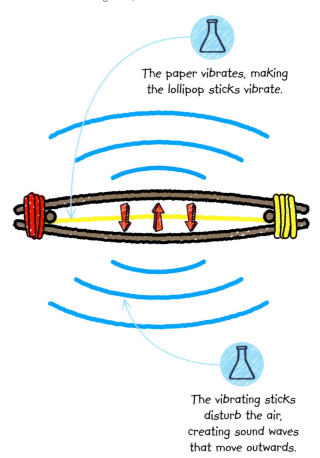

The paper vibrates, making the lollipop sticks vibrate.

The vibrating sticks disturb the air, creating sound waves that move outwards.

REAL WORLD: SCIENCE
VIBRATING REEDS

Real harmonicas work in a similar way to your lollipop harmonica. Instead of paper, they have metal sheets called reeds that vibrate when the player blows or sucks through a set of holes. There is at least one reed behind each hole, and each reed is tuned to a different note.

NUMBERS AND MEASUREMENTS

Whether you're working with weight, height, length, or depth, the projects in this chapter will show you how to master the art of measurements. Find out how scientists use measuring devices to record wind speed and the temperature. You'll learn how to tell the time on a colourful clock and a sundial, and use maths to measure the chances of something happening. You'll even find out how getting the measure of money can help you make a profit at your next school fair.

BRILLIANT BAROMETER

It may be hard to believe, but the air around you is pressing on you from every direction! This powerful push is called atmospheric pressure, and it's measured using a device called a barometer. Weather forecasters use barometers to help predict how the weather will change over the next few days, as the atmospheric pressure changes.

Record the straw's position on the scale every day. You will soon start to observe trends, and can then predict when those things will happen again.

The straw indicates changes in atmospheric pressure by moving up or down.

HOW TO MAKE A
BRILLIANT BAROMETER

This barometer is easy to make – you simply stretch a piece of rubber cut from a *balloon* over the opening of a glass jar. As atmospheric pressure increases, it pushes the rubber down against the air trapped inside, and as the pressure goes down, the rubber relaxes. Tape a straw to the rubber and watch it rise and fall as the pressure changes.

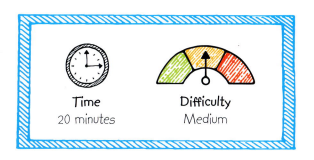

Time
20 minutes

Difficulty
Medium

WHAT YOU NEED

Biodegradable straw

Pencil

Balloon

Ruler

Coloured card

Coloured tape

Scissors

Rubber band

Glass jar

1 Cut the neck off the *balloon* and throw it away immediately. This will make it possible to stretch the rubber over the jar's opening. There's no need to blow up the balloon.

Make sure you have a smooth surface.

2 Stretch the rubber over the top of the jar, trapping the air inside. Pull the rubber tight, to get rid of any creases.

3 Secure the rubber in place with an elastic band. No air should be able to escape the jar.

Rain falls into the opening at the top of your rain gauge.

RAIN GAUGE

Meteorologists, or weather forecasters, measure and compare rainfall over time to find patterns in the weather. With the help of weekly, monthly, and yearly records, they can predict when there might be heavy rain, or if a drought is on the way – vital information for farmers and gardeners. To measure rainfall, meteorologists use a device called a rain gauge.

The rain gauge has a ruler stuck to the side, so you can easily measure how much rain has fallen.

STEM YOU WILL USE

• SCIENCE: Rain normally drains away, or collects on the ground if it is too dry.

• MATHS: A bar graph displays your results clearly to help you work out the wettest months.

HOW TO MAKE A
RAIN GAUGE

To make this simple rain gauge, you need to cut off the top of a bottle and make a flat surface at the bottom, inside the bottle, by adding gravel and modelling clay. There's a ruler stuck with tape to the side of the rain gauge that will allow you to measure and record how much rain falls in your local area.

1 Wrap the card around the bottle, to help you draw straight. Draw a straight line around the bottle, about 10 cm (4 in) down from the top.

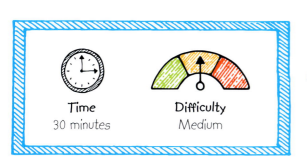

Time
30 minutes

Difficulty
Medium

Most plastic bottles are made of polyethylene terephthalate (PET).

WHAT YOU NEED

Scissors

Gravel

Felt-tip pen

Coloured tape

Modelling clay

Ruler

Large plastic bottle

Coloured card

2 Carefully cut along the line to separate the bottle into two parts. Be careful of any sharp edges and ask an adult to help you if you're finding it tricky.

3 Wrap tape neatly around the cut edges of the two parts, leaving enough to fold over. This will cover up any uneven cutting.

If your bottle has an uneven bottom, the layer of gravel will help to flatten it.

4 Pour gravel into the bottom part of the bottle, to weigh down your rain gauge so it won't fall over.

5 Press and mould the modelling clay into a thick, flat disc with the same diameter as the bottle. Make it as flat and smooth as you can.

6 Push the modelling clay disc down onto the surface of the gravel and press it against the sides of the bottle, to make a watertight seal.

The funnel covers the container, preventing the collected rainwater from evaporating (turning into vapour).

7 Attach the ruler to the outside of the bottle with tape. Make sure the zero at the end of the ruler lines up with the top of the modelling clay disc.

8 Put the funnel upside down in the bottom part. Place your rain gauge outside, away from buildings or trees. After the next shower, go outside to check the water level and make a note of how much rain has fallen.

TAKE IT FURTHER

Why not keep a diary of the rainfall over a year? If you empty out the rainwater from your gauge every week at the same time of day, you will have a set of weekly totals for the year. You could make a bar graph of your weekly totals to work out which are the wettest months – or you could compare your results with the average rainfall for other parts of the world, which you can find online.

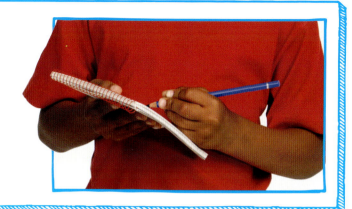

HOW IT WORKS

When rain falls, it normally runs away down drains, or it soaks into the soil. If rain couldn't run away like this, it would collect on the ground, and the more rain that fell, the deeper the water would be. That's the principle behind a rain gauge: you are collecting rainwater that falls on a particular area – in this case, the circular opening at the top of your gauge – to see how deep the water becomes. If you made a rain gauge with an opening twice the size, it would collect twice as much water, but the depth of water collected would still be the same because the area of the bottom part of the rain gauge would have doubled too. If you had a rain gauge the size of a football pitch, it would collect thousands of litres of water in a single rain shower, but the water would still be just a few millimetres deep.

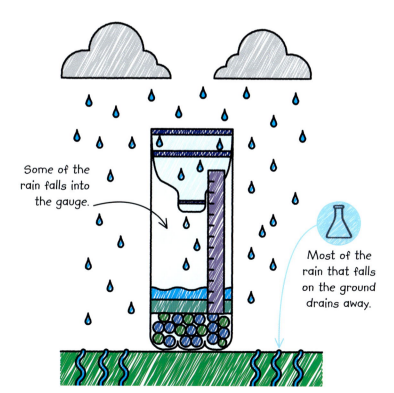

Some of the rain falls into the gauge.

Most of the rain that falls on the ground drains away.

REAL WORLD: SCIENCE
WEATHER WATCHERS

Rain gauges are a very important pieces of equipment for meteorologists and other scientists. They use the information they gather not only to keep track of how the weather in different places is changing over time, but also to predict what the weather is going to be like in the future. This can warn people about possible floods and droughts, and it also helps us to understand climate change. However, it's not just scientists that benefit from rain gauges. Farmers often use them to keep track of how much rain their crops are getting.

THERMOMETER

A thermometer measures temperature (how hot or cold something is). There are lots of different types, but one of the most common is the liquid thermometer, a tube in which a liquid rises and falls as the temperature changes. These steps show you how to make a simple liquid thermometer that works inside and outside.

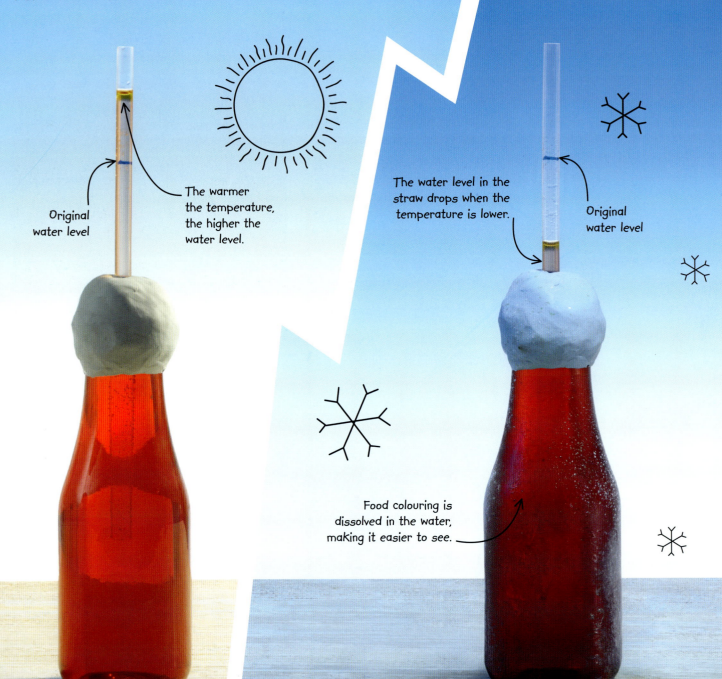

Original water level

The warmer the temperature, the higher the water level.

The water level in the straw drops when the temperature is lower.

Original water level

Food colouring is dissolved in the water, making it easier to see.

HOW TO BUILD A
THERMOMETER

It's easy to make your own thermometer, using coloured water as the liquid and a plastic straw as the tube. Once you've made your thermometer and tested that it's working well, you can create a temperature scale, in a process called "calibration".

Time	Difficulty	Warning
30 minutes	Medium	An adult is vital as this experiment uses hot water.

WHAT YOU NEED

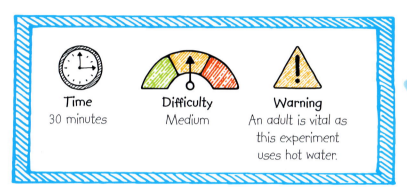

Modelling clay

Cooking oil

Food colouring

Clear biodegradable straw

Pipette

Felt-tip pen

Small bottle

Ruler

Glass bowl

1 Fill the bottle with water almost to the top and add a few drops of food colouring.

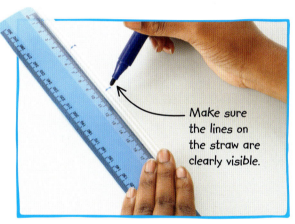

Make sure the lines on the straw are clearly visible.

2 Mark your straw with two lines, one 5 cm (2 in) from the end and one 10 cm (4 in) from the same end.

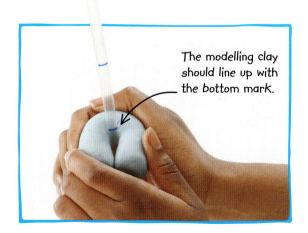

The modelling clay should line up with the bottom mark.

3 Roll the modelling clay into a sausage shape and wrap it around the straw, so that the top of it is level with the bottom line.

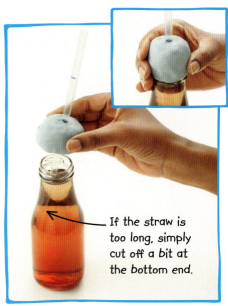

If the straw is too long, simply cut off a bit at the bottom end.

Add water into the straw until it reaches the top line.

The oil sits on top of the water because they are "immiscible" – they don't mix.

4 Manoeuvre the bottom half of the straw into the bottle (it shouldn't touch the base), and seal the opening with the modelling clay so it's airtight.

5 Mix more water and food dye, and use the pipette to add a few more drops of coloured water into the straw.

6 Add just a drop of oil to stop the water evaporating (turning into vapour).

With a tube half the diameter, the water would fall twice as far for the same drop in temperature.

8 Now put cold water into the bowl and see what happens.

At higher temperatures, the water level in the straw rises.

Be careful not to spill any hot water or scald yourself.

7 Your thermometer is complete and ready to use. To test that it's working, carefully place it in a bowl of hot water. The water level in the straw should rise.

The lower the temperature, the lower the water level falls.

You could add ice cubes into the bowl to make the water really cold.

TAKE IT FURTHER

The thermometer you've made only shows whether the temperature is high or low, but creating a scale by referring to a bought thermometer will give you more accurate temperature readings. This process is called "calibration". Start with hot water in the bowl and let it cool. Every so often, mark on your scale the water level and the temperature shown on the bought thermometer. To add lower temperature readings to your scale, put cold water into the bowl to bring down the temperature.

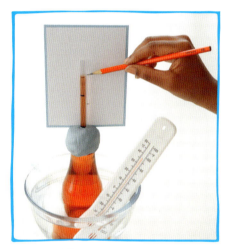

HOT WATER IN BOWL

COLD WATER IN BOWL

HOW IT WORKS

Water is made of tiny particles called molecules. The molecules are constantly moving about. The higher the temperature, the more vigorously they jiggle, causing the water to expand (take up more space). The only space into which the water can expand is in the straw – that's why the water level rises when your thermometer is put in hot water. As the temperature falls, the molecules move more slowly and take up less space, causing the water level to drop.

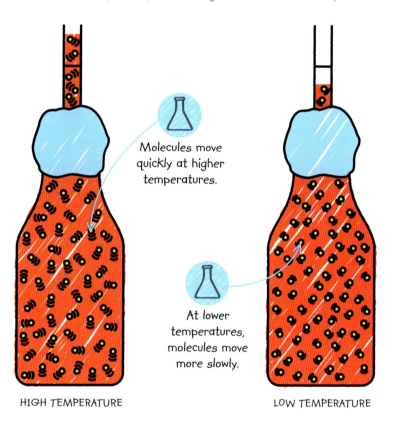

Molecules move quickly at higher temperatures.

At lower temperatures, molecules move more slowly.

HIGH TEMPERATURE   LOW TEMPERATURE

REAL WORLD: SCIENCE
BODY TEMPERATURE

A liquid thermometer can be used to measure the temperature of a room or check your body's temperature to see if you have an infection. Infections are caused by germs, such as bacteria and viruses,

that reproduce (breed) inside you. When you have an infection, your brain increases your body's temperature to try to slow down the rate at which the germs can reproduce.

ANEMOMETER

The wind can be anything from a gentle breeze to a very strong gale, but it is really just air in motion. Weather forecasters, or "meteorologists", use a device called an anemometer to measure the wind speed – the speed at which air is moving. You can measure the speed of the wind, too, by making your own anemometer using a ping pong ball and a shoebox.

MOVING AIR

The wind speed often increases when the weather is about to change from fine to unsettled, wet weather. Why not use your anemometer to keep a record of the wind speed over several days and see how the weather changes?

STEM YOU WILL USE

- SCIENCE: Wind is air in motion, and it exerts a force on objects.
- ENGINEERING: Weighting an object down with heavy materials can prevent it from toppling over.
- MATHS: A protractor is used to measure angles.

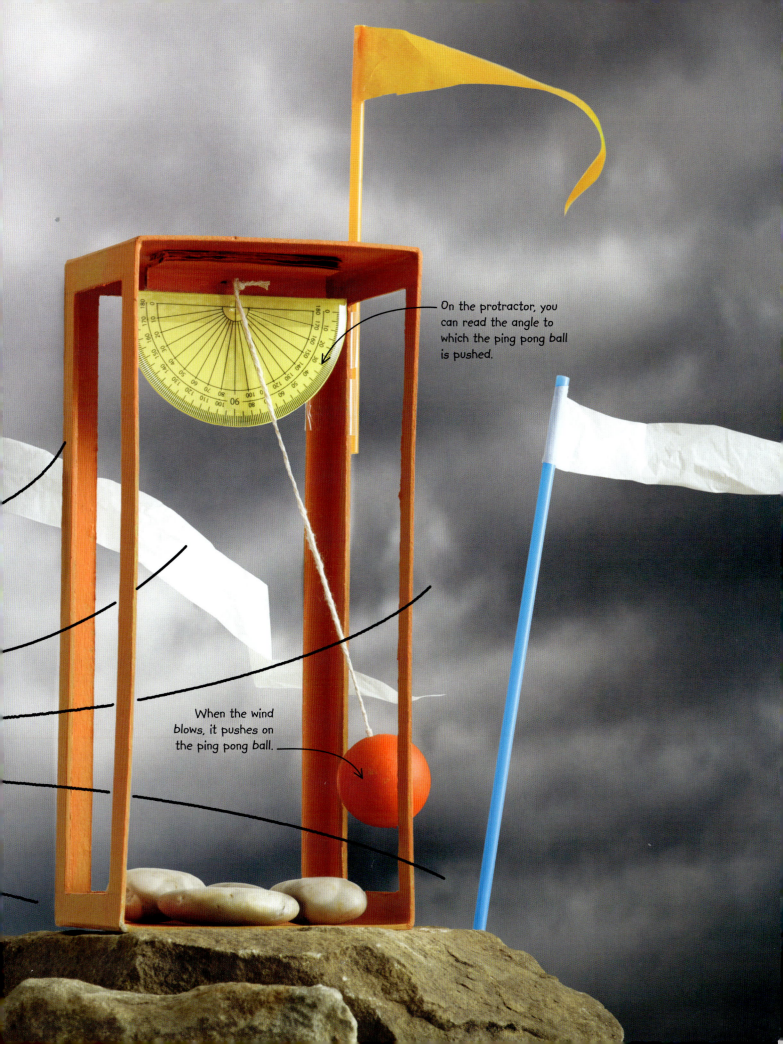

On the protractor, you can read the angle to which the ping pong ball is pushed.

When the wind blows, it pushes on the ping pong ball.

HOW TO BUILD AN
ANEMOMETER

This is quite a complicated project, so take your time and follow the instructions carefully. In this anemometer design, a ping pong ball is suspended on a string inside a cardboard frame made from a shoebox. You'll need to place it in a spot where the wind will push against the ball. The stronger the wind, the further the ping pong ball will move.

Time
1 hour plus drying time

Difficulty
Hard

WHAT YOU NEED

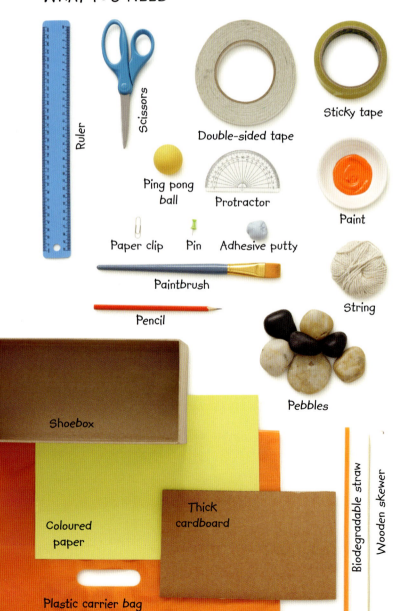

Ruler

Scissors

Double-sided tape

Sticky tape

Ping pong ball

Protractor

Paint

Paper clip   Pin   Adhesive putty

Paintbrush

Pencil

String

Pebbles

Shoebox

Coloured paper

Thick cardboard

Biodegradable straw

Wooden skewer

Plastic carrier bag

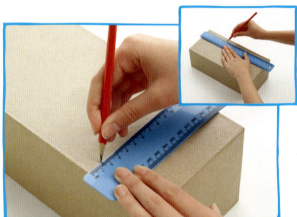

1 Make a mark 1½ cm (¾ in) in from each edge of the three long faces of the shoebox. Use these marks to draw a rectangle on each face.

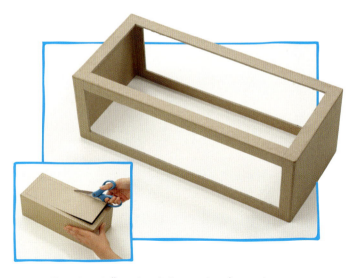

2 Carefully cut out the rectangle you have drawn on each of the three sides, to create an open frame.

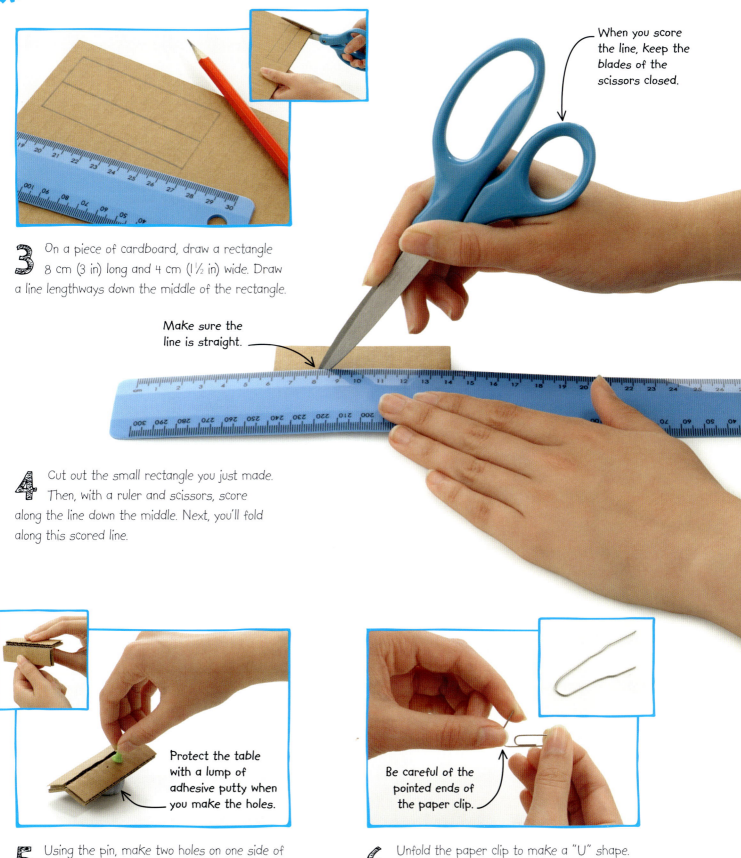

When you score the line, keep the blades of the scissors closed.

3 On a piece of cardboard, draw a rectangle 8 cm (3 in) long and 4 cm (1½ in) wide. Draw a line lengthways down the middle of the rectangle.

Make sure the line is straight.

4 Cut out the small rectangle you just made. Then, with a ruler and scissors, score along the line down the middle. Next, you'll fold along this scored line.

Protect the table with a lump of adhesive putty when you make the holes.

Be careful of the pointed ends of the paper clip.

5 Using the pin, make two holes on one side of your cardboard rectangle. The holes should be 3.5 cm (1¼ in) from each end of the rectangle and about 1 cm (½ in) apart.

6 Unfold the paper clip to make a "U" shape. This step is fiddly, so you might want to ask an adult to help you.

This small gap is where you will later tie the string.

Fold the ends to hold the loop in place – you could add tape to make it extra secure.

7 Push the paper clip ends through the holes you made and leave a small gap above to create a loop. Fold the two ends outwards.

8 Draw around the protractor onto coloured paper or use the template at the back of this book. Cut out the semi-circle shape.

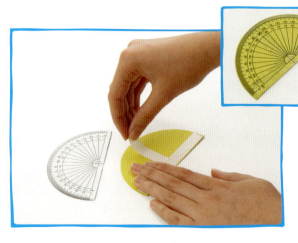

9 Stick two pieces of double-sided tape onto the semi-circle. Peel off the protective strips and secure the paper to the protractor.

Stick the straight side of the protractor just below the loop.

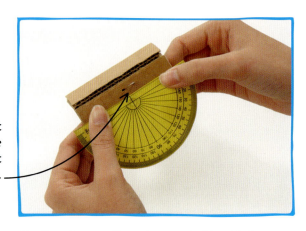

10 Use another piece of double-sided tape to stick the protractor onto the rectangle so the curved side hangs down.

11 Now you need one last piece of double-sided tape to make the other side of the cardboard rectangle sticky. Peel off the protective strip.

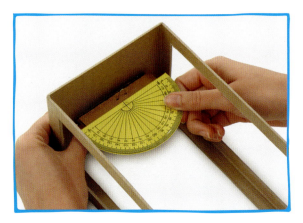

12 Attach the cardboard rectangle to the inside of one end of the box, as shown.

13 Paint the entire cardboard frame and then the ping pong ball. Don't paint the protractor! Leave them to dry.

Use a piece of adhesive putty to protect the table.

14 With string taped to its pointed end, poke the skewer through the ping pong ball and out the other side. When the string appears, keep hold of it, then remove the tape, and pull the skewer out. You can now throw the skewer away.

15 Cut the string so it is long enough for the ping pong ball to hang near the bottom of the frame. Tie a knot at one end of the string to stop the ball falling off.

If this bit is too tricky, ask an adult for help.

16 Tie the free end of the string around the paper clip loop.

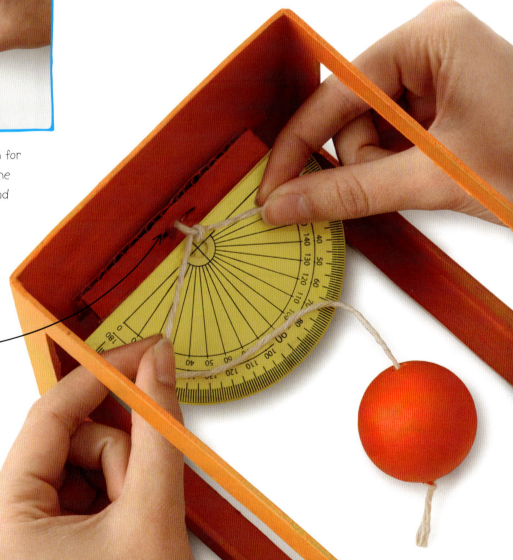

PAPER SUNDIAL

As the Sun moves across the sky during the day, the shadows cast by objects move too. With a sundial, you can use these shadows to tell the time. It's easy to make your own sundial using a drinking straw and a piece of paper, but you'll only be able to use it between spring and autumn. During winter, the Sun is too low in the sky for the straw to cast a shadow on the paper.

The Sun's daily movement east-to-west across the sky is actually caused by our planet's west-to-east rotation.

READING THE SUNDIAL

You may have to adjust the time the sundial shows for daylight saving time, a period when clocks are changed to give more daylight in the evening. Ask an adult if and when that applies to your location. When it does, you'll usually have to add an hour to the time shown on the sundial.

The Sun moves at an angle of 15° every hour, 360° every 24 hours.

This sundial shows the time is about half-past four in the afternoon.

6 P.M.

6 A.M.

70
65
60
55
50
40
30
20
15
10

5
4
3
2
1
12
11
10
9
8
7

HOW TO MAKE A PAPER SUNDIAL

First you'll need to trace or photocopy one of the templates at the back of this book. There is one template for use in the Northern Hemisphere and another for the Southern Hemisphere. Make sure you use the correct version. If you don't know which hemisphere you live in, ask an adult. You'll also need to find out a number called your latitude: you can ask an adult, look online, or make your own latitude locator to find out – see pages 256–261!

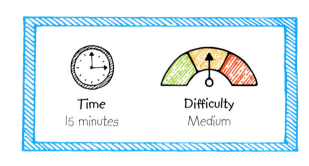

Time
15 minutes

Difficulty
Medium

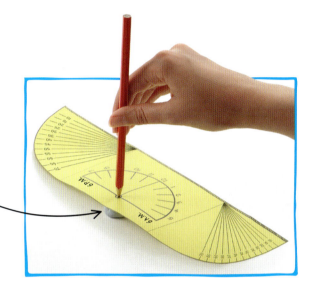

The adhesive putty helps to protect the work surface.

WHAT YOU NEED

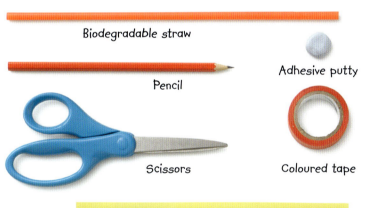

Biodegradable straw

Pencil

Adhesive putty

Scissors

Coloured tape

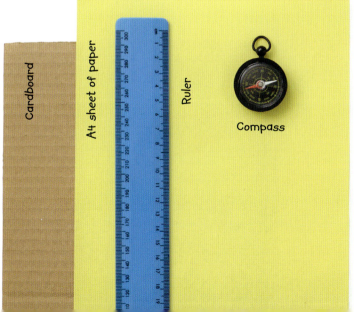

Cardboard

A4 sheet of paper

Ruler

Compass

1 Make sure you have a copy of the right template. Cut it out and put some adhesive putty under where the dot is at the top of the hour scale. Make a hole with the pencil through the dot.

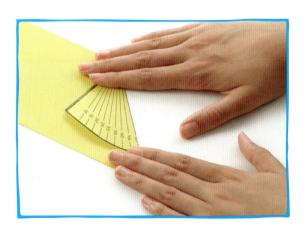

2 Find your angle of latitude along the scale at the side of the paper. Fold and crease along that angle (50° latitude in the example).

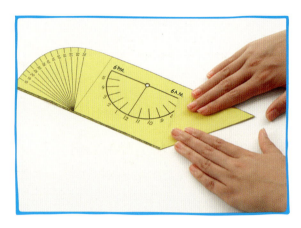

3 Turn the template over and fold again along the crease you created. Repeat steps 2 and 3 for the scale on the other side of the template.

The two corners of the sundial must be at a 90° angle.

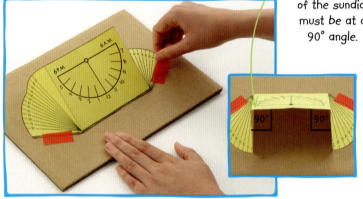

5 Using tape, attach the creased sundial template to the piece of cardboard. Make sure the sides of the sundial are vertical.

4 Now unfold the angled sides, then fold and crease along the dotted straight lines on either side of the sundial's main panel.

6 Cut a piece of the straw about 15 cm (6 in) long. This will be the "gnomon" – the piece of the sundial casting the shadow that tells the time.

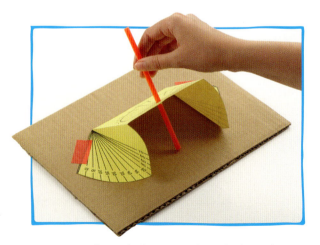

7 Carefully push the straw through the hole in the sundial's face, from the top down to the cardboard. Ensure it's at right angles to the face.

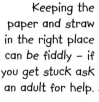

Keeping the paper and straw in the right place can be fiddly – if you get stuck ask an adult for help.

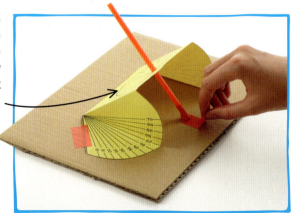

8 Secure the straw to the cardboard base, making sure that the sundial's face remains flat and that the straw is still at right angles to it.

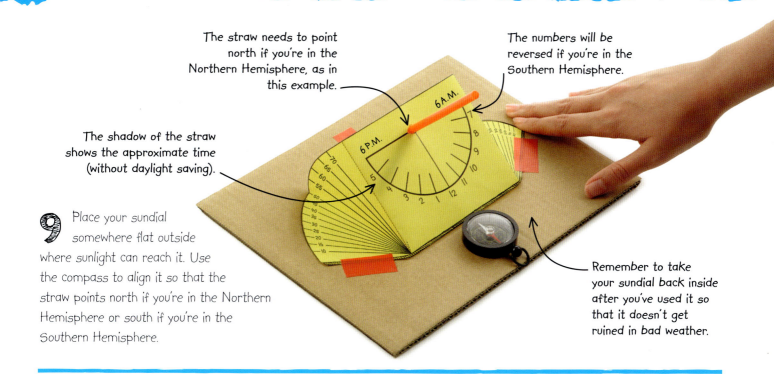

The straw needs to point north if you're in the Northern Hemisphere, as in this example.

The numbers will be reversed if you're in the Southern Hemisphere.

The shadow of the straw shows the approximate time (without daylight saving).

9 Place your sundial somewhere flat outside where sunlight can reach it. Use the compass to align it so that the straw points north if you're in the Northern Hemisphere or south if you're in the Southern Hemisphere.

Remember to take your sundial back inside after you've used it so that it doesn't get ruined in bad weather.

HOW IT WORKS

Planet Earth is spinning, and as a result, the Sun appears to move across our sky. It rises in the east, at noon it reaches its highest point, and then sets in the west. Earth takes 24 hours to make one complete rotation (360°) – so it turns 15° per hour, and the shadows created by the Sun shift by 15° per hour. The lines on the sundial are spaced 15° apart, so the space between each line represents one hour.

REAL WORLD: SCIENCE SHADOWS

Your own shadow is very long just after sunrise and just before sunset, when the Sun is low in the sky. Your shadow is shortest at noon. If you stood at the equator at noon on midsummer's day, you would have no shadow at all, because the Sun would be directly overhead.

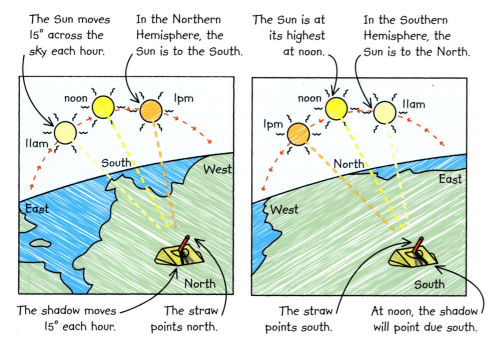

NORTHERN HEMISPHERE

The Sun moves 15° across the sky each hour.

In the Northern Hemisphere, the Sun is to the South.

The shadow moves 15° each hour.

The straw points north.

SOUTHERN HEMISPHERE

The Sun is at its highest at noon.

In the Southern Hemisphere, the Sun is to the North.

The straw points south.

At noon, the shadow will point due south.

STEM YOU WILL USE
• SCIENCE: The north and south celestial poles are fixed points in the sky.
• TECHNOLOGY: By using the stars and the right tools, you can work out where you are.
• MATHS: Latitude goes from +90° through zero to -90°.

To use your latitude locator, you'll have to go out at night and find a locator star or stars. These stars will be different depending on where you are in the world.

LATITUDE LOCATOR

Early sailors used the stars to figure out exactly where they were on Earth. In the system they created, a location is defined by just two numbers, called latitude and longitude. Your latitude is how far north or south of the equator you are, while your longitude is how far around the planet you are. In this activity you'll make a device that will give your latitude wherever you are in the world.

WHAT'S YOUR LATITUDE?
Around the middle of planet Earth, at an equal distance from the North Pole and the South Pole, is an imaginary line called the equator. If you live at the equator, your latitude is 0°. If you live at the North Pole, your latitude is 90° north (or +90°), while if you live at the South Pole, it's 90° south (or -90°). Chances are your latitude is somewhere in between. If you go on holiday to somewhere much closer to or further from the equator, you can use your latitude locator to record your new latitude.

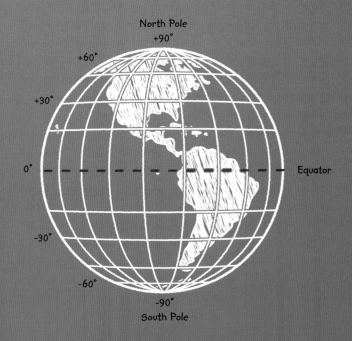

This kind
of device
is called a
mariners'
astrolabe.

The latitude is
read off the scale.

Gravity pulling
on a heavy nut
ensures that the
string is vertical.

0°   10°   20°   30°   40°   50°   60°   70°   80°   0°

HOW TO MAKE A
LATITUDE LOCATOR

It's really easy to make this latitude locator. First, turn to the back of this book to find the template for the scale you'll need. Trace the template onto a sheet of paper (or photocopy it) and cut it out. Then it just takes a bit more cutting and sticking.

Time
30 minutes

Difficulty
Medium

WHAT YOU NEED

String

Coloured tape

Felt-tip pen

Pencil

Double-sided tape

Scissors

Adhesive putty

Washer

A4 sheet of card

A4 sheet of paper

A4 sheet of card

The piece of card you use can be any colour.

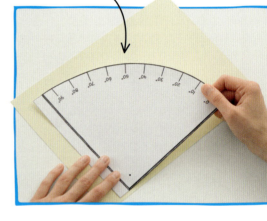

1 Stick several pieces of double-sided tape to the back of the paper. Peel off the protective strips, and stick down onto a piece of card.

2 Carefully cut the card around the edge of the paper with a pair of scissors. Remember to recycle any leftover pieces of card.

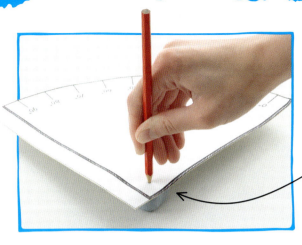

The putty makes it easier to push the pencil through the paper.

3 Put a piece of adhesive putty underneath the dot in the corner of your scale. Then use the sharp end of the pencil to make a small hole.

4 Cut a 20 cm (8 in) length of string. Thread one end through the hole and tie a double knot, near the end of the string at the back of the card.

Latitude affects how many hours of sunlight a location gets each day.

5 Roll the other piece of card tightly around the felt-tip pen, to make a narrow tube. This will be your sighting tube, which you will look through when measuring your latitude.

Make sure the card is wrapped tightly around the felt-tip pen to stop it from unravelling.

Rolling up a 2D rectangle of card results in a 3D shape called a cylinder, which forms your sighting tube.

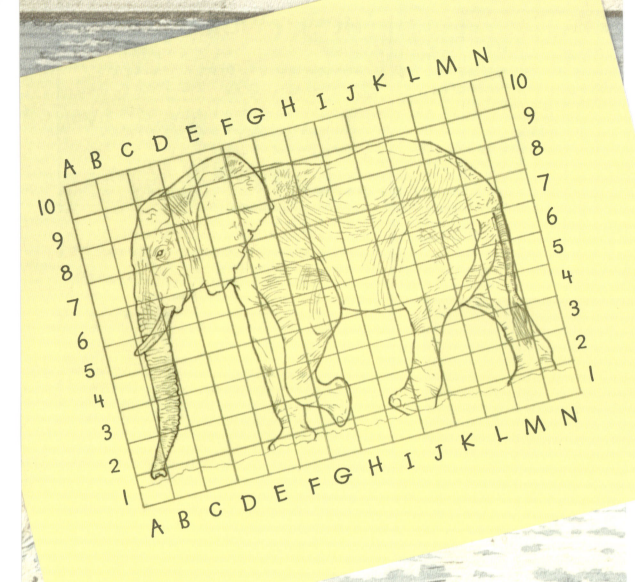

SCALING UP PICTURES

Using a grid is a handy way of enlarging a picture accurately while keeping the proportions the same. You can even make artworks big enough to hang on your wall – just choose your picture and prepare to go large.

A large image will give you space to add more detail.

HOW TO
SCALE UP
A PICTURE

For this project, you will need two separate grids. The difference in size between them is the scale – the larger the scale, the bigger the difference. You could copy your starting image from a book by making your first grid on tracing paper. Clip or stick the grid to the book so it doesn't move and then trace the picture.

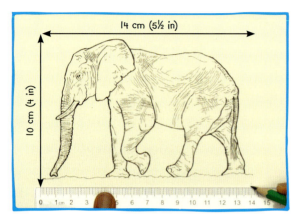

1 Choose an image you would like to enlarge and use a ruler to measure its height and width. Our image is 10 cm (4 in) in height and 14 cm (5½ in) in width.

Use a set square to ensure that your corners are right angles (90°).

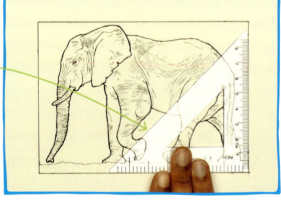

2 Draw a rectangle around the outside of your image. Leave a bit of space above, below, and to the sides of your drawing.

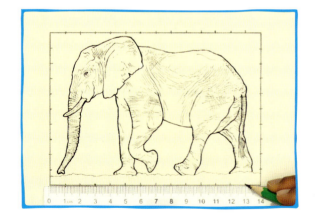

3 Use a ruler and pencil to make marks every 1 cm (½ in) along each side of the rectangle. Because of the size of our image, we have 14 marks along the top and bottom, and 10 along the sides.

Time
2 hours

Difficulty
Medium

WHAT YOU NEED

Ruler

A picture to copy

Black felt-tip pen

Pencil

Rubber

Scissors

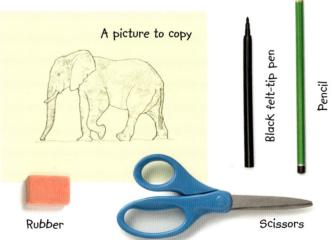

A3 white paper

Set square

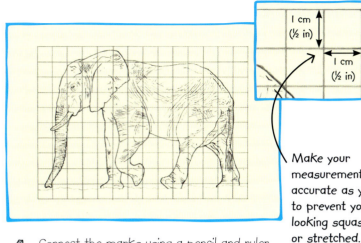

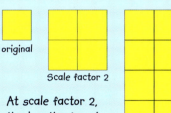

Make your measurements as accurate as you can to prevent your image looking squashed or stretched.

4 Connect the marks using a pencil and ruler to draw horizontal and vertical lines across the picture. You should now have a grid of 140 squares overlaying the original image.

5 Number the squares running up the sides of the grid from 1–10, then label the squares along the top and bottom A–N, as shown below. These labels are called grid references, and they will help you to find specific squares on your image.

SCALE FACTOR

Scaling is making something larger or smaller while keeping everything in proportion. The scale factor is the amount you increase or decrease the size by.

original

Scale factor 2

Scale factor 4

At scale factor 2, the length of each side is doubled.

Doubling the dimensions of the original image is equivalent to enlarging it by a scale factor of 2.

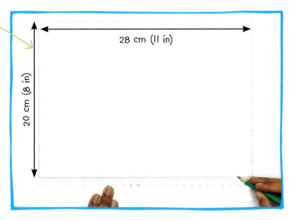

6 To double the size of the image, multiply both the height and width by two. On a blank piece of A3 paper, draw a rectangle with the new dimensions of 20 x 28 cm (8 x 11 in).

The grid for your pictures can have any number of squares, as long as they're equally sized.

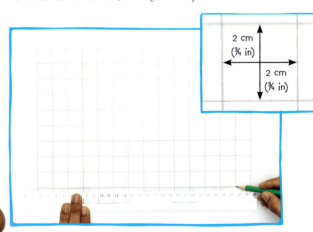

7 Repeat step 3 to create a new grid, but enlarging the squares by a factor of 2 – to 2 x 2 cm (¾ x ¾ in).

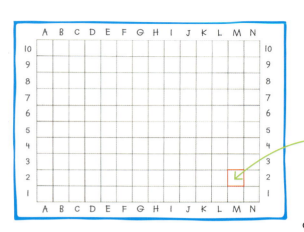

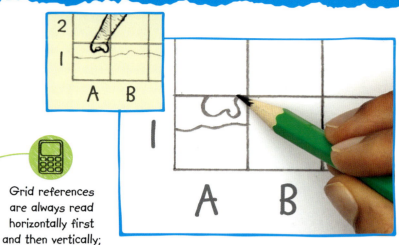

8 Add grid references to the columns and rows, as you did in step 5. You are now ready to copy the smaller elephant onto your larger grid.

Grid references are always read horizontally first and then vertically; for example this would be M2.

9 With a pencil, copy outlines from each small grid square to the same position on your large grid square, starting at A1.

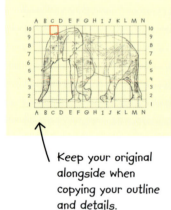

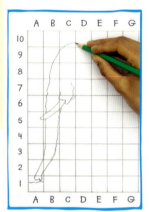

Keep your original alongside when copying your outline and details.

10 Work your way up and down the columns to transfer the picture to the larger grid. Keep it simple by starting with the outline image, and use the grid references to keep track of what you need to draw in each square.

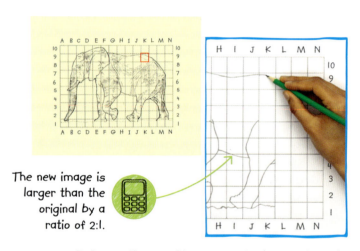

The new image is larger than the original by a ratio of 2:1.

11 Continue working across the large grid until you have transferred the whole outline from the smaller image. Check back over the squares to make sure you haven't missed any lines.

12 Repeat steps 9–11, this time copying the details from each small grid square to the same position on your larger grid until your drawing is complete!

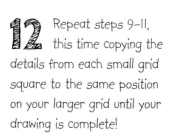

It is much easier to add detail and features once the outline is in place.

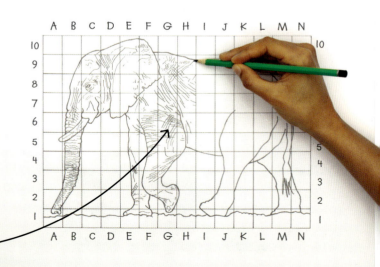

A B C D E F G H I J K L M N

10 9 8 7 6 5 4 3 2 1

A B C D E F G H I J K L M N

Use scissors to cut around the outer rectangle of your final image, to separate your drawing from the labelled grid.

13 Once you're happy with your drawing, go over the pencil lines with a *black felt-tip* pen. Rub out all of the pencil lines and then cut around the rectangle you drew in step 6.

SCALING 3D SHAPES

Scale factor can also be applied to 3D objects. In addition to height and width, this also affects the depth of an object.

The length of each of the larger cube's sides has been extended to three cubes.

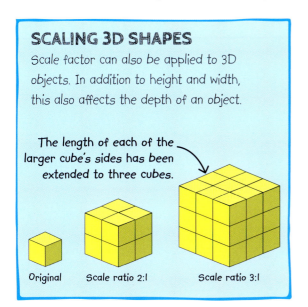

Original   Scale ratio 2:1   Scale ratio 3:1

REAL WORLD: MATHS
MINIATURE DOLL'S HOUSE

A doll's house is an example of a toy that is a detailed model of a real house, but shrunk to a fraction of the original size. To make the house and its objects look as realistic as possible, the scale has to be kept in proportion.

OPTICAL ILLUSIONS

Grab some pencils, paper, and your maths kit, and get ready to create some optical art! These clever pictures use colour, light, and patterns to trick our brains into seeing something that isn't really there. So although you are making flat drawings, mathematical magic makes the lines pop off the page so that the shapes look 3D.

Don't worry if your lines aren't perfect. It'll still look 3D.

Be bold with your shading. This is what gives your artwork the 3D look.

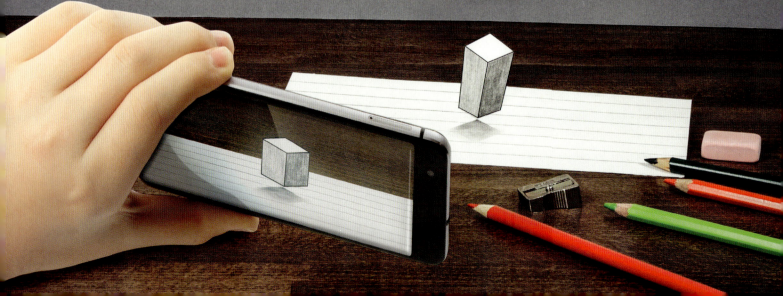

HOW TO CREATE
OPTICAL ILLUSIONS

Try your hand at two optical artworks. The first uses clashing colours and curved lines so that the shape bends off the page, while in the second, shading and cut-outs combine to make a cuboid float away! In both cases, shadow helps to create depth.

STEM YOU WILL USE

• MATHS: Angles and concentric circles are used to structure your drawing, and convex and concave lines make your drawing look like it's bending.

Time
1 hour

Difficulty
Easy

WHAT YOU NEED

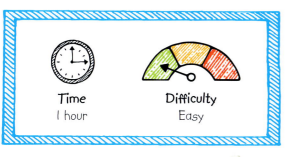

Ruler

Protractor

Compass and pencil

Black pen

Scissors

Contrasting coloured pencils (darker and lighter shades)

White paper

Rubber

Smartphone

PROJECT 1 – CIRCLE ILLUSION

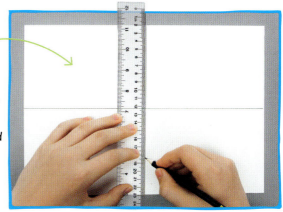

Marking the halfway point of all four edges will ensure that you find the exact centre.

1 Find the centre of your piece of paper by measuring its length and width and dividing each measurement by two. Draw a straight line across the paper from each of the halfway points.

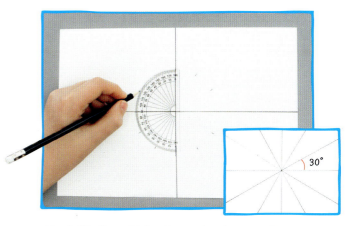

30°

2 With the middle of a protractor over the centre, mark out sections of 30°. Draw lines from the centre to the edge of the paper at 30° increments to create a "pie" of 12 equal slices.

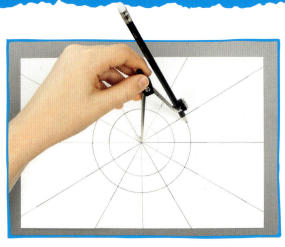

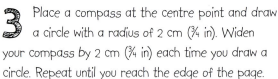

Lines like this are convex, which means they curve outwards, while concave lines curve inwards.

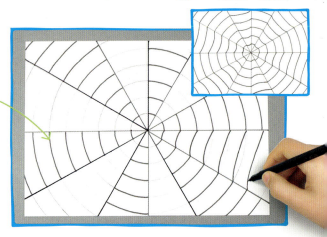

3 Place a compass at the centre point and draw a circle with a radius of 2 cm (¾ in). Widen your compass by 2 cm (¾ in) each time you draw a circle. Repeat until you reach the edge of the page.

4 With a black pen, draw over the straight lines. Go over the curved lines inside every alternate "slice". Finally, join the curves with concave lines that bend towards the centre of the circle.

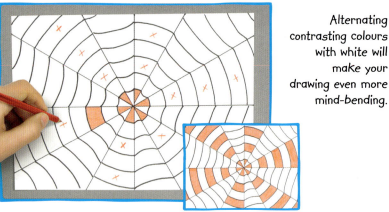

Alternating contrasting colours with white will make your drawing even more mind-bending.

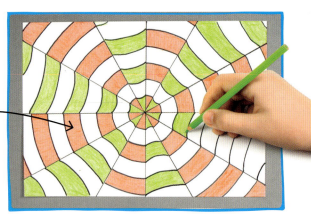

5 Take one colour and mark out every other "slice", and then every alternate section within each slice, to avoid mistakes once you start colouring in.

Make your shading darker at the edges and lighter in the middle to make your illusion look 3D.

6 Repeat step 5, but this time use your second, contrasting colour.

7 Lastly, use darker coloured pencils to shade the edges of the white areas and coloured sections. This will create the 3D effect.

REAL WORLD: MATHS
CONCENTRIC CIRCLES

Circles of different sizes that lie within each other but all share the same centre point are called concentric circles. You can find them on an archery target. Can you think of any other examples?

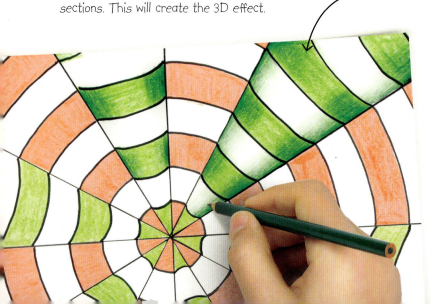

PROJECT 2 - FLOATING CUBE

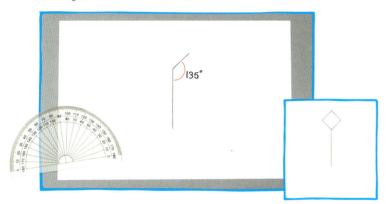

1 Draw a vertical line that is 9 cm (3½ in) long. Use a set square and a protractor to draw a 4 cm (1½ in) diagonal line at its top, at an angle of 135°. Add three 4 cm (1½ in) lines to form a tilted square.

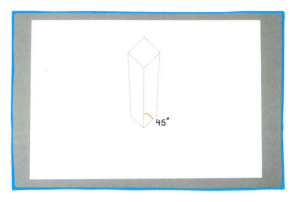

2 At the bottom of the vertical line, draw a 3 cm (1¼ in) line at an angle of 45°, then repeat on the other side. Connect these lines to those at the top to form a cuboid.

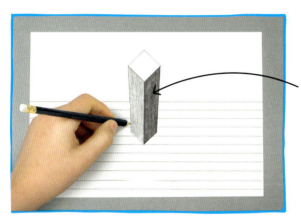

Shading one side of the cuboid darker than the other creates the illusion of depth.

3 Halfway down the page, draw horizontal lines on either side of the cuboid at 1 cm (½ in) intervals. Shade the two long sides of the cuboid.

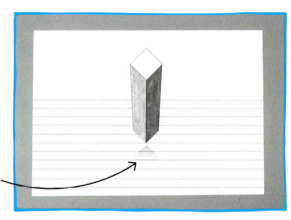

Make the bottom of the diamond a lighter shade.

4 Create a shadow effect by shading a diamond shape directly underneath the cuboid. It should look like it's hovering!

5 Draw around the outside of the cuboid with a black pen, then cut out the top and along the highest horizontal line. This makes the cuboid appear to jump off the page, giving the illusion that it is 3D.

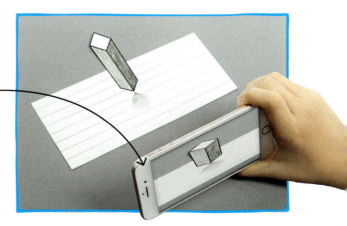

Try using the phone to film a shape-shifting video for your friends!

6 Look at your drawing through the camera of a smartphone, moving the phone's angle to watch what happens. The 2D drawing will appear to change size and shape!

Hang your feeder in your garden using a piece of string looped under the roof.

You can use coloured lolly sticks or you can paint plain ones with environmentally-friendly paint.

Different foods will attract different species. Robins love mealworms!

LOLLY STICK BIRD FEEDER

How would you like to have a garden busy with birds swooping in for a visit?
This colourful feeder will quickly become the new hotspot for local birds.
To put it together, you'll need to master the use of angles to make a strong
structure that can hold the bird food. Once you've built the feeder, you can
create a graph to help you work out what food your birds like best.

Birds will come to visit your
feeder, but you must be
patient. They may take a
few days to find it.

Some birds like perches,
others don't.

HOW TO MAKE A
LOLLY STICK BIRD FEEDER

This project might look a little complicated, but it is surprisingly simple and you will quickly find yourself with a brand new bird feeder. You may need to be a little patient with the birds while they find you, but once they do you can keep a tally of their visits to work out what kind of food they like best.

WHAT YOU NEED

Adhesive tape

String

Scissors

Coloured pencils

Marker pen

73 lolly sticks

Bird food

PVA glue (or a glue gun, operated by an adult)

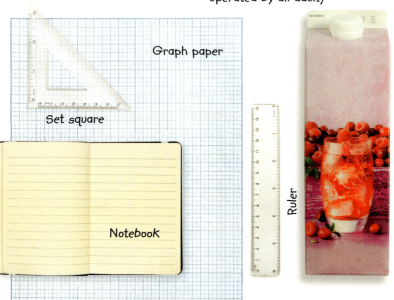

Graph paper

Set square

Notebook

Ruler

Empty drinks carton

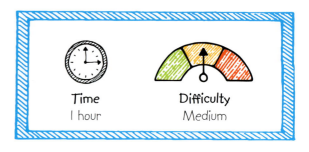

Time
1 hour

Difficulty
Medium

STEM YOU WILL USE

• MATHS: Use angles, halves, and parallel lines to build a bird feeder, and find out which food your visitors like the most by using tallies and graphs.

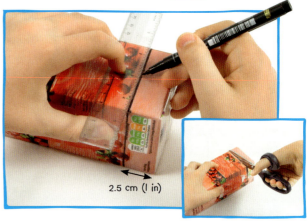

2.5 cm (1 in)

1 Start by making the bird feeder tray out of a drinks carton with a base 7 x 7 cm (2¾ x 2¾ in). Draw a straight line 2.5 cm (1 in) from the bottom of the carton and then cut along the line.

2 Place 12 lolly sticks next to each other and then put the bird feeder tray on top, making sure that you have two sticks on either side of the tray.

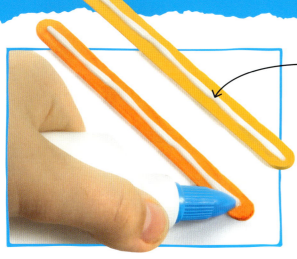

Make sure you glue along the whole length of the lolly stick.

3 Glue two lolly sticks from end to end. These two sticks will hold the 12 sticks on the bottom of the feeder's base together.

Use a set square to draw a right angle on paper as a guide for placing the sticks.

90°

4 Place the glued sticks 1 cm (½ in) from the edge of the feeder. The two sticks should be at right angles to the sticks that form the base.

Make sure the tray can fit on the base before building up the layers of sticks, but don't stick it down.

5 Repeat step 4, but this time only dab glue onto the ends of each lolly stick about 1 cm (½ in) in from the edge. Place the sticks so they form right angles with the two sticks you have just glued.

6 Repeat steps 4 and 5 to build up walls of sticks that can hold the bird feeder tray in place. Stop when you have three layers on two sides and two layers on the other two.

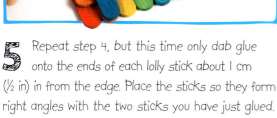

Half of 12 cm (5 in) is 6 cm (2½ in), so this is where to snap the stick.

6 cm (2½ in)

12 cm (5 in)

Divide the length of the whole lolly stick by two to work out how long the shortened one should be.

8 Glue a perch in the middle of one of the sides of the feeder with two layers of sticks so that it juts outwards and forms a right angle. Repeat so you have a perch on both sides.

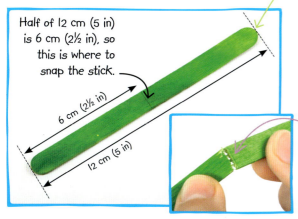

7 To make the perches, measure halfway along the stick and draw a line. Snap the stick in half neatly. Ask an adult to help if this is tricky.

To make your stick snap neatly, you could score a line with a craft knife first - ask an adult to help.

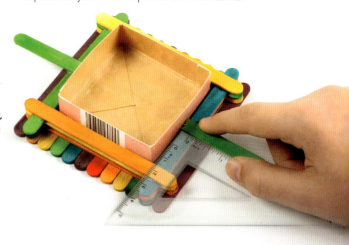

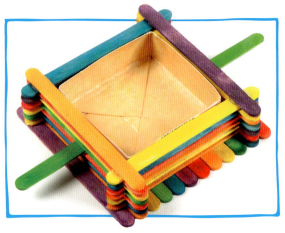

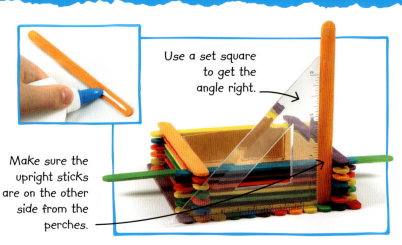

Use a set square to get the angle right.

Make sure the upright sticks are on the other side from the perches.

9 Continue to build up the layers of lolly sticks on each side of the feeder until the lower sides come up to the same height as the tray.

10 Glue one end of a stick and place it on an outside corner of the bird feeder so that it sticks up at a right angle to the base.

These horizontal sticks should be parallel to each other.

11 Repeat step 10 so that there are four vertical sticks – one at each corner of the tray.

12 Dab glue 2 cm (¾ in) from both ends of a stick and place it horizontally across the vertical sticks. Repeat on the opposite side.

13 To make the roof, place two columns of 12 lolly sticks next to one another and then join them together down the middle with adhesive tape.

The width of the roof should measure the length of one lolly stick.

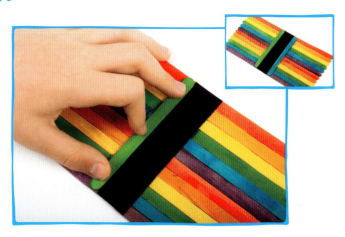

14 Glue another lolly stick, place it along the adhesive tape and press firmly. Repeat so there is a lolly stick either side of the adhesive tape.

15 Glue the length of another lolly stick and place it 0.5 cm (¼ in) in from the edge of the roof. Repeat on the other side.

This angle is less wide than a right angle. This is known as an acute angle.

16 Flip the roof over and gently fold it so that it forms a triangle with the adhesive tape on the inside.

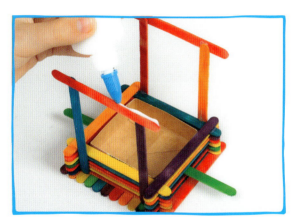

17 Dab glue along the top edge of the horizontal sticks.

ANGLES

Different types of angles have special names. An acute angle is smaller than a right angle, while an obtuse angle is larger.

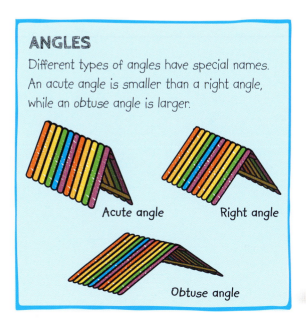

Acute angle

Right angle

Obtuse angle

18 Place the roof on top of the sticks and firmly hold in place. Leave until the glue is dry.

19 Glue along the top of the roof where the two sides meet. Place a lolly stick across the top of the roof and hold firmly until set. Your bird feeder box is now ready to attract birds!

20 Hang your bird feeder in the garden and fill the tray with tasty treats.

Place food in the tray and put the tray in the feeder.

TRACK YOUR BIRDS

To work out what food the birds in your garden like best, try a few different sorts to see how many birds come to visit. You can use a tally chart to record the visits, and once you've gathered the data, you can turn your tally into a graph. Use the graph to help you analyse what you've discovered and pick the food that your garden's birds prefer. For the most accurate results, make your observations at the same time each day.

Mealworms

Mixed bird seed

Make sure your nuts are chopped. Birds can choke on whole nuts!

Chopped nuts

1 You will have to try different foods over a few weeks to work out what the birds in your garden like to eat. We started with chopped nuts the first week, and then tried seeds and mealworms.

Use a ruler to draw a line between the points on your graph.

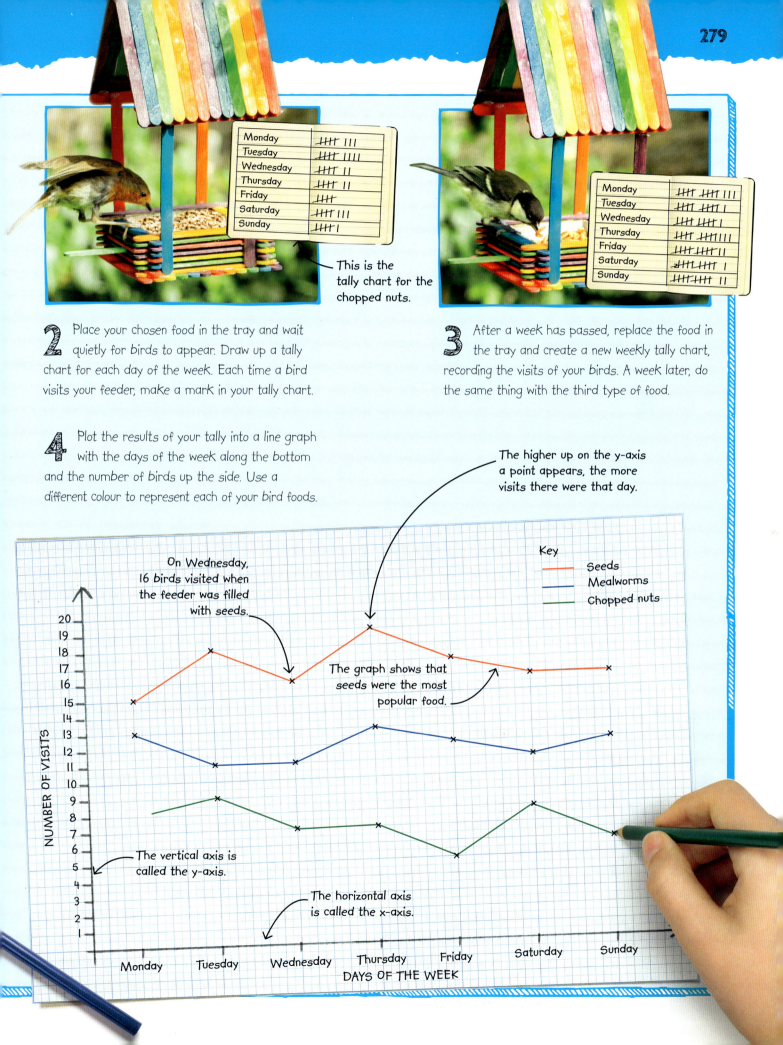

Monday	⊞ ⊞ ⊞ ⊞ III
Tuesday	⊞ ⊞ ⊞ ⊞ IIII
Wednesday	⊞ ⊞ ⊞ ⊞ II
Thursday	⊞ ⊞ ⊞ ⊞ II
Friday	⊞ ⊞ ⊞ ⊞
Saturday	⊞ ⊞ ⊞ ⊞ III
Sunday	⊞ ⊞ ⊞ ⊞ I

This is the tally chart for the chopped nuts.

Monday	⊞ ⊞ ⊞ ⊞ ⊞ ⊞ III
Tuesday	⊞ ⊞ ⊞ ⊞ ⊞ ⊞ I
Wednesday	⊞ ⊞ ⊞ ⊞ ⊞ ⊞ I
Thursday	⊞ ⊞ ⊞ ⊞ ⊞ ⊞ IIII
Friday	⊞ ⊞ ⊞ ⊞ ⊞ ⊞ II
Saturday	⊞ ⊞ ⊞ ⊞ ⊞ ⊞ I
Sunday	⊞ ⊞ ⊞ ⊞ ⊞ ⊞ II

2 Place your chosen food in the tray and wait quietly for birds to appear. Draw up a tally chart for each day of the week. Each time a bird visits your feeder, make a mark in your tally chart.

3 After a week has passed, replace the food in the tray and create a new weekly tally chart, recording the visits of your birds. A week later, do the same thing with the third type of food.

4 Plot the results of your tally into a line graph with the days of the week along the bottom and the number of birds up the side. Use a different colour to represent each of your bird foods.

The higher up on the y-axis a point appears, the more visits there were that day.

Key
— Seeds
— Mealworms
— Chopped nuts

On Wednesday, 16 birds visited when the feeder was filled with seeds.

The graph shows that seeds were the most popular food.

The vertical axis is called the y-axis.

The horizontal axis is called the x-axis.

NUMBER OF VISITS

20
19
18
17
16
15
14
13
12
11
10
9
8
7
6
5
4
3
2
1

Monday Tuesday Wednesday Thursday Friday Saturday Sunday

DAYS OF THE WEEK

STEM YOU WILL USE
• MATHS: Estimation helps you figure out how many jelly beans are in the jar. Use probability, shown as fractions, decimals, and percentages, to work out your chances of winning a jelly bean.

LUCKY DIP

Are you feeling lucky? You'll need to be to win this game! Pick a jelly bean at random from a jar and spin your brand-new spinner. If the colour on the spinner matches the colour of the bean, you get to eat the chewy treat. You can work out the likelihood that something might happen by using a maths technique called probability.

If the spinner picks the same colour you picked, you get to eat the bean! What are the chances of that happening?

HOW TO PLAY
LUCKY DIP

This project is pretty simple to do, but once you've made it you will have a game you can play again and again with friends. Make sure that you don't have too many different colours of jelly bean as you'll need to be able to colour your spinner to match the beans. We have used six colours.

Time
30 minutes

Difficulty
Easy

WHAT YOU NEED

Ruler

Protractor

Compass and pencil

Paper glue

Short pencil

Lots of jelly beans

Adhesive putty

Scissors

Paint brush

Empty jar

Paints or coloured pencils

White paper

Stiff card

Calculator

Weighing scales

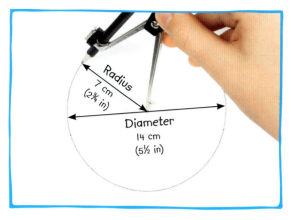

Radius
7 cm
(2¾ in)

Diameter
14 cm
(5½ in)

1 Set your compass to a width of 7 cm (2¾ in) and draw a circle with a 14 cm (5½ in) diameter on white paper. Note the centre of the circle.

A full circle is 360°, so to divide it into six segments each one must be 60°.

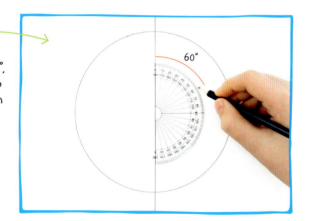

60°

2 You now need to divide your circle so you have one segment for each bean colour. Draw a line through the circle, then place the protractor over the centre and use it to measure each segment.

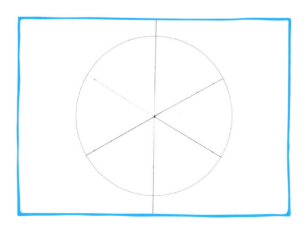

3 Use a ruler to draw lines from the angles you marked to the centre of the circle. This will give you a "pie" of six equal parts.

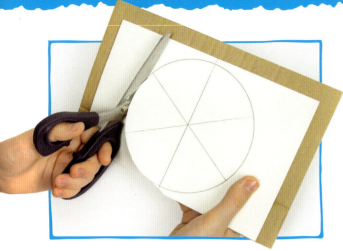

4 Glue the paper with the circle onto a piece of stiff card and then carefully cut around the outline of the circle.

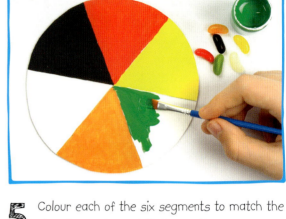

5 Colour each of the six segments to match the six colours of your jelly beans. You can use paints, pencils, or felt-tip pens.

6 Place a piece of adhesive putty under the centre of the circle, then push a short pencil through the circle to create a hole.

Try not to eat all of the jelly beans before you pour them into the jar.

PROBABILITY

You can use probability to measure how likely something is to happen. Probability is usually shown as a fraction.

Here, the probability of getting green is one in six, or ⅙.

Here, the probability of getting green is just one in two, or ½.

7 Pick a jelly bean from the jar and spin the spinner. If it matches the colour lying on the table when the spinner stops, you get to eat the jelly bean! If it doesn't match, return it to the jar.

The probability of the spinner landing on orange is 1/6.

PRESENTING PROBABILITY

If there were no green beans in a jar, the chance of picking one would have a probability of zero, while if there were only green beans, drawing one would have a probability of one. If there were some green beans, the likelihood of picking one would have a probability of between zero and one. You can use fractions, decimals, and percentages to represent probability.

DECIMALS

$$1/5 = 1 \div 5 = 0.2$$

If you were picking one of these five beans at random, you'd have a one in five chance of getting a red bean, that's a probability of 1/5. To turn this into a decimal, divide the top number of the fraction by the bottom number.

PERCENTAGES

$$2/5 = 2 \div 5 = 0.4$$
$$\times 100 = 40\%$$

In this example, you'd have a two in five chance of picking a red bean. To change the fraction to a percentage, you first work it out as a decimal and then multiply it by 100.

HOW MANY JELLY BEANS ARE IN THE JAR?

Why not challenge your friends to guess how many jelly beans are in the jar? Using some clever maths you'll be able to reveal how close their guess is. You can work out the number of jelly beans by finding the weight of a single one and dividing that by the weight of all the jelly beans that you can fit inside the jar.

2 Place your jar on the scales and set them to zero. Fill the jar with jelly beans and note the weight. Guess how many jelly beans are in the jar.

To make it easier to find the weight, assume that each of these 10 jelly beans weighs the same amount.

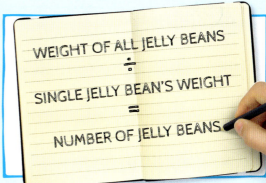

WEIGHT OF ALL JELLY BEANS
÷
SINGLE JELLY BEAN'S WEIGHT
=
NUMBER OF JELLY BEANS

1 Take 10 jelly beans and weigh them on the scales. Divide the weight by 10 to give you an accurate estimate of the weight of one jelly bean.

3 Divide the weight of all the jelly beans by the weight of one jelly bean to work out how many jelly beans are in the jar. How close were you?

BAKE AND SHARE A PIZZA

If you are having friends over for tea, why not make them some yummy pizza to share. As you make the dough and the sauce, you will learn how to measure out ingredients, and once your pizza is ready, fractions will help you to work out how much pizza each of your friends will get. Enjoy!

Divide your pizza into equal slices or there may be trouble!

STEM YOU WILL USE
• MATHS: Measurements are important in cooking and baking. Divide your pizza equally between friends with the help of fractions.

HOW TO
BAKE AND SHARE A PIZZA

Making a pizza is a great way to understand fractions, as you will need to divide up a whole pizza into equal parts so there's some for everyone. This recipe will make enough for two pizzas and you can add toppings of your choice.

Time
30 minutes plus 1 hour of resting time

Difficulty
Easy

Warning
Hot stuff! Adult supervision required.

FOR TWO PIZZAS YOU NEED

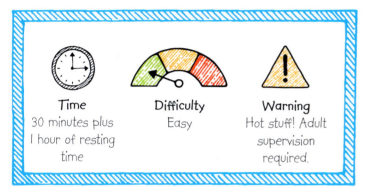

450 g (16 oz) strong white bread flour

275 ml (9 fl oz) water

Sugar

Dried yeast

Salt

Two balls of mozzarella

Red wine vinegar

Garlic

Dried basil

Other toppings of your choice

Tablespoon and teaspoon

Fresh basil (optional)

Tea towel

400 g (14 oz) tin of plum tomatoes

Weighing scales

Mixing bowl

Pizza baking tray

Blender

Rolling pin

1 Mix 450 g (16 oz) of strong white bread flour with a teaspoon each of salt, sugar, and dried yeast. Make a well in the middle of the mixture and pour in 275 ml (9 fl oz) of water.

2 Use a spoon to stir the water into the flour. When a ball of dough starts to form, use slightly damp hands to bring the mixture together.

3 Sprinkle flour onto your work surface to prevent sticking. Take the ball of dough and start to knead it by pushing and stretching it until it is smooth and less sticky.

5 While the dough is resting, make the tomato sauce. Pour the 400 g (14 oz) tin of tomatoes into a blender. Add a pinch of salt, some pepper and dried basil, the clove of garlic, and a tablespoon of red wine vinegar. Ask an adult to help you whizz the ingredients to form a smooth sauce.

When the dough expands, its volume is increasing.

4 Shape the dough into a ball and put it back into the bowl. Cover with a damp tea towel and leave for an hour, or until it has doubled in size.

There is no need to slice your clove of garlic. Just peel it.

6 Remove the tea towel and knock the air out of the dough by punching it lightly. Tip it out of the bowl and give it a final knead. Split the dough into two equal-sized pieces.

FRACTIONS

A fraction is a portion of something larger. Here, the two balls of dough that you split apart are both fractions – halves – of the larger ball. If you split the ball into three, they would be thirds.

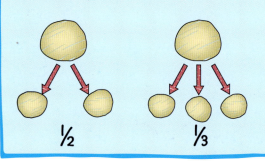

½   ⅓

Temperature is measured in different units, Celsius or Fahrenheit, in different parts of the world.

7 Preheat the oven to 220°C (430°F/Gas 7). Lightly dust your work surface with flour and then roll each piece of dough into a circular shape.

8 Lift your dough onto the baking tray. Fold the edges over if it is too big – this will make a nice crust. Spread half your sauce over the dough.

9 Tear one ball of mozzarella into pieces and scatter it over the pizza. You can add any other toppings you want, such as onions, peppers, or salami. Repeat to make a second pizza. Ask an adult to put the pizza into the oven and bake for 10–15 minutes.

10 When the cheese is bubbling and golden, take the pizza out. Ask an adult to help you as the oven will be hot. Wait for the pizza to cool down a bit. Divide it up and enjoy!

You could divide your pizza into two halves by putting one topping on half of its surface and another topping on the other half.

DIVIDING UP YOUR PIZZA

Sharing a pizza equally between friends is a useful way to understand how fractions work.

1 If there are three of you sharing a pizza and you each want one slice, the pizza needs to be divided into three equal parts. One divided by three is ⅓, so split the pizza into thirds.

⅓   ⅓

⅓

$$1 \div 3 = ⅓$$

2 If three more friends turn up and you all want one slice, then you'll need to divide the pizza into six equal parts. One divided by six is ⅙, so cut the pizza into sixths. The larger the bottom number of the fraction, the smaller each slice of pizza will be.

⅙   ⅙

⅙   ⅙

⅙   ⅙

$$1 \div 6 = ⅙$$

Garnish your pizza with fresh basil if you like.

POPCORN SALE TRAY

If you have a playground charity sale or school fair coming up, why not make a sale tray bursting with yummy popcorn cones to raise money? Or turn a movie night with friends into a cinema experience by bringing out some popcorn cones. Whatever you decide, this fun project will show you how to design a 3D tray, create cones, and calculate how to price your popcorn to make a tasty profit!

STEM YOU WILL USE

• MATHS: To draw the correct-sized holes for the popcorn cones you'll need to measure the radius and diameter. Use calculation to work out the cost of making each cone and the price they need to be to make a profit.

Fill each cone with delicious buttery, salty, or sugary popcorn. What will you choose?

The ribbon around your neck will keep your hands free for serving customers.

POPC

HOW TO MAKE A
POPCORN SALE TRAY

The key to this project is to make the cones before you begin work on the tray. You don't want the cones to be too big to fit inside! The size of the sale tray we have made here allows space for 12 popcorn cones.

Time
3 hours

Difficulty
Hard

WHAT YOU NEED

Ruler

Rubber

Compass and pencil

Felt-tip pen

Adhesive tape

PVA glue

Scissors

Adhesive putty

Large bowl of popcorn

A2 thick card (420 × 594 mm, 16½ × 23⅖ in)

A4 coloured or plain white paper

200 cm (80 in) of red ribbon

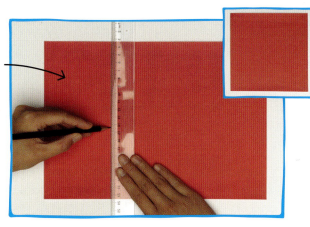

Why not make cones of different colours? We used eight red and four white squares.

1 To make each cone, take a sheet of paper and use a pencil and ruler to measure a square 21 × 21 cm (8¼ × 8¼ in). Cut out the square and repeat another 11 times to make 12 squares in total.

2 Rotate the paper square by 45° so it looks like a diamond and then roll it up into a cone with a point at one end. Stick tape where the edges meet so the paper does not unravel. Repeat to make 12 cones.

A cone is wide at one end and narrows to a point at the other end.

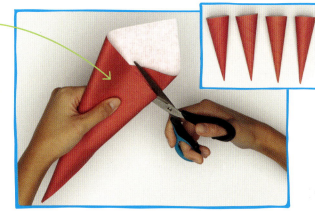

3 With a pair of scissors, carefully cut the pointy tops off all 12 cones. The open end should be level all the way around the circumference.

PROPERTIES OF A CONE

A cone is a 3D shape with one circular face and curved sides that taper to a point known as the vertex.

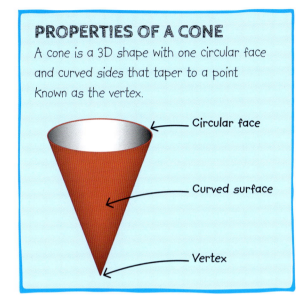

Circular face

Curved surface

Vertex

The diameter of a cone is at its widest at the opening and becomes narrower the closer it is to the vertex.

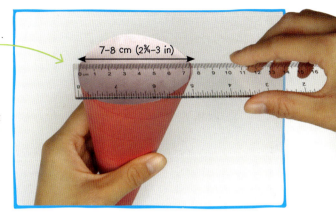

7–8 cm (2¾–3 in)

4 Check all 12 cones have roughly the same diameter of 7–8 cm (2¾–3 in) at the opening. This ensures each one will hold the same amount of popcorn when filled. Place your cones to one side.

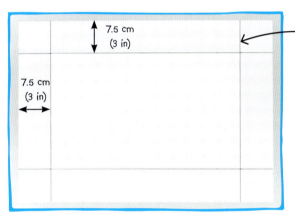

7.5 cm (3 in)

7.5 cm (3 in)

These lines will be your fold lines when you assemble the tray.

5 To make the tray, turn your piece of thick A2 card and draw a line 7.5 cm (3 in) in from each of the four sides of the card.

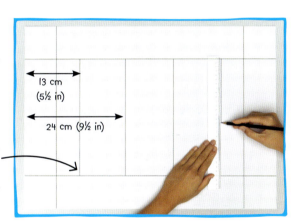

13 cm (5½ in)

24 cm (9½ in)

Draw the vertical lines in between the top and bottom horizontal lines.

6 Then draw two vertical lines, 13 cm (5½ in) and 24 cm (9½ in) in from the left side. Repeat on the right-hand side, so you end up with four new lines.

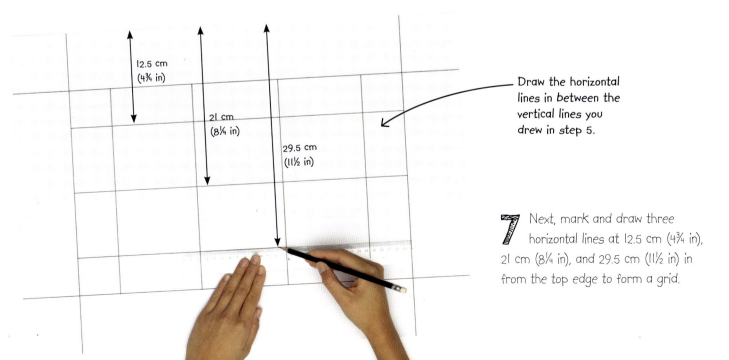

12.5 cm (4¾ in)

21 cm (8¼ in)

29.5 cm (11½ in)

Draw the horizontal lines in between the vertical lines you drew in step 5.

7 Next, mark and draw three horizontal lines at 12.5 cm (4¾ in), 21 cm (8¼ in), and 29.5 cm (11½ in) in from the top edge to form a grid.

8 In the top corners, make a pencil mark along the side 1 cm (½ in) above the horizontal line. Then draw a diagonal line connecting this point to where the horizontal and vertical lines meet. Repeat for the bottom corners, but make the mark below the horizontal line. These will be your glue tabs.

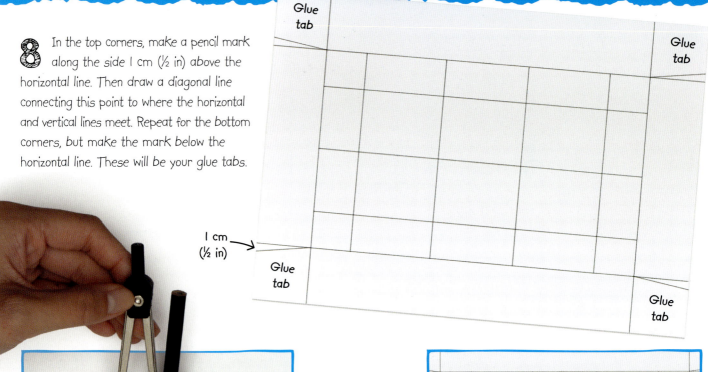

1 cm (½ in)

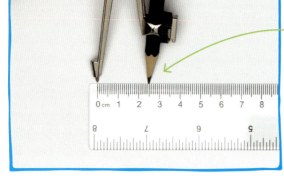

A circle with a radius of 2.5 cm (1 in) will have a diameter of 5 cm (2 in).

9 To make holes for the cones, set your compass to a radius of 2.5 cm (1 in). The diameter of the widest part of your cone is 8 cm (3 in), so don't make the holes too big or your cones will fall through them!

10 Place your compass point where one of the horizontal and vertical lines intersect to form a cross, then draw a circle. Repeat for each cross until you have drawn 12 circles of equal size.

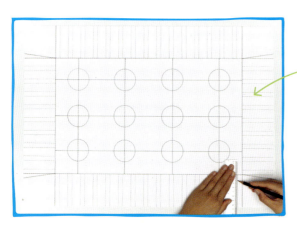

When the net of the tray is folded to make a 3D shape, the stripes will be on the outside.

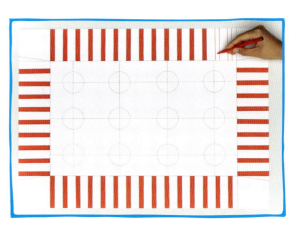

11 Decorate the outside of your box with stripes. Use a ruler and pencil to draw 1 cm- (½ in-) wide vertical lines with 2 cm (¾ in) in between.

12 Carefully colour in your stripes using a bright red felt-tip pen or a colour of your choice.

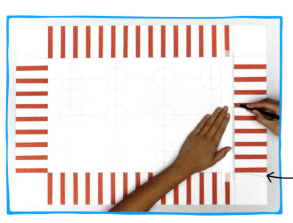

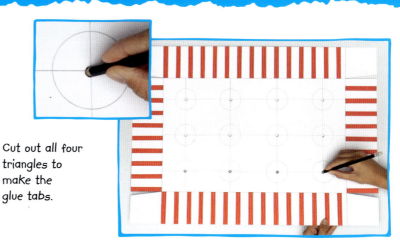

Cut out all four triangles to make the glue tabs.

13 Score along the four fold lines using a ruler and pencil. Then use scissors to cut out the small triangle glue tabs in each corner.

14 One by one, punch a hole in the centre of each circle by pressing a pencil into some adhesive putty on the underside.

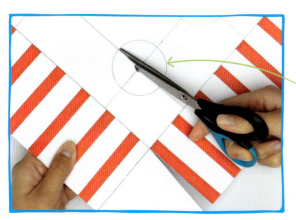

The line around the outside of a circle is called the circumference.

Make sure the glue tabs are on the inside.

15 Place scissors inside one of the pierced holes and snip along the lines inside the circle. Then cut around the circle's circumference. Repeat until all the circles have been cut out. Rub out the pencil marks.

16 Turn your card over and fold the four sides upwards. Bend the tabs in at the corners so they are on the inside of the tray. Dab PVA glue on each tab and stick the sides together firmly.

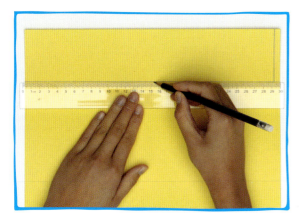

18 Flip over the tray so the holes are at the top, then add glue to the back of your sign and stick it in the centre of one of the longer sides. Press down and allow to dry.

17 Now make a sign for your tray. Draw a rectangle 6 x 29 cm (2¼ x 11½ in) on a piece of card. Write "Popcorn" and cut out the sign.

POPCORN

19 Cut two 100 cm (40 in) lengths of ribbon. Turn your tray over, and measure and mark on the inside 13.5 cm (5¼ in) from the front along both sides. Tape one end of each ribbon to the sides where you made the marks.

20 Turn the tray over again and hold it in front of you. Ask someone to tie the two ribbons together around your neck. Now place the 12 empty cones into the holes in the tray. Fill a bowl with popcorn and then carefully spoon it into each cone until they are all full. You're now ready to sell your popcorn!

You could add a price tag here.

REAL WORLD: MATHS
SHOP PRICES

The price of food in shops is calculated to cover not only the cost of the food and its packaging, but also the expense of transporting it, staff wages, and the rental of the shop. If the price is too high, no one will buy the food, so it must be worked out very carefully.

HOW TO PRICE YOUR POPCORN

If you want to sell your popcorn, you will need to work out what you should charge for each cone, based on the cost of the popcorn, and the price of making your cones and tray. You will need to cover your costs, but not make the price so expensive that you put people off. Add a little bit extra on top of the overall cost to make a profit from your sale. When you have decided on the price to charge, make a tag with the cost and glue it to the tray.

ITEM	COST	NUMBER	TOTAL COST
Popcorn	£1.52	1	£1.52
Cone	£0.10	12	£1.20
Tray	£4.00	1	£4.00
		OVERALL COST	£6.72
		COST PER CONE (OVERALL COST DIVIDED BY 12)	£0.56

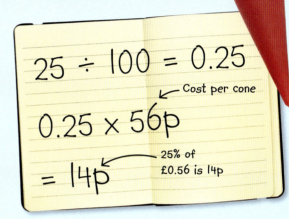

1 List the cost of the popcorn, the paper for one cone, and materials for making the tray. Add up the total (multiply the cone paper cost by 12) to work out your overall spending. Divide this by the number of cones to work out the cost of one cone. You now know the minimum price you need to charge for each cone to make back what you spent.

2 To make a profit, you will have to charge a bit more for each cone. To work out how to make 25 per cent profit, divide 25 by 100 and multiply by the cost per cone. A 25 per cent profit on one cone is £0.14. To increase the profit, you would need to use a higher percentage.

25% PROFIT PER CONE	£0.14	TOTAL INCOME	£8.40
COST PER CONE	£0.56	TOTAL COST	£6.72
PRICE PER CONE (COST PLUS PROFIT)	£0.70	TOTAL PROFIT (INCOME MINUS COST)	£1.68

3 If each cone costs £0.56 and you add a profit of £0.14, you can charge £0.70 per cone. If you sell 12 cones at £0.70, your income will be £8.40. To work out the profit, subtract your total spend of £6.72 from this figure, which will give you a profit of £1.68.

4 Once you have worked out what to charge for your popcorn, make a circular badge with a diameter of 8 cm (3¼ in) out of card. Use a felt-tip pen to write out the price per cone so it stands out, then glue the price tag to the front of your sale tray.

MATHS BINGO

This is a great game for practising quick calculations in your head. The faster you can answer the questions, the quicker you will cover your card and the more likely you are to win! It's great for groups of any size, as you can play with as many friends as you can make bingo cards for.

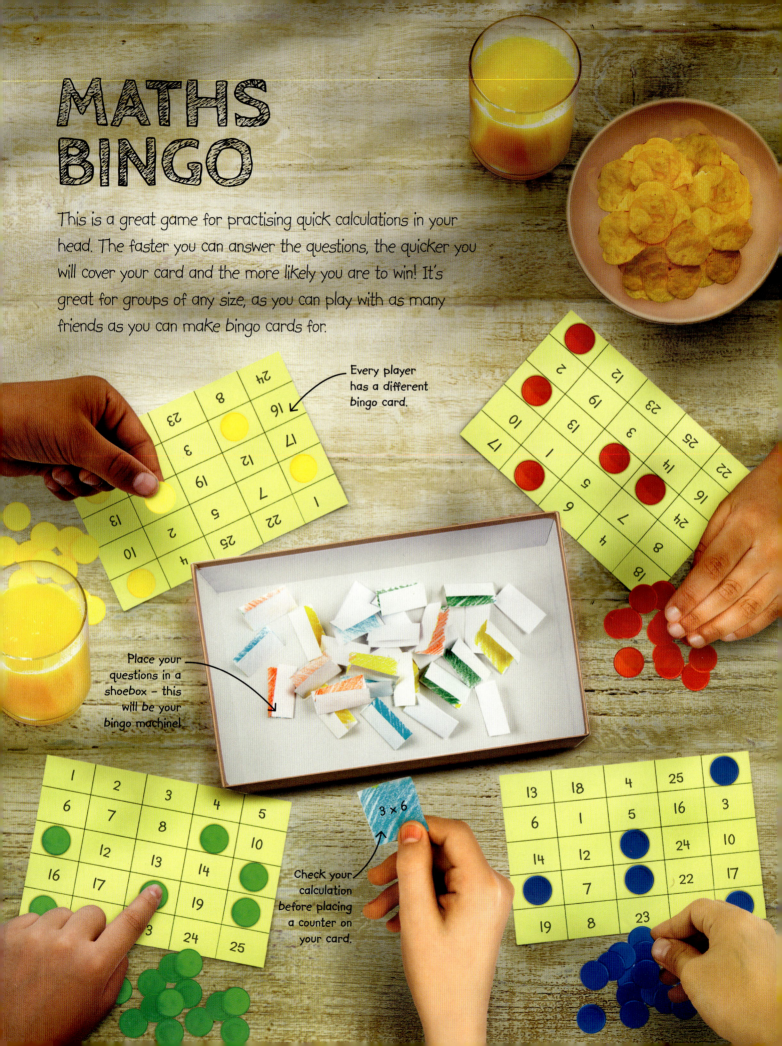

Every player has a different bingo card.

Place your questions in a shoebox – this will be your bingo machine!

3 × 6

Check your calculation before placing a counter on your card.

HOW TO
PLAY BINGO

To keep your game of bingo exciting, each player needs their own bingo card with numbers in a random order. That means that even though everyone hears the same questions, you'll all cover different squares and score points at different rates.

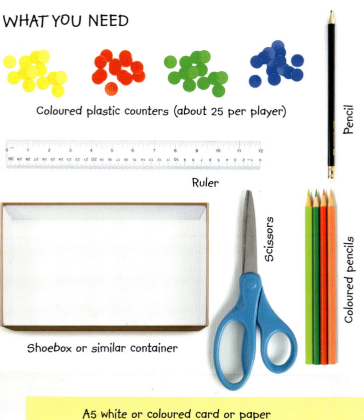

Time
I hour

Difficulty
Easy

WHAT YOU NEED

Coloured plastic counters (about 25 per player)

Ruler

Pencil

Scissors

Coloured pencils

Shoebox or similar container

A5 white or coloured card or paper

Measure the full width of your card and divide it by five to make sure you get equal columns.

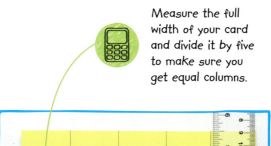

1 Take a piece of A5 card and create a 5 × 5 grid by drawing four vertical lines from the top to the bottom of the page. Make sure that the lines are equally spaced.

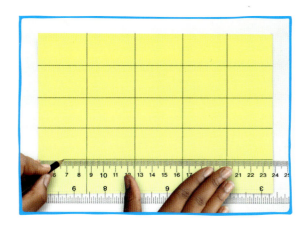

2 Divide the height of the card by five and draw four equally spaced horizontal lines down the page so you have a grid with five columns and five rows.

1	2	3	4	5
6	7	8	9	10
11	12	13	14	15
16	17	18	19	20
21	22	23	24	25

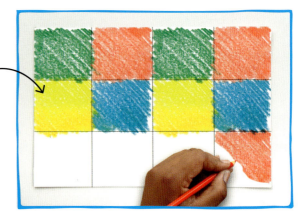

You could colour each square in the grid a different colour.

3 Number the grid from 1 to 25, starting at the top-left and ending at the bottom-right corner. Repeat steps 1–3 to make more bingo grids, but put the numbers on those grids in a random order.

4 On another piece of card, create a 4 x 3 grid by drawing three equally spaced vertical lines from the top to the bottom of the page and two equally spaced lines crossing the width of the page.

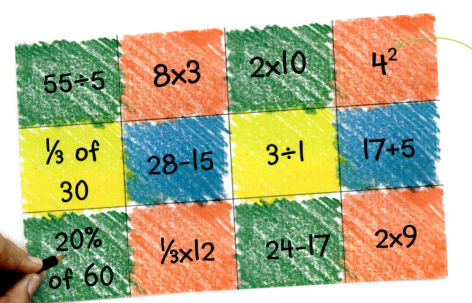

55÷5	8x3	2x10	4²
⅓ of 30	28-15	3÷1	17+5
20% of 60	⅓x12	24-17	2x9

This small 2 is called a power. It tells you how many times to multiply the number below it by itself. To work this out you need to do 4 x 4.

5 Fill each square of the grid with questions then repeat steps 4–5 to create more maths calculations until you have 25 plus a few spare for another game. Make sure that each of the 25 questions has a different answer. Each answer should be between 1 and 25.

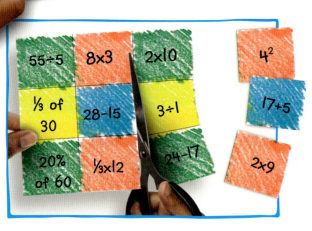

Make sure the caller puts the question away after reading it out so there are no repeats.

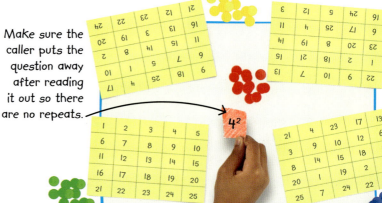

6 Use a pair of scissors to cut out the questions, then fold them up and place them in a shoebox or similar container.

7 Give every player but one a set of counters and a bingo card. The other player is the "caller", who picks questions from the box and reads them out.

If you win, you'll have to prove that your covered answers are all correct!

Your counters are discs: thin 3D shapes with a circular cross section.

8 Each time you figure out the answer to a question that the caller reads out, place a counter over the number matching the answer.

9 You can use the examples on the right to work out how to score the game. Keep playing until one person reaches 15 points.

BINGO SCORING

There are two ways to score in this version of bingo: covering all the answers in a column or row, or completing a cross from one corner to the other. A horizontal or vertical line is worth 5 points, while a cross is worth 10 points. The first person to get 15 points or more is the winner!

Column – 5 points

Row – 5 points

Cross – 10 points

REAL WORLD: MATHS BINGO MACHINES

In a bingo hall, it's important to ensure that the numbers called are completely random. To do that, transparent machines such as this one hold the bingo balls in a chamber that rotates as the handle is turned. This mixes the balls up, before a random ball is scooped out into the tube – or "runway" – below.

FIBONACCI SPIRAL COLLAGE

Follow in the footsteps of Leonardo da Vinci and create a masterpiece all of your own using the Fibonacci sequence. By fitting together ever-increasing squares, you can draw a perfect spiral and produce a collage fit to hang on your gallery wall.

STEM YOU WILL USE

• MATHS: Sequences and patterns create ideally sized squares. Use ratio to draw a perfect triangle and right angles to ensure your squares fit neatly next to each other.

Eye-catching beads make the Fibonacci spiral pop out of the collage.

HOW TO MAKE A
FIBONACCI SPIRAL COLLAGE

The key to this project is to create the template first by using a number pattern called the Fibonacci sequence to find the size of each square. Fibonacci was an Italian mathematician living 800 years ago who discovered a number sequence common in nature.

Time
2 hours

Difficulty
Medium

WHAT YOU NEED

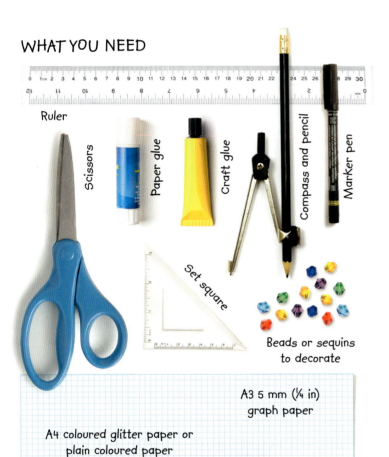

Ruler

Scissors

Paper glue

Craft glue

Set square

Compass and pencil

Marker pen

Beads or sequins to decorate

A3 5 mm (¼ in) graph paper

A4 coloured glitter paper or plain coloured paper

FIBONACCI SEQUENCE

The Fibonacci sequence is a pattern of numbers in which the next number in the series is the sum of the two numbers that come before it.

$$1 + 1 = \boxed{2}$$
$$1 + 2 = \boxed{3}$$
$$2 + 3 = \boxed{5}$$
$$3 + 5 = \boxed{8}$$
$$5 + 8 = \boxed{13}$$
$$8 + 13 = \boxed{21}$$
$$13 + 21 = \boxed{34}$$

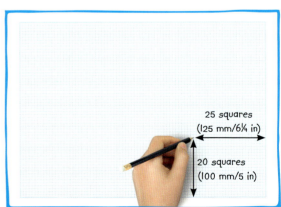

25 squares
(125 mm/6¼ in)

20 squares
(100 mm/5 in)

1 On an A3 sheet of 5 mm (¼ in) graph paper, make a pencil mark 25 squares left from the right edge and 20 squares up from the bottom edge.

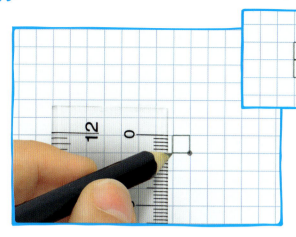

Use the Fibonacci sequence to work out the number of squares needed for the size of the next square.

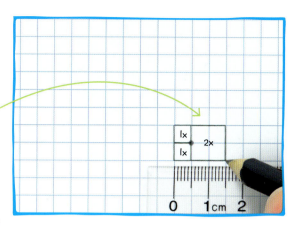

2 Trace a square to the left of the mark. This is a 1 × 1 square because it is one length on each side. Trace another square below the first square, so the mark is between them.

3 The next square needs to be 2 × 2 squares. Draw this square to the right of the two squares you have just drawn.

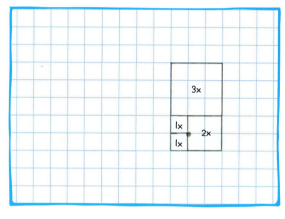

Each time you add a new square, you turn the shape into a larger rectangle.

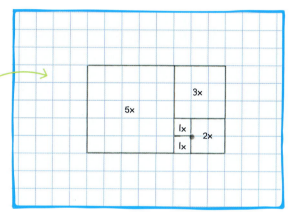

4 The following number in the sequence is 3, so draw a square 3 × 3 immediately above the squares you have already drawn.

5 Five is the next number in the Fibonacci sequence, so draw a square 5 × 5 to the left of the group of smaller squares.

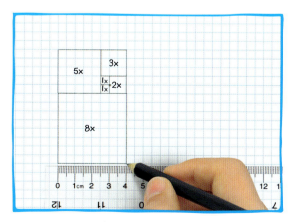

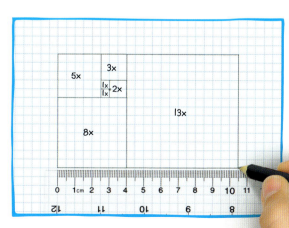

6 Next comes 8, so draw an 8 × 8 square immediately below the rectangle.

7 Thirteen is next, so draw a 13 × 13 square to the right of the rectangle.

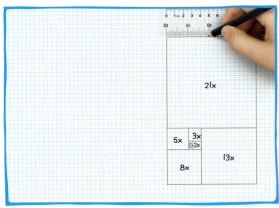

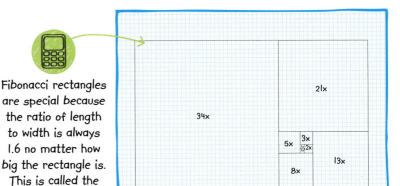

Fibonacci rectangles are special because the ratio of length to width is always 1.6 no matter how big the rectangle is. This is called the Golden Ratio.

8 And next is 21, so draw a square 21 x 21 immediately above the rectangle.

9 Next up is 34. Draw a square 34 x 34 to the left of the rectangle. Your Fibonacci template is now ready!

You can multiply the Fibonacci numbers by 5 mm (¼ in) to calculate the size of each coloured square to cut.

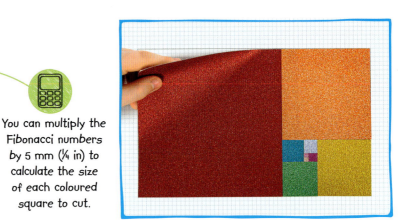

10 On different coloured paper, measure and cut out squares the same size as the ones you have just drawn. Use a set square and a ruler to ensure the corners are right angles.

11 Glue the squares into position on the template. Start with the smallest squares, then move onto the next biggest until the template is covered. Trim off any excess graph paper.

FIBONACCI SPIRAL
You can use the Fibonacci sequence to draw a spiral by linking the opposite corners of each square with a curved line.

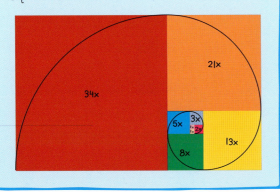

Position the compass point on the very first mark you made in step 1.

12 Set a compass to 5 mm (¼ in) and place it at the top-right corner of the first square. Draw a curve across the two smallest squares.

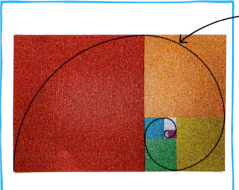

You can use a pencil or black marker pen to draw the curve.

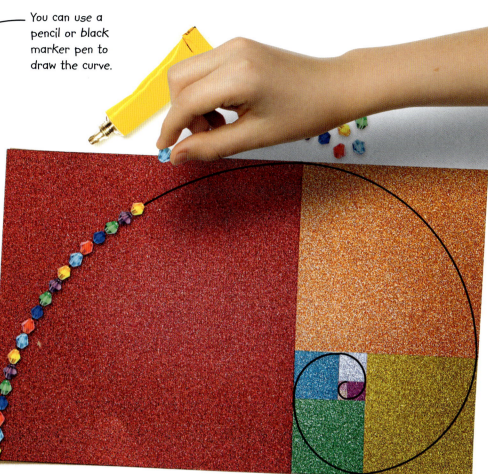

13 Repeat step 12, but each time adjust the compass to the length of the next square and place the compass point on the corner opposite where you will draw your curve. Then use your compass to continue the spiral.

14 Decorate the collage by sticking beads or sequins along the contours of the spiral. Can you create a pattern or sequence using the beads?

REAL WORLD: MATHS

FIBONACCI IN NATURE

Fibonacci spirals don't just occur in maths, they are also found in the natural world. Pine cones and pineapples arrange their scales in a Fibonacci spiral, and the number of petals on a flower are often Fibonacci numbers. For example, Michaelmas daisies like these usually have 34, 55, or 89 petals, all of which are Fibonacci numbers.

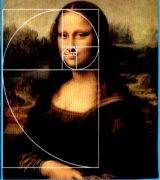

GOLDEN RATIO IN ART

As well as cropping up in nature, the Fibonacci sequence also appears in the art world. As shown above, the famous Italian artist Leonardo da Vinci is thought to have used golden rectangles to make the proportions of some of his most famous paintings, including the *Mona Lisa*, more harmonious.

MAKE YOUR OWN CLOCK

What better way to keep your day on track than by making your own clock? You'll need a working clock mechanism for this activity (you can find these in craft shops and online), along with some modelling clay and colourful paints to decorate your timepiece just the way you like it. Painting the clock face is also the perfect chance to practise your fractions, as it's divided into 12 equal sections. Ready? It's time to start!

Each time the short hand passes one of these marks, a new hour begins.

TIDDLES

We have decorated our clock with coloured wedges, but you can use any pattern you like.

Use a black marker pen to draw the numbers clearly on your clock.

LUNCHTIME

HELP TIDY THE KITCHEN

DO SOME HOMEWORK

BEDTIME

DINNER

FEED TIDDLES

Stick reminders on the different hours so you remember when to do things!

HOW TO
MAKE YOUR OWN CLOCK

The clock mechanism will make your finished product tick, but it's important to measure the sections of the clock carefully to make sure the numbers are in the right place. Once the clay is set, decorate the clock by copying our painted pattern or make up your own.

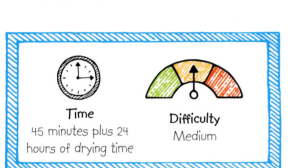

Time
45 minutes plus 24 hours of drying time

Difficulty
Medium

WHAT YOU NEED

Plate

Ruler

Sticky notes

Air-drying modelling clay (check drying time)

Acrylic paints and brush

Protractor

Clock mechanism and battery

Dinner Knife

Pencil

Black marker pen

Detachable pen lid

Rolling pin

1 Roll your clay out into a rough circle that is larger than your plate and approximately 0.5 cm (¼ in) thick. Try to make it nice and flat.

The plate you choose will determine the size of your finished clock face.

2 Place your plate on top of the clay and cut around it with a dinner Knife to make a circle shape. Gently lift the plate off the clay.

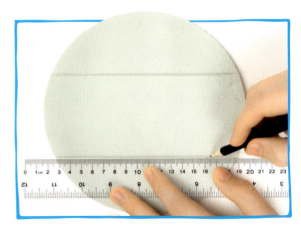

3 To find the centre of the clay circle, use a pencil to lightly draw two parallel lines across it. Make sure that the lines are equal in length.

Check that your pen lid is wider than the shaft at the front of the clock mechanism.

4 Draw two diagonal lines joining the two opposite corners of the parallel lines. The point where they meet is the centre of the circle.

5 Push the pen lid through the centre point of the circle to make a hole. Leave the clay to dry on a flat surface. It may take a few days.

A circle is 360°, and 360 divided by 12 (for each hour of a 12-hour clock) is 30°.

6 Once it has fully dried, flip your clay circle over. Draw a line across the middle of the circle and place a protractor over the hole. Mark with a pencil every 30°. Rotate your protractor 180° and repeat on the other half.

7 Use a ruler to draw straight lines out from the centre of the circle to create 12 segments. Each of these will represent one hour.

8 Paint the clock in different colours with your acrylic paints, using any pattern you like. Allow the paint to fully dry – this could take up to two hours.

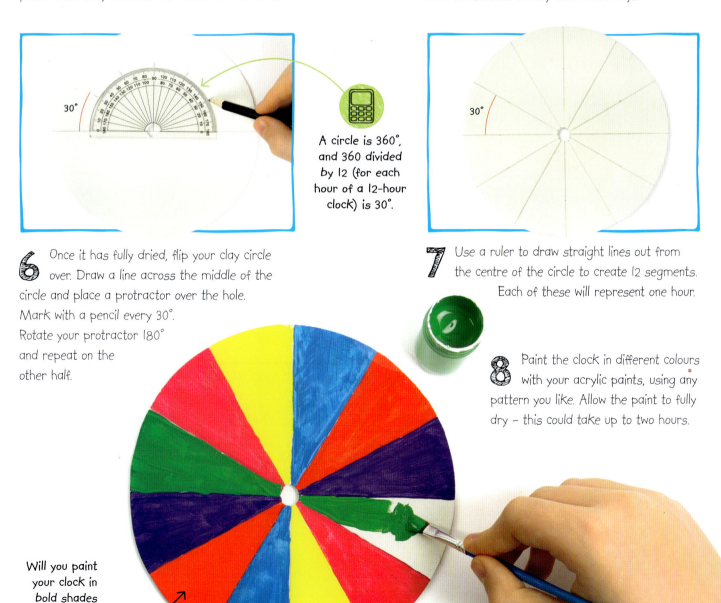

Will you paint your clock in bold shades or pretty pastels?

9 Using a pencil, draw numbers from 1 – 12 around the clock face. Then go over the numbers with a black marker pen to make them stand out.

10 Push the *base* of your clock kit through the hole in the centre of the face. Make sure the hook for hanging up the clock is aligned with number 12.

11 Place the circular *brass* washer onto the clock shaft and then tighten the hexagonal nut on top of it. Don't over-tighten the nut in case you crack the clay.

12 Carefully push the clock hands onto the shaft of your clock kit, starting with the small hour hand, then the longer minute hand, and finally the thin second hand.

Starting all three hands at 12 ensures they will be set correctly.

13 Align all three hands at 12 o'clock. Insert the battery and set the time by moving the minute hand round until you reach the correct time.

Push the second hand onto the shaft last of all. Be careful not to use too much force or you might bend it.

Draw a mark by each number so you can see clearly when the clock hand reaches it and the hour passes.

14 To help remind you of the things you need to do at certain times, you can write them on sticky notes and put them on the clock face. You can move these around depending on what you are up to each day. Trim the notes to size if they are too large.

LUNCHTIME

HELP TIDY THE KITCHEN

DO SOME HOMEWORK

FEED TIDD

TELLING THE TIME

There are two types of clock, analogue – like the one you've just made – and digital, which displays the 24 hours in a full day and night on a screen. The clocks here show the same time – 5 minutes to midnight – but in different ways. To convert a 24-hour time to a 12-hour format, if the hours are more than 12, simply subtract 12 from the hours. So 23.00 would be 11.00, because 23 - 12 =11.

On this analogue clock, Roman numerals mark the hours.

On a digital 24-hour clock, midnight is 00.00. The first two figures show the hour, the next two the minutes, followed by the seconds.

23:55 59

The numbers on this analogue clock mark the hours, while the small dashes represent the minutes past the hour.

TEMPLATES

These are the templates you need for the anemometer, twirling helicopter, water rocket, latitude locator, and sundial. You can either trace the lines onto a piece of paper or photocopy the page you need. For the sundial, make sure you use the correct template - one is designed for use in the Northern Hemisphere, and the other is designed for use in the Southern Hemisphere.

Twirling helicopter p.12

Anemometer p.244

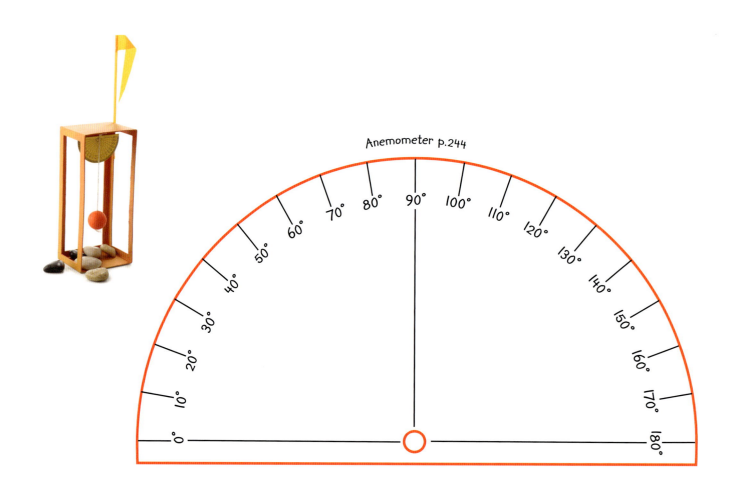

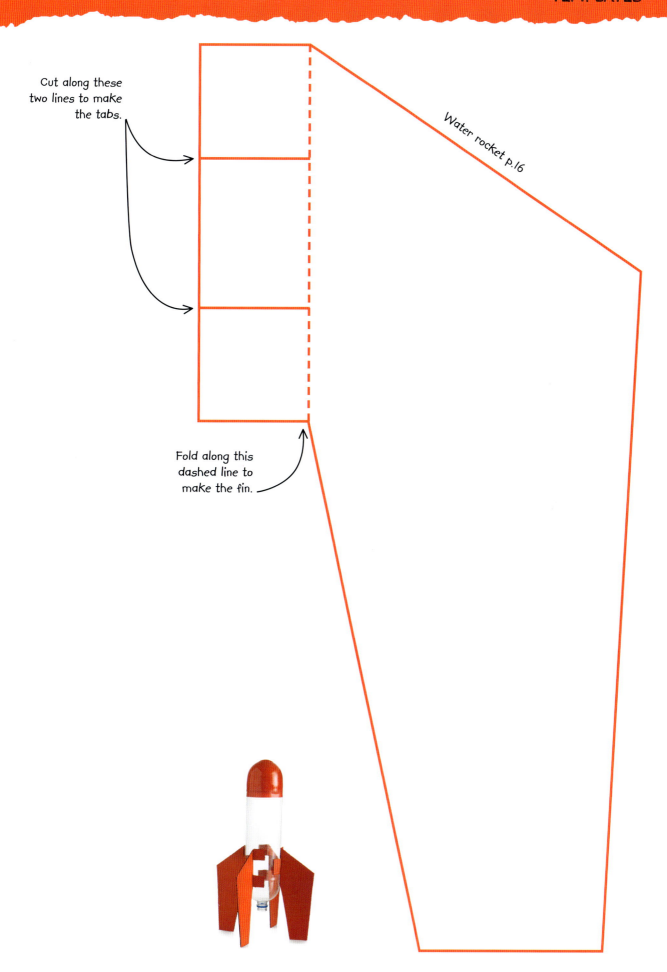

Cut along these
two lines to make
the tabs.

Water rocket p.16

Fold along this
dashed line to
make the fin.

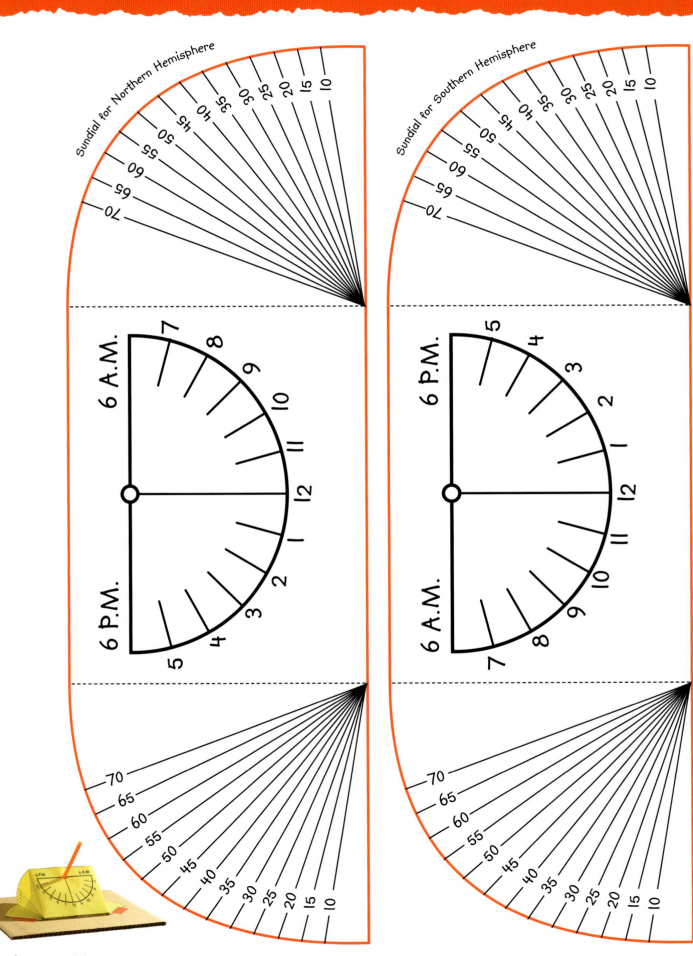

Sundial for Northern Hemisphere

Sundial for Southern Hemisphere

6 A.M.
7
8
9
10
11
12
1
2
3
4
5
6 P.M.

6 P.M.
5
4
3
2
1
12
11
10
9
8
7
6 A.M.

Paper sundial p.252

Fold along this dashed
line to make a tab that
will attach the locator to
the viewing rod.

Latitude locator p.256

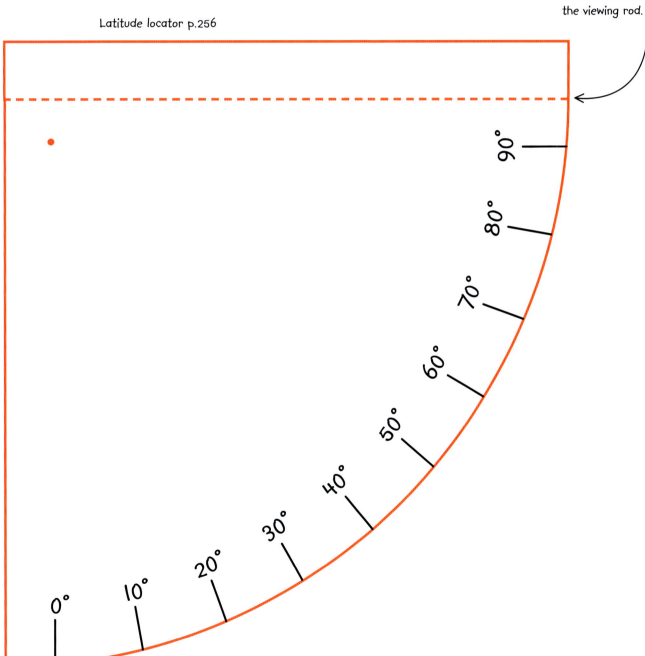

90°

80°

70°

60°

50°

40°

30°

20°

10°

0°

GLOSSARY

AIR RESISTANCE
A force that slows down moving objects as they travel through air, such as rockets.

ANGLE
Measured in degrees, an angle is the amount of turn from one direction to another. You can also think of it as the difference in direction between two lines meeting at a point. *See degree.*

ATTRACTION
A force that pulls things together, such as the opposite poles of two magnets.

AVERAGE
The typical or middle value of a set of data.

AXIS
(1) One of the two main lines on a grid, used to measure the position of points, lines, and shapes. (2) An axis of symmetry is another name for a line of symmetry.

BOND
A force that holds together tiny particles such as molecules.

CAM
A machine part that turns rotation into back-and-forth or up-and-down motion.

CHEMICAL
A compound or element that can change when combined with another substance. Chemicals can be liquids, solids, or gases.

CIRCUIT
A complete and closed path, around which an electric current can flow.

CIRCUMFERENCE
The distance all the way round the outside of a circle.

COMPRESSION
A squashing force, such as that experienced by weight-bearing materials in buildings.

COORDINATES
Pairs of numbers that describe the position of a point, line, or shape on a grid, or the position of something on a map.

CRANK
A machine part that can turn rotation into to-and-fro motion or do the opposite.

DATA
Any information that has been collected and can be compared.

DEGREE
A measure of the size of a turn or angle. The symbol for a degree is °. A full turn is 360°.

DENSITY
A measure of how much mass (stuff) is present in a certain volume. Rock is much more dense than water, for example.

DIAGONAL
A straight, sloping line that isn't vertical or horizontal.

DIAMETER
A straight line from one side of a circle or sphere to the other that goes through the centre.

ELECTRIC CURRENT
Movement of electric charge.

ELEMENT
A substance made of just one type of atom that cannot be broken down into a simpler substance by chemical reactions.

ENERGY
The ability to make things happen. Energy has different forms, such as electrical energy, kinetic energy (movement), and potential energy (stored energy).

EROSION
Wearing away. Rocks and soil can be eroded by wind and rain.

ESTIMATION
The process of finding an answer that's close to the correct answer, often by rounding numbers up or down.

FORCE
A push or a pull. Forces change how an object moves: by causing it to start or stop moving, speed up or slow down, or change direction. Forces can also change the shape of an object.

FRACTION
A number that is not a whole number, such as ½ , ¼ , or ⅓.

FRICTION
A force between surfaces that are in contact. Friction between a tyre and the ground pushes a bicycle along as the wheels turn.

GRAVITY
A force that pulls objects towards the centre of the Earth. It keeps you on the ground, instead of floating around.

INTERSECT
To meet or cross over (used of lines or shapes).

LATITUDE
A measure of how far north or south of the equator you are. The latitude of the equator is 0°, while the North Pole has a latitude of +90° and the South Pole, -90°.

LEVER
A rigid bar that modifies force or motion when it swings around a fixed point known as a pivot, or fulcrum.

LINE OF SYMMETRY

An imaginary line through a shape that divides it into two halves. Some shapes have no line of symmetry, while others have several.

MASS

A measure of the amount of matter in an object.

MIXTURE

A substance made of two or more compounds or elements.

MOLECULE

Two or more atoms held together by bonds.

PARALLEL

Running side by side without getting closer or further apart.

PERCENTAGE (%)

A proportion expressed as a fraction of 100. For example, 25% is the same as $\frac{25}{100}$.

PERPENDICULAR

Something is perpendicular when it is at right angles to something else.

PRESSURE

A measure of how much a force pushes on a surface.

PROBABILITY

The chance of something happening or being true.

RADIUS

Any straight line from the centre of a circle to its circumference.

RATIO

Ratio compares one number or amount with another. It's written as two numbers, separated by a colon (:).

RIGHT ANGLE

An angle of 90° (a quarter turn), such as the angle between vertical and horizontal lines.

ROTATION

Turning around a central point or line.

ROTOR

The spinning part of a helicopter, which produces an upward force called lift as it moves through the air.

SEQUENCE

An arrangement of numbers one after the other that follows a set pattern, called a rule.

SPECTRUM

A spread of colours produced by splitting white light into the colours of which it is made, as happens in a rainbow.

STATIC ELECTRICITY

The build-up of electric charge on an object that has lost or gained electrons.

STREAMLINED

Describes an object shaped in a way that offers very little resistance to the flow of liquid or gas.

SURFACE TENSION

A force that stretches the surface of a liquid tight. It is the result of attraction between atoms or molecules.

TENSION

A pulling force, such as that exerted by the steel cables used in parts of buildings or bridges.

THREE-DIMENSIONAL (3D)

Having length, width, and depth. All solid objects are three-dimensional – even thin paper.

TURBINE

A device with rotating fan blades that are driven by the pressure of gases, liquids, or steam. Turbines powered by the wind or by moving water are often used to generate electricity.

ULTRAVIOLET RADIATION (UV)

A form of radiation given off by sun. It's a type of light that's invisible to human eyes.

UNIT

A standard size used for measuring, such as the metre (for length).

VERTEX

A point where two lines meet.

VISCOSITY

The resistance of a liquid to changing shape. A thick, sticky substance like honey flows slowly because it has a high viscosity.

VOLUME

The size of a 3D space occupied by something or enclosing something.

VERTEX

A point where two lines meet.

WEIGHT

The downward force on an object caused by gravity. The more mass something has, the more it weighs.

INDEX

ACKNOWLEDGMENTS

DK would like to thank the following people for their contribution:
Rakesh Kumar, Gayatri Menon, and Joe Lawrence for design assistance; Helen Peters for the index; and Jane Parker for proofreading.

DK would like to thank the following people for their contribution in Home Lab, Maths Lab, Outdoor Maker Lab, and Science Lab:
Laura Gardner, Ashwin Khurana, Nicola Erdpresser, Ann Baggaley, Dave King, Lisa Gillespie, Mary Slater, Michelle Crane, Sam Kennedy, Rachel Thompson, Mik Gates, Jim Green, Simon Tegg, Fran Baines, Phil Letsu, Alex Lloyd, Branka Surla, Stefan Podhorodecki, Michael Wicks, Michelle Staples, Amanda Wyatt, Sean Ross, Edward Byrne, Jacqui Swan, Steven Carton, Ben Morgan, Chrissy Barnard, Gus Scott, Gregory McCarthy.

DK would like to thank the following for their kind permission to reproduce their photographs:
(Key: a-above; b-below/bottom; c-centre; f-far; l-left; r-right; t-top)

8 Alamy Stock Photo: Jim Reed / RGB Ventures / SuperStock (cla). Dreamstime.com: Ukrit Chaiwattanakunkit (cra); Ian Klein (ca); Toldiu74 (ca/Windmill). 15 123RF.com: aleksanderdn (crb). 23 Alamy Stock Photo: Newscom (br). 37 123RF.com: epicstockmedia (bl). 43 Alamy Stock Photo: Jeff Rotman (bl). 51 Dreamstime.com: Toldiu74 (bl). 59 Dreamstime.com: Andrei Shupilo (br). 69 Dreamstime.com: Vladislav Kochelaevskiy (br). 77 Alamy Stock Photo: PA Images / David Davies (crb). 83 Getty Images: Mmdi / DigitalVision (crb). 87 Alamy Stock Photo: NASA Photo (crb). 89 Alamy Stock Photo: Cultura Creative RF / Rodrigo Friscione (crb). 97 Alamy Stock Photo: Science History Images (bl). 103 Alamy Stock Photo: Jim Reed / RGB Ventures / SuperStock (br). 107 Alamy Stock Photo: Simon Perkin (br). 109 Shutterstock.com: AP (br). 113 Dreamstime.com: Sean Pavone (crb). 117 Dreamstime.com: Ivangelos (br). 123 Getty Images: Sebastin Crespo Photography / Moment (ca). 129 Dreamstime.com: Jarrun Klinmontha (crb). 133 Dreamstime.com: Horseman82 (cb). Science Photo Library: Steve Lowry (crb). 141 123RF.com: Songquan Deng (crb). Dreamstime.com: Ian Klein (clb). 147 Science Photo Library: Laguna Design (bl). 153 Dreamstime.com: Travelling-light (br). 159 123RF.com: Maria Wachala (cr). 165 Dreamstime.com: Suljo (br). 173 Dreamstime.com: Ukrit Chaiwattanakunkit (br). 185 Dreamstime.com: Hayati Kayhan (br). 195 Alamy Stock Photo: Sipa US / Kristoffer Tripplaar (bc). 199 Getty Images: Inti St Clair / Tetra images (bl). 205 NASA: ESA / Hubble (bl). 217 Dreamstime.com: Mrchan (br). 225 Dreamstime.com: Katja Nykanen (crb). 229 Dreamstime.com: Elitsa Lambova (br). 235 123RF.com: Adrian Hillman (bl). 239 Alamy Stock Photo: Joel Douillet (cr). 243 Alamy Stock Photo: sabphoto / YAY Media AS (br). 251 Depositphotos Inc: Wongsaphat Suknachon / Flypix (bl). 255 Alamy Stock Photo: Sergio Azenha (crb). 261 Alamy Stock Photo: Dino Fracchia (crb). 294 Getty Images: Westend61 (bl). 299 Getty Images: Jonathan Kitchen / DigitalVision (bc). 305 Getty Images: UniversalImagesGroup (crb). 311 Getty Images / iStock: chasmer (crb)

All other images © Dorling Kindersley

For further imformation see: www.dkimages.com.

MORE GREAT STEM PROJECTS...

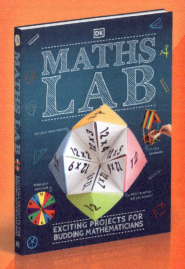

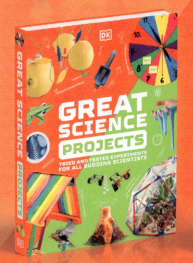

 For the curious